RANDOM HOUSE

LARGE
PRINT

POLITICS LOST

Also by Joe Klein
available from Random House Large Print

The Running Mate

POLITICS LOST

★ ★ ★ ★ ★ ★ ★ ★ ★ ★ ★ ★ ★ ★ ★ ★ ★ ★ ★

How American Democracy
Was Trivialized by People Who
Think You're Stupid

Joe Klein

RANDOM HOUSE
LARGE PRINT

**The Library of Congress has established a
Cataloging-in-Publication record for this title.**

ISBN-13: 978-0-7393-2614-5
ISBN-10: 0-7393-2614-7

www.randomlargeprint.com

FIRST LARGE PRINT EDITION

10   9   8   7   6   5   4   3   2   1

This Large Print edition published in accord
with the standards of the N.A.V.H.

FOR VICTORIA, OF COURSE,

and

IN MEMORY OF DANIEL PATRICK
MOYNIHAN

If you agree with me on nine out of twelve issues, vote for me. If you agree with me on twelve out of twelve issues, see a psychiatrist.

—EDWARD I. KOCH, RUNNING FOR MAYOR OF NEW YORK IN 1989

Contents

★ ★ ★ ★

Contents

POLITICS LOST

Prologue

★ ★ ★ ★

On the evening of April 4, 1968, about an hour after Dr. Martin Luther King Jr. was assassinated, Robert F. Kennedy responded with a powerfully simple speech, which he delivered spontaneously in a black neighborhood in Indianapolis. Nearly forty years later, Kennedy's words stand as a sublime example of the substance and music of politics in its grandest form, for its highest purpose—to heal, to educate, to lead—but also, sadly, they represent the end of an era: the last moments before American political life was overwhelmed by marketing professionals, consultants, and pollsters who, with the flaccid acquiescence of the politicians, have robbed public life of much of its romance and vigor.

Many people believe Kennedy was standing on top of a car, in the midst of angry chaos, when he addressed the crowd that night. Actually, he spoke from a podium on the back of a flatbed truck, and the crowd was quiet and orderly and unaware, until Kennedy told them, that King was dead. It was a cold and extremely windy night. The only light came from floodlights trained on the podium, illuminating a smoky stand of oaks behind the stage. No one knows how many people were gathered in the small park—maybe a thousand, not much more. There was no police estimate of the crowd, because there was no police presence in the park that night. Robert Kennedy was unprotected as he was lifted onto the stage: no secret service, no local police. The Indianapolis police chief, a man who was actually named Winston Churchill, had warned Kennedy against going into the ghetto. The police were cordoning off the area to prevent the expected violence from spilling over into the rest of the city; they wouldn't be able to protect a visiting, showboating politician. And Kennedy's aides were worried that the crowd—which had been waiting in the park for more than an hour—would explode as soon as the senator told them that King was dead. But there was no chance Kennedy would beg off, play it safe, disappoint the people. None of his aides even thought to dissuade him. "Ladies and gentlemen," the senator began, tentatively, clearing his throat. "I'm only going to speak to you for one or two minutes tonight because I have sad news for all of you . . ."

Robert Kennedy's presidential campaign was two weeks old at that moment, and it was a wild, passionate, frightening thing—part insurgency, part restoration, a portable mob scene. The crowds were unbelievable from the start, larger and more intense than any since in American politics. Almost every evening on the television news, there were scenes of Kennedy—a small, taut, diffident man—swarmed and crushed by throngs of loving supporters. At the time, his words and policies almost seemed superfluous. What mattered was that he was a Kennedy, that he seemed so much like his brother in looks and ideals and Boston accent, that his candidacy promised the resumption of a violently truncated American public romance.

Indiana was Robert Kennedy's first primary campaign; April 4 was one of his first full days on the stump. He began with a rally at the University of Notre Dame, then another at Ball State. He spoke about race and poverty at both schools; at Ball State, he was confronted by a black student who was skeptical about white America's willingness to address those issues. "I think the vast majority of white people want to do the decent thing," Kennedy said.

Afterward, at the Muncie airport, word came that King had been shot. "That was all the information we had," Frank Mankiewicz, Kennedy's press secretary, later recalled. "There were no cell phones in those days, no way to find out more while we were in the air to Indianapolis. But I remember that Bob's eyes went vacant when he heard the news; he became very quiet and withdrawn, which was not unusual for him. We talked a bit about what he should say in Indianapolis. I suggested that he ask everyone to say a prayer for the King family, also that he remind them of King's nonviolence and plead with them not to retaliate. He told me that sounded good, that I should write it up."

Apparently Kennedy was still thinking about what he'd said to the black student at Ball State. "You know, it grieves me," he said to John J. Lindsay of **Newsweek** on the short flight to Indianapolis. "I just told that kid this and then walk out and find out some white man has just shot their spiritual leader."

And then, in Indianapolis, word that King was dead. Lindsay saw Kennedy recoil at the news "as if he had been struck physically." Kennedy got into a car with Fred Dutton, a campaign strategist. "What should I tell them, Fred?" he asked. Dutton didn't know what to say; Kennedy was staring out the window, a million miles away. Finally Dutton told him, "You know what to say, Bob. Just speak from your heart," knowing that the advice was banal, but sensing that's what Kennedy was going to do anyway.

Mankiewicz was thinking the same thing, but he wrote some notes for Kennedy as he rode downtown on the press bus. He noticed—everyone noticed—that the police escort dropped off as they entered the black neighborhood. The motorcade shattered in the traffic near the rally, the press bus cut off from the candidate's car. By the time the bus arrived, Kennedy was onstage, beginning to speak, and Mankiewicz had no chance to give the senator his notes.

Adam Walinsky, Kennedy's young speechwriter, had

preceded the campaign staff to Indianapolis and was having dinner downtown when he heard that King had been shot. He immediately started drafting remarks for Kennedy on a yellow legal pad, then jumped in a car and headed for the rally. The police had already set up blockades, and Walinsky's car was stopped as he entered the black neighborhood. "You can't go in there," the cop said.

Walinsky asked, why not? "Because we can't protect you in there," the cop replied. "**We're** not going in there tonight."

"Hey, it's okay, I'm with Senator Kennedy. He's in there. I'm going in," Walinsky said, and the policemen gave him a be-my-guest-but-you're-nuts look.

Walinsky arrived at about the same moment as Kennedy. He noticed, from a distance, that Kennedy wasn't moving side to side, working the crowd as he normally did; he was plowing straight ahead, head down. "Senator," Walinsky shouted, and pulled the notes from his pocket.

Kennedy, who was wearing a dark-blue raincoat, gave Walinsky a grim look and a quick, curt hand signal: no, he wouldn't be needing any words that night. Walinsky saw Kennedy pull some notes from his pocket, which he'd probably scribbled in the car on the way in from the airport. Mankiewicz, in the back of the crowd, saw Kennedy up on the podium and wondered if Bobby could keep it all together, keep his composure, say the right thing and calm the crowd, which still—

remarkably—wasn't aware of King's death. And then, for the next four minutes and fifty-seven seconds, Robert Kennedy spoke . . .

"Ladies and gentlemen," he began, rather formally, respectfully. "I'm only going to speak to you for one or two minutes tonight because I have sad news . . ." His voice caught, and he turned it into a slight cough, a throat-clearing. The crowd hadn't quite settled in yet; his supporters were still waving signs. He couldn't go on if they were celebrating. "Could you lower those signs over there?" he asked, and the crowd quieted. "I have sad news for you, for all of our fellow citizens and for people who love peace all over the world—" he paused, his voice still uncertain, then gathered himself up and said—"and that is that Martin Luther King was shot and killed tonight in Memphis, Tennessee."

There were screams, wailing—just the rawest, most visceral sounds of pain that human voices can summon. As the screams died, Kennedy resumed, slowly, pausing frequently, measuring his words: "Martin Luther King . . . dedicated his life . . . to love . . . and to justice between fellow human beings and he died in the cause of that effort."

There was total silence now. Rather than exploding, rather than indulging their anger, the crowd was rapt. One senses, listening to the tape years later, a trust and respect for the man at the podium, a man who knew all about assassinations, as well as a yearning to be reassured, to be comforted.

"In this difficult day, in this difficult time for the

United States, it is perhaps well to ask what kind of nation we are . . . and what direction we want to move in . . .

"For those of you who are black—considering the evidence," he stumbled here, "evidently there were white people who were responsible." A shudder went through the crowd at the powerful unadorned word: responsible. "You can be filled with bitterness, with hatred, and a desire for revenge.

"We can move in that direction as a country, in great polarization—black people amongst blacks, and white amongst whites, filled with hatred toward one another.

"Or we can make an effort, as Martin Luther King did, to understand and comprehend," he paused, perhaps considering whether or not to take the next step, whether to lay himself bare before that crowd—the next few phrases seemed to be placeholding, preparation as he gathered himself emotionally, "and to replace the stain of bloodshed that has spread across our land, with an effort to understand, with compassion and love."

Then he plunged ahead: "For those of you who are black, and are tempted to be filled with hatred and distrust of the injustice of such an act, against all white people," he paused again, "I can only say that I feel"— his voice broke—"in my own heart the same kind of feeling. I had a member of my family killed, but **he** was killed by a white man." Walinsky's head snapped up: he had been working for Kennedy for five years and had never heard him speak before—publicly or even

privately—of the death of his brother. It was just too
painful, a place Kennedy would not go, a topic skidded
away from whenever anyone came close to raising it.
No one who knew him ever spoke of it in his presence.
And yet here he was, tentatively—he still could not
say the words "my brother," it was "a member of my
family"—and somewhat confusedly (why did the race
of his brother's assassin matter?) stripping himself
before strangers, evaporating the distance between
himself and the crowd. They were suffering together
now; you could hear it in the quality of the silence,
which seemed a conscious, cooperative thing, a group
achievement. "We have to make an effort in the United
States, we have to make an effort to understand, to get
beyond these rather difficult times."

And now, he drew them closer still: "My favorite
poem, favorite poet was Aeschylus. He once wrote:
Even in our sleep, pain which cannot forget, falls drop
by drop upon the human heart," he paused, still speaking softly, his voice shaking a bit as he caressed every
word. Again, the silence of the crowd was stunning.
"Until . . . in our own despair, against our will, comes
wisdom through the awful grace of God."

He proceeded briskly from there, with a poetic lilt to
his phrasing:

What we need in the United States is not division;
what we need in the United States is not hatred;
what we need in the United States is not violence
or lawlessness but love and wisdom, and compas-

sion toward one another, and a feeling of justice for those who still suffer within our country, whether they be white or whether they be black.

So I ask you tonight to return home, to say a prayer for the family of Martin Luther King—yes, that's true—but more importantly, to say a prayer for our own country, which all of us love, a prayer for understanding and that compassion of which I spoke.

We can do well in this country. We will have difficult times; we've had difficult times in the past. And we will have difficult times in the future. It is not the end of violence; it is not the end of lawlessness; and it is not the end of disorder.

But the vast majority of white people and the vast majority of black people in this country want to live together, want to improve the quality of our life, and want justice for all human beings who abide in our land.

Someone shouted, "YAY!" There were other shouts, which melted into a warm, buttery round of applause.

Kennedy seemed to exhale. "Let us dedicate ourselves to what the Greeks wrote so many years ago: to tame the savageness of man and make gentle the life of this world.

"Let us dedicate ourselves to that . . . and say a prayer for our country, and for our people."

Over the next few days, there were riots in seventy-six American cities.

Forty-six people died, 2,500 were injured, 28,000 jailed.

Indianapolis remained quiet.

I was a senior in college when Kennedy delivered that speech; he passed away the week I graduated. His death was, for me, the saddest of the trinity of killings that punctured my youth. I had been shocked by President Kennedy's death and outraged by Martin Luther King's; but Bobby's passing marked not only the end of my schooldays but also the beginning of a darker, less idealistic time. Having come of age in a decade breathless with nobility—the incredible courage of the Freedom Riders and other civil rights workers; the soaring rhetoric of the Kennedys and King—I entered the world of work bereft, heroless. A year later, I began my career as a political reporter. I have covered all or part of eight presidential campaigns since then. I tried to quit the business after the endless, depressing 2000 race, but—somewhat to my dismay, and very much to my family's—I was back on the trail four years later. When people ask why I keep coming back for more, I try to make a joke of it: "They don't have twelve-step programs for political junkies."

But that's not it, not entirely. There's also the memory of Robert Kennedy. Not that I expect to see another campaign as gracious, eloquent, and true as his brief flight. Kennedy's situation was unique. He had been liberated by suffering and family legacy. The personal doubts and rigorous internal moral colloquy that had burdened him throughout his life suddenly became a sword. He was able to take chances—to challenge his audiences and himself—in a way most politicians never would. A few weeks before his Martin Luther King speech, Kennedy confronted students at the University of Oklahoma about the unfairness of their military draft deferments; service, he told them, should be required of the educated and the uneducated alike. A week later, he was discussing heath care with doctors in Indiana and was asked who was going to pay for his health-care proposals. "You are," he replied. Indeed, there was a freshness, an unpredictability, often a naked emotional intimacy to Kennedy's transactions with the public—an intimacy that was more than the sum of the public grief, especially among the poor, for the gaping wound of his suffering; it also was about the visceral recognition, among the white working class, of Kennedy's innate toughness, of his effulgent Roman Catholicism, of his eleven children. It had to do with the fact that he was an aristocrat who had taken the trouble to understand and respect the exhausting routines and difficulties, the tragedies and occasional pleasures of everyday life. It was quite unique, the most **personal** presidential campaign I've ever witnessed.

Thirty-five years later, I still find myself hoping for Kennedy-like moments of spontaneity and courage from the politicians I trail after—moments when they deviate from their script and betray a real emotion. Moments when they tell their supporters an inconvenient truth, or force their detractors to think in a different way; moments when they stumble across a new and gorgeous locution, when they inspire a crowd without high-flown or overblown or pretested words. I've been lucky enough to experience a few such moments in each of the presidential campaigns I've covered, but they come less frequently now, almost always in the early primaries, when the crowds are sparse and human contact is unavoidable; practically never in a general-election campaign, when the entire nation is watching and any wisp of unscripted humanity—a gesture, a sigh (as Al Gore found out in 2000)—can prove disastrous. This is a book about that loss of spontaneity, and what it has cost us.

Listen to Kennedy's Indianapolis speech and there is a deep respect for the audience, which is not present in modern American politics. It isn't merely that he quotes Aeschylus to the destitute and uneducated, although that is remarkable enough. Kennedy's respect for the crowd is not only innate and scrupulous, it is also structural, born of technological innocence: he doesn't know who they are—not scientifically, the way postmodern politicians do. The audience hasn't been sliced and diced by his pollsters, their prejudices and policy priorities cross-tabbed, the turns of phrase most efficient to their ears focus-grouped. He hasn't been told what **not** to say to them. (Aeschylus would never survive a focus group.) The crowd has not been fragmented and objectified by all those numbers and data. They are not part of a demographic sliver to be courted in a certain way; nor is the candidate specifically aware of the words and issues he has to avoid in order not to alienate other such slivers. He knows certain things, to be sure: they are black, they are poor, they are aggrieved and quite possibly furious. But he doesn't know too much. He is therefore less constrained than subsequent generations of politicians, freer to share his extravagant humanity with them.

"I had a member of my family killed, but **he** was killed by a white man," he says. One of Kennedy's speechwriters—Walinsky or Mankiewicz—might have made it more direct: "My brother was killed by a white man, too." No doubt, the gratuitous "by a white man" would have been eliminated. But because of its diffidence and awkwardness, the line remains one of the most memorable and revealing of that speech. It sticks in the mind because it is so raw, so imperfect, so real.

"There's something about the sound of the genuine," the Reverend Jesse Jackson once told me. "You know it when you hear it. I remember once in South Carolina, way back when I was a kid, a singing group, the Five Blind Boys of Mississippi, came to our church. They had a tenor named Archie Brownlee with a really sweet voice. And before they sang that day Archie Brownlee said, 'This is my last tour through the South. And I hope you'll forgive me if there's a little liquor on my breath'—now this was in a church and so there was some rustling in the pews—'but I'm not using it for pleasure. I have the cancer and I need it to ease the pain . . . But don't worry about me, because I'm going cross the river. I hear there's a man on the other side who cures cancer and can make the blind to see.' Well, the place just went crazy. The power of a simple truth."

I asked Jackson who was the first politician to move him that way. "Well, the politicians were all white, and we couldn't vote," he said. "When Kennedy was getting elected in 1960, I was getting arrested for trying to integrate a library. But I do remember, some years later, I was coming out from the jail in Greenville and I heard Robert Kennedy's voice on the radio. He was talking about Birmingham. And I remember him saying, 'We will defeat segregation because we have the legal right and the moral right, and segregation is legally and morally wrong.' I'd never heard a white person say it so plainly, so powerfully. I've never forgotten it."

Compare that, if you will, with this:

All my life I have stood up for people who do the right thing and play by the rules.

Respect for the law, respect for others and respect for property: these values are at the heart of a successful society.

These are my values.

And they are the values of the forgotten majority—the hardworking men and women who make up the backbone of our country.

These families abide by the law, they take responsibility for themselves and they teach their children to respect others.

Like me, they are appalled that today too many

people who do the wrong thing are allowed to get away with it.

These words could have been uttered by . . . anyone. As it happens, they were written for Michael Howard, the leader of Britain's Conservative Party, for delivery on April 19, 2005, in the midst of his dismal campaign for prime minister—by which time they seemed hilariously banal. Why? Because they smack of the synthetic, market-tested language peddled by two generations of political consultants. Michael Howard's "forgotten majority" is an amalgam of Richard Nixon's "silent majority" and Bill Clinton's "forgotten middle class." It was Clinton, I think, who first spoke of "people who do the right thing and play by the rules." Words like "responsibility" and "respect" and "values" are beloved by focus groups everywhere. They may have been effective once, but they are easily spotted now—they are, in fact, rhetorical snooze buttons: clear signals that the politician speaking has absolutely nothing of interest to say. And they are what passes for political discourse on both sides of the Atlantic in the early twenty-first century.

There are perils to writing a book about the decline and trivialization of American politics. The good old days weren't so terrific, either. Political greatness has always been the exception to the rule. After a founding generation populated by geniuses, the majority of American presidents have been overmatched mediocrities. Happily, the greatest of leaders—Washington,

Lincoln, Franklin Roosevelt—rose to the occasion at the most crucial moments; indeed, it is inherent in our extremely conservative system of checks and balances that "greatness" is near impossible absent a crisis. In any case, eloquence and honor have rarely been the coin of the realm; bloviation and expediency were more like it. And while there has been nonstop bleating in recent years about how politics has gotten so much worse because of the vast sums of money and the smarmy influence of lobbyists, there have always been toads and rodents like Jack Abramoff—poster boy of the 2006 congressional scandal—eager to spread money about to morally retarded elected officials. Indeed, we have moved past the days of cash-on-the-barrelhead bribery; politicians solicit contributions mostly to fund the television advertising in their next campaign, not—with certain appalling exceptions—to aggrandize their lifestyles. Doubters should compare latter-day power brokering with the nineteenth-century Washington described in the wonderful novel **The Gilded Age**, by Mark Twain and Charles Dudley Warner.

The intellectual elite's pristine disdain for the tawdriness of politics and disgust with the egomania of politicians has been a running American theme since the early nineteenth century. A hundred years ago, Henry Adams dreaded the pure gust of testosterone that marked the arrival of Theodore Roosevelt, who often walked across Lafayette Park for dinner at the adjoining town houses of Adams and John Hay. The disdain has always been mutual, and politicians usually came up with the better names for their detractors: "mugwumps" in the late nineteenth century, "goo-goos" and "nattering nabobs of negativism" in the twentieth.

I don't know about you, but I've always found rogues more fun, and often more useful, than reformers. The efforts of reformers—especially their muddled attempts to cleanse and regulate the campaign-finance system—have resulted, as often as not, in unintended consequences that have made public life more perverse and corrupt. A vibrant democracy is a messy spectacle, dependent on grease, horse manure, and prestidigitation. Furthermore, and to lay all my cards on the table, I am a pro-peccadillo journalist. I want a president who has intimate, personal knowledge of human frailty, who has been humbled by what Woodrow Wilson once called his own "imperious passions," who has the wisdom that comes from failing, falling down, and getting up again. Consequently, I have usually taken the side of the fox and not the hounds in the post-Watergate run of scandalettes and circuses, regardless of partisan disposition—from Justice Clarence Thomas to President Bill Clinton, from Speaker Jim Wright to Speaker Newt Gingrich. These witch hunts threaten to drive everyone interesting, and anyone you'd want to have over for dinner, from our public life. This will not be a book proposing the sterilization of politics; quite the opposite, in fact. I abhor the prospect of government by goody-goodies.

Another problem with books lamenting the sad state of American public life is that they are mostly written by losers. That means they've tended to be written by Democrats in recent years, especially by academic sorts blind to the achievements of the conservative revolution led by Ronald Reagan (which is not to say Reagan was perfect, or even close, but he did get some very important things right). Inevitably, such books decry the shallowness of American public life because mainstream candidates refuse to talk about such high-minded, vegetarian notions as state-run health care and the imperialistic cruelty of the American empire. There are plenty of issues that have been insufficiently or stupidly discussed in recent years, but the covert thesis of this book is not that American politics has fallen on hard times because the last thirty-five years have been dominated by conservatives. Some of the finest moments I've witnessed in politics—the moments of passion and courage and conviction—were provided by Republicans.

But this book **is** a lament, nonetheless—and perhaps a bit of a screed, too. I am fed up with the insulting welter of sterilized speechifying, insipid photo ops, and idiotic advertising that passes for public discourse these days. I believe that American politics has become overly cautious, cynical, mechanistic, and bland; and I fear that the inanity and ugliness of postmodern public life has caused many Americans to lose the habits of citizenship. This lack of interest may have been understandable during the half century of unprecedented

prosperity that followed World War II, although public lassitude **was** briefly replaced by passionate involve-
ment during the civil rights movement and the war in
Vietnam: Robert Kennedy's time. But lassitude is not
an option now. Big changes are afoot—the economic
changes wrought by globalization, the demographic
changes made possible by miraculous medical develop-
ments, the probability of a long-term, slow-burning
war against Islamist extremism—and big decisions have
to be made about the nation's future. In order to make
the right decisions, we are going to need citizens who
see politics as something more than a distant cloud
marring the eternal sunshine of the American day.

A final caveat: this book should be regarded as a sub-
jective and somewhat quirky tour of the battlefield, a
compendium of my prejudices, a reflection of the things
I've seen and learned over the past thirty-five years. It is
a book about the aesthetics, not the mechanics, of politics. It is not meant to be comprehensive—although
someone should haul off and write a full-fledged history of politics in the television age.

"Television," Adam Walinsky said many years after
his apprenticeship with Robert Kennedy, "has ruined
every single thing it has touched." There was some
puckishness to this—he was talking about professional
basketball, if I remember correctly—but Walinsky is a
serious man, an Old Testament prophet given to brilliant diatribes about the slovenliness of modern life,

and he wasn't really joking. Yes, yes, television has been a wondrous thing. Vast numbers of people now watch presidential debates, State of the Union messages, prime-time press conferences, not to mention terrorist attacks, hurricanes, assassinations, and wars in real time (and dedicated nerds like me can watch the proceedings of Congress, or presidential hopefuls on the stump, on C-SPAN).

But television also set off a chain reaction that transformed the very nature of politics. Suddenly, a politician's ability to perform in public became his or her most important asset (Abe Lincoln's screechy voice, it is commonly said, just wouldn't fly nowadays). Suddenly, politicians were able to use televised advertising to communicate in a more powerful and intimate (and negative) way than ever before—and suddenly politicians had to raise vast sums of money to pay for those ads. The hours they had spent studying issues, chatting with colleagues, or napping in the past were now devoted to working the phones and trolling for dollars. The need for money empowered the special interests of left and right: they provided the bulk of campaign contributions and campaign workers. An enormous special-interest industry seemed to sprout instantaneously in Washington, starting in the late 1960s— lobbyists and researchers and fund-raisers for corporate America, labor unions, environmentalists, abortion advocates or opponents, you name it. In presidential election years where no great issues were at stake—1984,

1988, 1996, and 2000, for example—politics almost seemed to be the special interests' private game.

At the same time, the secret ceremonies of politics were no longer viable: 1968 was the last year that the Democratic Party chose a candidate, Hubert Humphrey, who hadn't captured the nomination by winning the most delegates in the primaries. Television demanded transparency and the rules of presidential politics were changed. The voters took control, selecting the candidates in a maddening chaos of state-by-state campaigns. By 1976, the process had been turned upside down: a politician most Americans had never heard of—Governor Jimmy Carter of Georgia—won the nomination to the bemusement of the Democratic Party's leaders (and Ronald Reagan nearly unseated the sitting Republican president, Gerald Ford). Presidential politics was now a matter of self-promotion rather than smoke-filled selection by political experts. Over time, journalists found convenient, and often foolish, ways to quantify the anarchy: money raised, standing in the polls, endorsements. These, rather than a sober assessment of character and leadership ability, became the yardsticks for presidential plausibility.

Gradually, the languorous, and often bipartisan, deliberation that marked the discussion of serious issues in Washington slipped into history as well. Partisanship—the more fervent, the better—became the easiest way to gain the attention of the media and the support of the special interests, and thereby the

money necessary to get reelected. Those who were reluctant to play this game, moderates mostly, either
were defeated by better-funded fanatics or saw the
handwriting on the wall and left Congress voluntarily.
A new generation of TV politicians—the Republican
congressman Newt Gingrich was a brilliant pioneer—
displayed electronic impatience with the dainty traditions and glacial pace of the legislative process. They
were soon joined by a new class of journalists and para-
journalists—that is, people whose main function was
not to report but to perform—whose bilious on-air
patter required immediate, simplistic answers to complicated questions . . . if complicated questions were
discussed at all. More often, serious stuff was avoided
and journo-performers were rewarded for their ability
to construct clever lines about the prurient political
trivia of the moment. A generation of Americans came
to believe that political discourse consisted mostly of
rabid hyperbole: Rush Limbaugh ridiculing Bill Clinton, Michael Moore ridiculing George W. Bush, frothing packs of journalists screaming questions at evasive
or discursive officials, or yelling at each other on **The
McLaughlin Group**, **The Capital Gang**, or **Crossfire**.

"Can you imagine sending Lincoln out with the
Gettysburg Address in this atmosphere?" the Republican consultant Mike Murphy once mused to me. "My
biggest worry would be: What sound bite would you
get on the evening news? And whatever you got, it
would be immediately subsumed by some blowhard
reporter saying, 'Lincoln campaign insiders said the

speech was an attempt to win support from veterans groups and a test of a new, shorter speaking format.' Why should any politician even try for eloquence in those circumstances?"

Most politicians tend to be cautious, straitlaced people. Confronted by the raging television torrent, by the strange new theatrics of public performance which transformed every last word or handshake into a potentially career-threatening experience, they sought creative help to navigate the waters. And so, the pollster-consultant industrial complex was born.

Politicians had been communing with advertising and public relations specialists for decades. According to Sidney Blumenthal—whose 1980 book, **The Permanent Campaign**, was one of the first to describe the impact of consultants on politics—"the first overt act initiated by a media adviser for a President" was a pancake breakfast with vaudevillians that the public relations specialist Edward Bernays arranged to make the dour Calvin Coolidge seem more human. The **New York Times** headline: ACTORS EAT CAKES WITH THE COOLIDGES . . . PRESIDENT NEARLY LAUGHS. By the 1950s, politicians were routinely hiring advertising experts to make their TV and radio ads, and pollsters to tell them how the race was going. But these were peripheral advisers; they didn't run the campaigns. "The relationship was much different from what it later became," the pollster Peter Hart told me. "When Lou Harris was polling for John F. Kennedy, he once said, 'Here are the numbers. Let me tell you what they mean.' And Kennedy replied, 'Just give me the numbers. I'll figure them out for myself.' "

Robert Kennedy had Lou Harris, too, and he also had people to make his television ads. But the campaign was run by his staff and a core group of longtime family retainers like Ken O'Donnell, Ted Sorensen, Larry O'Brien. In a way, Kennedy's candidacy was every bit as old-fashioned as that of his establishment rival, Vice President Hubert Humphrey. Eugene Mc-Carthy's coalition of college students, women, academics, white-collar professionals (especially lawyers), teachers, and other public employees was a harbinger of the new, post–New Deal Democratic Party that would stagger through the next thirty-five years.

But it was Richard Nixon who really represented the future in 1968. He ran a campaign rife with consultants who had greater power than in any previous presidential candidacy. They "rebranded" him—to use a later, loathsome marketing term—as the "New Nixon," a supposedly more amenable edition of the mingy, petulant Nixon who'd lost to Kennedy in 1960 and to Pat Brown for governor of California in 1962. After the latter race, Nixon had undressed himself memorably in a press conference: "You won't have Nixon to kick around anymore." Unscripted moments of that sort would have to be controlled in 1968. Equally important for the long-term interests of his party, the Nixon campaign intended to move the Republicans downmarket from their Wall Street/Main Street business base into more fertile demographic fields, making a coded racial appeal to working-class whites, especially in the South. An angry populist third-party candidate, George C. Wallace of Alabama, would win the Confederacy in 1968, but Nixon began the tectonic shift of the South from fervently Democratic to fervently Republican (apparently, Southerners don't do tepid)—a landmark political transformation caused, at bottom, by the Democratic Party's honorable decision to support the civil rights legislation that desegregated the region. The Democrats have been swimming upstream ever since, which has probably made them more dependent on the consulting industry than the Republicans. Their attempts to communicate with voters—with the exception of an occasional public genius like Bill Clinton—have been less comfortable, more opaque, more tortured.

Actually, Nixon's 1968 campaign seems quaint and relatively honorable now. Joe McGinniss's groundbreaking book **The Selling of the President, 1968** begins with a scene meant to be shocking (and it was, at the time): Richard Nixon sitting in a New York television studio, filming television ads, repeating the same words—more or less—over and over. McGinniss's intent is to convey the robotic vacuity of the New Nixon. He quotes from Daniel Boorstin's book **The Image**: "The qualities which now commonly make a man or woman into a 'nationally advertised' brand are in fact a new category of human emptiness."

But the scene in the television studio looks different thirty-five years later. The reason why Nixon is repeating the words over and over is because they're **his own words**. To the dismay of his handlers, he's not reading from a script. "I wish he'd use a TelePrompTer," says Harry Treleaven, one of his media advisers.

"That's been bugging me for a year," replies another hired gun, Al Scott. "People think he's reading, anyway."

Nixon insists, however, on what would soon become an entirely radical concept in the world of politics: inventing his own words. In fact, toward the end of the session he decides to try a completely unplanned ad, a local spot discussing the New York City teachers' strike and the teachers' right to impose discipline in the classroom. His handlers hate the idea, but Nixon riffs it, off the top of his head—and impressively so: the words are coherent and on message, if looser than a professional might have written them. "Yep, this hits it right on the nose," Nixon says afterward, Nixonially. "It's all about law and order, and the damn Negro–Puerto Rican groups out there."

The other memorable scenes from **The Selling of the President, 1968** concerned the staging of Nixon's town meetings, which were choreographed by a young television producer named Roger Ailes, who would invent the Fox News Channel thirty years later. Ailes packed the town-meeting audiences with Nixon supporters. This soon became standard operating procedure for Republicans. The 2004 George W. Bush campaign made some news by kicking out people who tried to attend the president's fake public question-

and-answer sessions without the prior approval of local party officials.

Nixon's 1968 town meetings were far more compelling than Bush's 2004 charades, though. Ailes insisted that Nixon face panels of hostile questioners—it made for better television. After staging a particularly raucous joust between Nixon and an anti–Vietnam War interrogator in Philadelphia, Ailes told McGinniss, "Boy, is [Nixon] going to be pissed. He'll think we really tried to screw him. But critically, it was the best show we've done."

Nixon had been awkward and—this almost seems impossible, given his public formality—near human during the confrontation. At one point, the hostile questioner asks the candidate why he won't appear on **Meet the Press**. "I've done those quiz shows, Mr. McKinney. I've done them until they were running out of my ears." Nixon, it seemed to McGinniss, was skating the edge, very close to losing his temper. Ailes loved it: Nixon was strong, pummeling a nitpicking peacenik. "This is the beginning of a whole new concept," Ailes later said. "This is it. This is the way they'll be elected forevermore. The next guys up will have to be performers."

Ailes was right, of course, about the need for politicians to be performers in the future. But the messy emotions he coaxed from Nixon would soon be bleached from the process: unscheduled—un-market-tested—humanity would be deemed too risky. In the future, almost all performances would be staged.

. . .

Some of my best friends are consultants. They tend to be the most entertaining people in the political community: eccentric, fanatic, creative, violently verbal, often extremely funny—the sort of people who sat in the back of the room in high school and tossed spitballs at the future politicians sitting up front. But their impact on politics has been perverse. Rather than make the game more interesting, they have drained a good deal of the life from our democracy. They have become specialists in caution, literal reactionaries—they react to the results of their polling and focus groups, they fear anything they haven't tested.

In early 2003, I had dinner with several of the consultants who had advised Al Gore in the 2000 presidential campaign. I asked them why Gore, a passionate environmentalist, had spent so little time and energy talking about the environment during the campaign.

Because we told him not to, the consultants said. Why? I asked. Because it wasn't going to help him win. "He wanted to talk about the environment," said Tad Devine, a partner in the firm of Shrum, Devine and Donilon, "and I said to him, 'Look, you can do that, but you're not going to win a single electoral vote more than you now have. If you want to win Michigan and western Pennsylvania, here are the issues that really matter—this is what you should talk about.' "

Gore won Michigan and Pennsylvania, but lost an election he should have won—and he lost it on intangibles, on qualities that it was difficult to quantify. He lost it because he seemed stiff, phony, and uncomfortable in public. The stiffness was, in effect, a campaign strategy: every last word he uttered had been market-tested in advance. I asked Devine if he'd ever considered the possibility that Gore might have been a warmer, more credible and inspiring candidate if he'd been able to talk about the things, like the environment, that he'd really wanted to talk about.

"That's an interesting thought," Devine said.

Bob Shrum, who was Devine's partner and one of the very best speechwriters in the Democratic Party, once told me about the quality that made Harry Truman a memorable speaker even though he lacked Franklin Roosevelt's confidence, John F. Kennedy's eloquence, and Ronald Reagan's dramatic modulations. "He never sang, but goddamnit his off-keyness touched people," Shrum said. "For example, in the midst of his acceptance speech at the 1948 convention, as he's challenging the 'do nothing' Republican Congress, he says that he's going to call them back to Washington on 'the 26th of July, which out in Missouri we call Turnip Day.' " Shrum paused, and shook his head in admiration, "Turnip Day!"

Actually, Truman was a day off. The old Missouri adage was, "On the 25th of July, sow your turnips wet or dry." But then, Harry Truman was **riffing**! He was working without a text. He was accepting the nomination of his party, one of the most hallowed moments in the life of any politician, without a prepared speech.

He had decided to speak from the heart at, arguably, the most desperate moment in his political career. His stand-in presidency, after the death of the beloved Franklin Roosevelt, was considered a complete failure. His Republican opponent, Governor Thomas Dewey of New York, was the front-runner; his Democratic base was shattered by the candidacy of Henry Wallace on the left and Strom Thurmond's Dixiecrats on the right. The Democratic convention had been dull and dispirited, and he was to deliver his speech well past midnight. "Considering the time, the fatigue of the crowd, it was a scene made for failure," Truman's biographer David McCullough wrote. "Any radio or television audience that Truman might have hoped for was long since asleep." And then McCullough continues:

> He advanced to the microphones, his natty white suit gleaming now in the full glare of the lights . . . Wasting no time with pleasantries or grand phrases, his head up as he spoke without a script, his voice strong, hands chopping the air, he brought the convention immediately to its feet cheering.
>
> "Senator Barkley and I will win this election and make these Republicans like it—don't you forget that." Not until this moment had anyone used the word "win" as though he meant it . . .
>
> For the first time since 1945 he was speaking not as a leader by accident, by inheritance, but by the choice of his party. He was neither humble nor elegant nor lofty . . . He was cracker-barrel plain,

using words like "rotten" (for the Republican tax bill) and "poppycock" (for the Republican platform promise to increase Social Security benefits) . . . It was exactly in the spirit of the vehement backcountry politics that he loved, and where he knew he belonged . . .

The Turnip Day moment was the climax of the speech. He was calling the Republicans' bluff.

On the 26th of July, which out in Missouri we call Turnip Day, I am going to call Congress back and ask them to pass laws to halt rising prices, to meet the housing crisis—which they say they are for in their platform . . . I shall ask them to act upon . . . aid to education, which they say they are for . . . civil rights legislation, which they say they are for . . .

Truman's support for civil rights legislation was particularly courageous. It was the reason why the solid, Southern wing of the Democratic Party was splitting off to support Thurmond's segregationist candidacy. "The cheering and stomping in the hall was so great he had to shout to be heard," McCullough writes. And then the conclusion:

Now, my friends, if there is any reality behind the Republican platform, we ought to get some action from a short session of the 80th Congress. They

can do this job in 15 days, if they want to do it.
They will still have time to go out and run for
office.

After the speech, the president demonstrated for reporters how he had sowed his turnips as a boy, with a
broad sweep of the arm: "A half-pound of seed sows
a couple of acres of turnips," he told them. In the
process, Truman was able to remind the voters who he
was—an average guy, a man of the soil, who was plainspoken often to a fault. The mention of Turnip Day
was a throwaway, a tiny gesture, perhaps an unwitting
one, a small seed of humanity planted in the public
mind—but the seed blossomed into the "Give 'em
Hell, Harry" persona that won one of the greatest up-
sets in American presidential history that November.
"He walked out there," recalled Clark Clifford, Truman's closest adviser, as quoted by McCullough, "and
reached down within himself, found the strength and
the inspiration to make that fiery speech which was
necessary to put him over."

Bob Shrum understands the music of oratory as well as
anyone I've met in politics. He knows that awkward,
seemingly extraneous touches like "Turnip Day" have
great subliminal power. And yet he has spent much
of his adult life smoothing out the rhetoric of the
politicians he works for, taking out the bumps and
spontaneity, and in his latter years as a professional

consultant—long after he left Ted Kennedy's staff—eliminating the risky ideas . . . and, in the process, dulling the passion of politics.

But thanks, Bob, for Turnip Day: it offers a handle on the ineffable. For the purposes of this book, it will represent all those tiny and not so tiny things—not just the intermittent bolts of unmassaged oratory but also the spontaneous moments of honor and cowardice, the gestures, the body language, the smirks and sighs—that give us real insight into those who would lead us. It encompasses Bobby Kennedy quoting Aeschylus and Richard Nixon saying that we won't have him to kick around anymore. In **The Reasoning Voter**, the political scientist and sometime pollster Samuel Popkin argues that these intangibles, which he calls "low-information signaling," are what many civilians use to make up their minds about politicians. A truckload of academic studies have proven that voters have only a vague sense of the issues; they don't sweat the big stuff. But they do have fierce antennae for phoniness. They sense courage, they honor principle, they love humor and common sense.

If you're going to ask them to make a sacrifice—to pay higher taxes, to go to war—you'd best have your act together. If you're going to lead, you'd best be willing to show them something of yourself, something that hasn't been pureed by pollsters. If you want them to take a risk, you're going to have to take one yourself. Sadly, most politicians are neither risk-takers nor leaders. They are followers—of convention, of public opinion—and while leadership is an art, followship has become a science, measured in polls and focus groups.

Turnip Day is an appropriately inelegant shorthand for everything I love about politics. It represents a good deal of what we have lost—and a quality of humanity that I hope we can recover.

1

The Burden of Southern History

★ ★ ★ ★

As Robert Kennedy campaigned through Indiana in the days after Martin Luther King was killed, a precocious and passing-strange high-school senior named Patrick H. Caddell was going door-to-door in the working-class neighborhood of north Jacksonville, Florida, asking the residents about their presidential preferences for a poll that he had devised as a class project. There was a lot of support for Alabama governor George C. Wallace, which was no surprise: north Jacksonville was deep, deep South, pickup-truck-with-a-gunrack country. But Caddell was stunned by the number of people who said they supported Robert Kennedy or "Wallace or Kennedy, either one."

Caddell had no precise sense of what pollsters did—what sort of questions they asked or, more important, didn't bother to ask (in fact, very few people did at that point)—and so he invented his own rules as he went along, asking open-ended questions, having conversations really, digging deeper, probing the nuance and intensity of the responses. **Why** did they support Wallace? Was it because he had supported "segregation forever" in Alabama? And what was it about Kennedy that they liked? And what on earth did they think Wallace and Kennedy—who had battled each other, famously, over the admission of black students to the University of Alabama, and who now were taking opposite sides on Vietnam—had in common? The answers came in blunt, simple sentences:

"They're tough guys."

"They protect the little guy."

"You can believe 'em."

Hmmm. Caddell began to understand that there was more to the Wallace phenomenon than racism—although there was certainly plenty of that. Wallace voters also were classic, gutbucket Southern populists, angry at the bureaucrats and stuffed shirts and big corporate guys and the intellectual elites who ran the show. "But, you know," Caddell told me years later, "the thing that really blew me away in north Jacksonville was when I'd ask them about the war. They didn't see themselves as hawks or doves. They weren't part of the elite conversation that was taking place in the media. It was **their** kids who were over in Vietnam bleeding to death. And so it was, 'Stop this horseshit! Either go all out and win the damn thing, or get out and bring the boys home.' It was mind-blowing, and it made perfect sense. The people who were polling the war had it all wrong. 'Are you in favor or are you op-posed' just wasn't the right question."

And so, even before he had graduated from high school, Pat Caddell had begun his quest: to find a way to speak to those alienated Southern populists, to lure them back to the Democratic Party despite their essen-tial cultural conservatism. This would also become a central question in the life of the Democratic Party, which began to experience a deep electoral swoon as it was abandoned by middle-class white voters, first in the South in the 1960s, then across the country in the 1980s. Furthermore, Caddell had intuitively grasped an aesthetic truth about the sampling of public opin-ion: "It is not a scientific process," he told me thirty-seven years after he had first walked the north Jacksonville precinct. Poll results were not to be taken literally; they were to be read—and there could be a va-riety of readings. "I could get a fucking monkey to draw a sample. But that's the end of the science," he said, referring to the statistical models used to approx-imate the demographic composition of the public. "The rest is . . . is . . . I mean, it's a crude tool. You're trying to apply a linear measurement to something nonlinear: how people think, their emotions, the whole thing."

Crude or not, it was a powerful tool—almost magic. And fun, an incredible parlor trick. On election night in 1968, Caddell had entertained the local political crowd by sitting in the Duval County courthouse with a big old adding machine, cranking in the data precinct by precinct, and announcing—in advance of the final tallies—who had won. A crowd of candidates who were looking for the latest results gathered around him as he peremptorily delivered thumbs-up and -down: "You're in," he told one Democrat. "You just carried the most Republican precinct in town." Every one of Caddell's projections turned out right that night ("Some within half a percentage point!" he later said), and the story about the high-school kid with the political magic show spread quickly. The local newspaper featured Caddell a few days later: "Meet Mr. Prediction."

Mr. Prediction was soon hired by a local politician named Fred Schultz, who was about to become Speaker of the Florida House of Representatives; within the year, Caddell—who pretty much took up residence in Schultz's home—was summoned to Tallahassee where he solved a major political dispute by concocting a redistricting plan for Duval County that somehow satisfied both Republicans and Democrats. Then he was hired by the local **Washington Post**-owned television station to poll a special referendum held to determine whether Jacksonville and its surrounding communities would combine as one governmental unit. "The station sent me up to New York to have Lou Harris check me out and see if I knew what I was doing," Caddell recalled. "He said yeah, I was doing fine."

Caddell pretty much looked the part of a wizard— especially a few years later when a lightning bolt of white hair prematurely struck his goatee and completed his thunderous visage: dark hair, dark lowering brows over dark eyes, a hawklike nose, a splutter of words, a thermonuclear temper. He crackled with static jitters; he seemed to exist in a perpetual state of self-electrocution. The brilliance was manifest, though, the thoughts and ideas torrential. He seemed old for his age—his wisdom was well beyond his years—but there was a stubborn puerility as well: the lack of social experience that came with being a classic outsider, a nomad, the son of a Coast Guard officer who moved from base to base along the East Coast. Caddell seemed, in fact, just barely civilized—sloppy, rude, forgetful, tempestous. It was as if he had been raised by wolves. Idealistic wolves: he was ferociously in favor of the civil rights movement, ferociously opposed to the war in Vietnam. He loved baseball statistics—he didn't know much about the game or the players, but he loved the stats—and he had loved politics ever since he and his mother had made pilgrimages to the PX at Otis Air Force Base on Cape Cod where they would occasionally see John F. Kennedy landing in Air Force One. And so it seemed natural, when confronted with the need to do a senior math project, that he combine his two loves—stats and politics—and do a project on polling. He convinced his classmates to go door-to-door with him on weekends (within the year, he was paying them $20 for their services).

On to Harvard. By late 1969, the middle of sophomore year, Caddell had his own polling firm—started with two classmates, John Gorman and Daniel Porter, and funded by a $25,000 loan from Fred Schultz—

with clients in Ohio and Florida. "Pat was taking a seminar with Helen Keyes, who had been treasurer of the 1960 John F. Kennedy presidential campaign," Gorman recalled, years later. "The course was an excuse for Keyes to bring a lot of her old pals to Harvard, to gossip about politics. John Gilligan, who was running for governor of Ohio, spoke to the class and afterward Pat starting telling him about the sort of stuff he had done in Florida. Gilligan decided to hire us—as did John Glenn, who was running for the Senate from Ohio that year."

Caddell's talent wasn't statistical. Gorman and Porter did all the number crunching and regression analysis—usually late at night when they could get access to Harvard's Aiken Computer Laboratory. ("The Gilligan polling took three hours to process," said Gorman. "Nowadays it would take three seconds.") Caddell's real expertise was in sales, in political strategy, and in the front end of polling: figuring out which questions to ask and how to ask them. Over the next eight years, he would be the front man for Cambridge Survey Research, while Gorman served as the designated adult, managing the company and riding herd on Caddell. (Porter—universally described as "the sane one" and the most natural politician of the three—was murdered, along with his girlfriend, on a camping trip in 1973.)

A good deal of Caddell's intellectual energy early on was devoted to finding new ways to burrow beneath the apparent apathy of middle-class Americans. He would not take "undecided" or "no opinion" for an answer—he needed to know exactly who the undecideds were, how wealthy they were, how much education they'd had, their marital status, race, religion. He was curious about the intensity of their feelings and the general quality of their moods. He liked to use the "ladder" methodology: Is this year better or worse than last year for your family? Are you optimistic or pessimistic about the future? He used a seven-point scale to measure intensity ("On a scale of one to seven, with seven being the highest, how do you feel about . . ."). Working for Westinghouse Corporation on a study of attitudes toward nuclear power in California, he and Gorman were able to figure out, for example, that while black women were opposed to nuclear power, they felt more intensely about the need for cheaper energy—an angle that proved the best way to change their opinion.

But Caddell's real innovation was a newly aggressive type of questioning, designed not only to test existing attitudes but also to figure out ways to change them. He would test different versions of the precise wording that a candidate might use. On abortion, for example, the winner was: "Abortion is a decision of a woman, her clergyman, and her doctor." In essence, Caddell helped transform the nature of polling from the mere reporting of public opinion into an active, strategic weapon. His purposes were evangelical, not scientific:

he was probing for new ways to frame the debate and, ultimately, to move his beloved "alienated" voters back to the Democratic Party.

While George Gallup had been conducting public opinion surveys since the 1930s, and a handful of others—Louis Harris, Oliver Quayle—had done national polling on presidential preferences and broad questions like the popularity of the war in Vietnam, the sort of intensive local, and highly partisan, polling that Caddell offered candidates like John Gilligan and John Glenn (and Fred Schultz, who was running for the Senate from Florida) was practically unknown in 1970. "Most of our clients, even in 1972, had never done a poll—and these were statewide candidates, for senator and governor," Gorman recalled. Caddell and Gorman were not alone, of course. The Republicans Bob Teeter, Richard Wirthlin, and John Deardourff were testing new methods as well. "I was working with Deardourff in New Jersey in the 1960s, and we were asking those same sort of probing, predictive questions," recalls Andrew Kohut, who later became the director of the Pew Research Center, "but Caddell was the first to really take this stuff to the national level, to a presidential campaign."

As it happened, Mr. Prediction reached the pinnacle of his profession before he graduated from college. He was polling for George McGovern's presidential campaign, hanging out with celebrities, and blowing away everyone he met with a gale-force spew of data and ideas. "He was a rock star," recalls Dotty Lynch, a young political researcher for NBC who was introduced to Caddell in the spring of 1972 by McGovern campaign manager Gary Hart. "Gary said I had to meet this guy—and so I go to dinner, and there's Pat, sitting with Warren Beatty and Shirley MacLaine, holding forth. Gary clearly thought he was a genius." And more, Caddell seemed the embodiment of the idealistic college kids who were running McGovern's guerrilla campaign in New Hampshire and around the country—the veterans of the antiwar and civil rights campaigns, the first wave of the demographically enormous generation born after World War II, the baby boomers, to get involved in politics. It was absolutely clear to Hart—a matter of faith, not even worth debating—that these kids were going to change the world. (As one of those kids, I can say that it was absolutely clear to us, too.) They certainly were changing the Democratic Party: McGovern was the first nominee in history not chosen by the party's leaders.*

Caddell was also telling the McGovern advisers something that they were desperate to hear: that the

---

*John Kennedy probably wouldn't have been chosen by the Democratic Party leaders, either, were it not for his performance in the Wisconsin and West Virginia primaries—but in 1960, primaries were only glorified straw polls; most of the delegates at party conventions were held by leaders like Chicago's Richard Daley, who could be swayed by primary results—or not, if they chose. After the riots at the 1968 Democratic National Convention, the party decided to put the delegate-selection process in the hands of primary and caucus voters; the Republicans followed suit in 1976.

senator's appeal wasn't merely to the college-educated elites, that he also could move working-class folks. Indeed, the morning after McGovern shocked the world by winning the New Hampshire primary, Caddell called a press conference at the Queen City Motor Inn in Manchester to explain the miracle. "It was, shall we say, a **selective** briefing," Gorman would recall. "McGovern **had** cut into Ed Muskie's strength in some working-class districts but the truth is, he won New Hampshire because of the support he got from middle-class white women. But then, the actual data were never so important to Pat as Pat's reading of the data."

Gorman was being snippy but, in the end, Caddell agreed with him. "The data was a prop," he would later say. "I **surfed** the data." In the New Hampshire primary, Caddell was more excited by a possibility—that McGovern could attract working-class voters—than the already proved reality that McGovern was popular among peaceable women. Evangelism, as always with Caddell, trumped science.

Gorman was beginning to understand that he and his partner were very different breeds of political cats. Gorman came from Illinois and was steeped in traditional "Chicago school" politics. The game was about concrete issues: who gets what, who pays for it—solid stuff like taxing the rich and employing the poor. The basic political question was "Where's mine?" Caddell was something new under the sun—a political Freudian, or maybe Jungian, or something like that—a luftmensch, a man of the air rather than of the pavement.

For Caddell, politics was all about moods and symbols, about manipulating emotions and changing attitudes. It was about **feelings** rather than "where's mine?" Gorman kept trying to pin Caddell down on alienation—define it, quantify it, come up with a typology. "Was someone who was alienated because he hated racial preferences for blacks in the same category as someone who was alienated because he hated the military-industrial complex?" Gorman wondered. "It was something Pat and I argued about throughout the 1970s, until we stopped talking to each other."

Gorman, embittered by his eventual split with Caddell, was being slightly unfair here: by the 1976 Florida primary—in which Jimmy Carter confronted George Wallace on Caddell's home ground—Caddell had sliced and diced and segmented the Wallace vote to a fare-thee-well.

Pat Caddell would later spread the story, and perhaps believe, that it was love at first sight between him and Jimmy Carter, the candidate who seemed his fantasy come to life: the liberal Southerner who could win the confidence of Wallace voters. The truth was, Cambridge Survey Research was involved in an elaborate mating ritual with several candidates—the liberal Morris Udall, the Kennedy heir Sargent Shriver, Carter, perhaps others—keeping its options open, waiting to see who would pop the question. Carter had come to Caddell through the side door—through a sister firm,

Cambridge Reports, which was established in 1973 to handle corporate clients. ("We suddenly realized they didn't have elections every year," Gorman recalled.) The firm was approached by Carter associates Bert Lance and Charles Kirbo, allegedly on behalf of Lance's Calhoun National Bank. But the bank was fronting for the Carter campaign, and the job was a full-scale investigation of Carter's viability as a presidential candidate.

Jimmy Carter—peanut farmer, Annapolis graduate, naval engineer, governor of Georgia, born-again Christian—had eyes the color of an aquamarine swimming pool at noon in July and a great, down-home, one-on-one sell. He spoke softly. He was humble. He came from Plains, Georgia. He taught Sunday school (and still does). "I went down there and we spent a night talking," Caddell recalled. "And you know what we talked about? We didn't talk about numbers and stuff. We didn't talk about issues. We talked about . . . the country."

Caddell, apparently, did a fair amount of the talking. He had been thinking a lot about the country. While Gorman and Porter had been taking statistics courses, Caddell had fallen in love with Southern history. He was especially struck by C. Van Woodward's elegant essay "The Burden of Southern History," which argued that the South was different from the rest of the nation because it was the only part of the United States that had lost a war. The sense of loss made Southerners more nostalgic, more romantic, less optimistic than other Americans. And now—in 1975—the rest of the country was catching up to the South. Vietnam and Watergate had changed America in ways that were only beginning to be understood. Previously, the nation's defining characteristic had been optimism: America was the one country in the world where a majority of people always believed next year would be better. But that changed abruptly in the mid-1970s. For the first time, nonpolitical, trend-oriented pollsters like Daniel Yankelovich were finding that more Americans were pessimistic than optimistic. Nostalgia became a craze. (I wrote a piece for **Rolling Stone** about a man named Jim Matson who had created the first corporate granola, Heartland Natural Cereal, and packaged it—the genius was all in the packaging—as a nostalgia item, in a sepia-toned box.)

Caddell had learned a lot from David Garth, the brilliant, combative New York political consultant who had figured out how to sell the aristocratic John V. Lindsay as mayor of New York to the Yankee equivalent of rednecks: the brusque, tough-talking, blue-collar ethnics residing in the city's outer boroughs. "Garth told me that all the national myths had been shattered," Caddell recalled. "You know, America always fights just wars and always wins the wars it chooses to fight. And presidents might not always be so swift, but they're always honest. They always try to do the right thing. And you know, all of those beliefs—those core American beliefs—had just been chucked out the fucking window. I was running around saying the country was falling apart and everyone thought I was crazy."

But not Jimmy Carter.

"He had it," Caddell recalled. "He had spent a year living in people's homes in Iowa and New Hampshire, and he understood what was going on—the need for healing, the damage that the war and Watergate had done. We didn't talk numbers or issues. We talked about **themes**. It was all about the culture. It was all about the land. The need for honesty and trust. People up at Harvard—all the people I knew—made fun of this Southern guy going around the country saying things like, 'I'll never lie to you . . .' But by the spring of 1976, he was the finest-tuned candidate in history because he'd been living it."

But also, in part, because he was receiving the finest-tuned polling in history.

The mid-1970s saw a revolution in public opinion sampling. The most important breakthough, by far, was that pollsters discovered the telephone. They no longer had to pay women—and poll-takers were mostly women—to go door-to-door. Phone interviews were, of necessity, shorter; at most twenty-five minutes, as opposed to forty-five minutes the old-fashioned way. They were also much cheaper. "We were still going door-to-door in 1976," Gorman recalled. "In fact, we had a room full of maps. We had every block in the United States, so we could copy a map and send it out to a poll-taker in the field, anywhere in the country. But we were also doing nightly telephone tracking polls"—these were brief interviews, seven minutes long, using smaller groups of respondents, designed to pick up gross movements in the horse race. "The amount of data was staggering," Gorman continued. "We had a truck and every evening we'd fill it with boxes of computer cards, send it out to the computer center in Waltham, and get the results the next morning."

As telephone polling supplanted door-to-door interviews, pollsters began to miss the qualitative information that could only be gleaned from an extended, face-to-face encounter, and so the use of "focus groups" was borrowed from the world of advertising. These were small, carefully selected groups of people—no more than fifteen or twenty—who would be paid to sit around a table and respond to questions. There were perils here if the group wasn't conducted with a fair amount of sophistication. People who were willing to sit for several hours munching chocolate-chip cookies, allowing themselves to be probed by professionals, were, by definition, atypical: they were talkers, less private than most voters (and less busy, too, one imagines). And then there was the notion—often mistakenly referred to as the Heisenberg uncertainty principle—that observation changes the nature of any phenomenon. The focus groupers were not just sitting around the kitchen table having a chat, they were **performing**. They were, therefore, reluctant to seem mean-spirited or prejudiced in front of people they didn't know. There was the tendency to become a civics class—please, please stop all the negative advertising, the focus groupers would plead. Please talk more about the issues. We are dying to hear every last detail of your health-care plan. (Of course, the negative ads were, inevitably, what people remembered best.)

But there was real value to focus groups, especially early on while the concept was still fresh. You could show people things in focus groups—ads, logos, speeches, your opponent's ads—and see how they'd respond. Sometimes the civilians inadvertantly divulged real insights. One of the very first focus groups Caddell and Gorman did was of working-class voters in Pittsburgh in the spring of 1976. They showed a video of Carter's standard stump speech, and then asked the group what it thought. "There was a lot of support from people who were opposed to forced busing [to achieve school integration]," Gorman recalled. That was mystifying: Carter was **in favor** of busing. He had said so in the speech. But the focus group refused to believe it. "They said, 'He's a Southern governor. He's really opposed to busing. He's just saying that now to get black votes,'" Gorman recalled.

Actually, the focus group was essentially correct. In the Florida primary, Carter was using his position on busing as a wedge issue to secure the black vote—both his main opponents, Wallace and Washington senator Henry "Scoop" Jackson, were opposed to busing. As for the white vote, Carter's Georgia ad man, Gerald Rafshoon, had come up with a brilliant idea based on Caddell's polling. In 1968, Wallace's slogan had been "Send Them a Message." But Caddell knew there was a wellspring of regional pride to be tapped. The folks in north Jacksonville knew that Wallace was a protest vote (especially in 1976, after he had been crippled in an assassination attempt), and they knew that Carter, who had already won the New Hampshire primary, might actually have a chance to become the first president from the South since the Civil War. Caddell didn't think Carter could actually beat Wallace in places like north Jacksonville, but if he could scrape about ten points off Wallace's margin in redneck precincts, Carter could win Florida. And so, Rafshoon's slogan: "This time, don't send them a message. Send them a president."

Carter beat Wallace in Florida, and then he beat Scoop Jackson in Pennsylvania, and the nomination was his. It seemed an entirely preposterous turn of events. Carter was barely known by the party poo-bahs. His campaign had been managed by a tight circle of loyal, and very young, advisers who'd been with him from the start in Georgia. In 1972, right after the McGovern debacle, the strategist Hamilton Jordan, then all of twenty-eight years old, had written a memo that accurately laid out Carter's path to the White House. Jordan and press secretary Jody Powell displayed breezy, fresh, and often hilarious down-home smarts. They set the tone for a generation of mouthy, wild-ass Southern political handlers to come, from South Carolina's Lee Atwater to Louisiana's James Carville to the Texas troupe that elected George W. Bush.

Flush with their early victories in the primaries, and barely controlling their populist disdain for the self-righteous Yankees who ran the Democratic Party, the Carterites set about introducing their man to the Washington establishment. At a dinner party after the New Hampshire primary, hosted by the columnist Clayton Fritchie and his formidable wife, Polly, Carter was blistered by the assembled liberals for not being more vocal in his opposition to the Vietnam War. "You're scarred," he said to them, simply. The table fell silent. Had he said **scarred** or **scared**? And where did this pissant peanut farmer from Georgia get off talking to them, the grandees of D.C., like that? Here they were, offering to show him the ropes and he was almost acting like he had something to teach **them**. At the very least, he was refusing to be patronized. "You're scarred by Vietnam," Carter continued. "You may be permanently damaged by the war. But if you can't get past that, you're not much use to me. I'm going to win this presidency. The train is leaving the station. If you're too scarred to climb aboard, then that's too bad—but it's your problem, not mine."

Nearly everyone at the dinner climbed aboard, but the seeds of what would become an extremely tetchy relationship between the Georgians and the Washington establishment were sown. In any case, Carter's confidence about his own prospects seemed justified. The Republicans were ripping themselves to shreds in an intense primary battle between former governor Ronald

Reagan of California and the unelected incumbent president, Gerald Ford. Those few Republican political professionals who were paying attention to the Democratic primaries noticed a striking thing about Jimmy Carter's campaign: "The close connection between the candidate and his pollster has already had important tactical results," the Ford campaign staff noted in a memo preparing their candidate for the general election. "On an institutional basis [Caddell's methods are] a generation ahead of most other techniques. No one has yet devised a system protecting the incumbent from the Caddell-style alienation attack."

Carter beat Ford, of course, but he let a thirty-two-point lead slip away in the general-election campaign. It turned out that broad themes—"a government as good as its people"—weren't enough; before long, the folks had begun to notice that Carter was, well, fuzzy on the issues facing the country. He won much of the Deep South, and the public did have a vague sense that he was a nice guy (at least he smiled a lot—even if the smile seemed a frozen rictus), but he remained something of a stranger. According to Caddell's postelection polling, 50 percent of the public still didn't know where Carter stood on the issues, or what he was intending to do as president. The left wing of the Democratic Party was privately more obsessed than the public: What on earth did this guy stand for? Caddell had gotten a job on Carter's campaign staff for one of his friends from the McGovern crusade, a young speechwriter named Robert Shrum. Shrum quit after ten days and sent a withering letter to Carter: "I don't believe you stand for anything other than yourself."

"[Carter] stood," Rafshoon would later say, "for getting elected."

Pat Caddell was twenty-five years old. He had elected a president. And more, he had helped to change the way presidents would be elected in the future. Now there was a country to run. On December 10, 1976, he dropped a 10,000-word, 62-page memo entitled "Initial Working Paper on Political Strategy" on the president-elect's desk. It was an extraordinary document, prescient in many ways—especially in defining the problems that Democrats would face in the future. But most important, Caddell successfully defined the presidency in the television age. "Essentially," he wrote, "it is my thesis that governing with public approval requires a continuing political campaign."

Thus, the Permanent Campaign was born. It proved a radical change in the nature of the presidency, a significant dumbing-down of the office. All future presidents would run their administrations from a consultant's-eye view. Short-term tactical success would be emphasized over long-term strategic planning. There would be constant polling. The pressure to "win" the news cycle—to **control** the news—would overwhelm the more reflective, statesmanlike aspects of the office.

An over-caffeinated and under-discerning press would be quickly corrupted by the horse-race presidency: new policies would now be judged politically rather than substantively. Success would be judged in days rather than years or decades. It is no small irony that some of Jimmy Carter's best moves as president—a strict monetary policy to combat inflation, an arms buildup against the Soviet threat—would bear fruit years after he left office, and be credited to his successor, Ronald Reagan. But then, Carter was among the least-skilled of recent presidents as a permanent campaigner.

Caddell's memo was divided into two parts: first, an elaborate tour of the most recent polling data, and then suggestions for "specific political strategies for early stages of government." It was the second half of the memo that would become notorious when it eventually was leaked to the press. No pollster, indeed no hired political consultant, had ever taken so active a role in determining the style and content of a presidency. But the first half of the memo was significant, too. It demonstrated the rigor with which Caddell (and Gorman, who edited the memo) read a poll, and also the sophistication of Cambridge Survey Research's methods. There was no fawning; the memo was frank about Carter's weaknesses. The public believed the president-elect was "inexperienced," a person who often "flip-flops," who "overpromised," who posed a "risk" as president because he was "unknown." (Carter underlined each of the above quoted words with a felt-tip pen when he read the memo.) Caddell was equally frank about Carter's personal strengths as a "practical anti-politician."

In a section called "Strategies and Constituencies," Caddell laid out the nuts and bolts of Carter's victory ("The secret to Carter's success in Pennsylvania, Ohio and Wisconsin . . . was his ability to cut into traditional Republican margins in rural areas and small-town communities"). On the downside, Caddell worried about "non-working housewives. They were the bulk of women with doubts. In the end, many of them followed their instinct for change and selected Governor Carter—cautiously."

Carter had run well with Catholics, but "the ties that have traditionally bound Catholics to the Democratic Party are weakening." And later Caddell elaborated about blue-collar ethnics in general: "Unfortunately, these voters are no longer solely motivated by economic concerns—which have traditionally made them Democrats. They are now concerned with social issues, particularly those relating to change in society. This is one of the most vulnerable groups in the Democratic coalition."

Although this sort of public opinion analysis quickly became common—every subsequent president would have access to this type of data—it is difficult to overestimate how revealing it seemed at the time. Even now, Caddell's clear-eyed prescience about the problems that would plague the Democrats is impressive—although other pollsters, particularly Richard Scammon, had already noticed how wobbly the traditional, white Democratic constituencies had become. Still, Caddell had taken the magic he'd performed at the Duval County courthouse to the national level, and to the eyes of the president. And then he took it one step further.

The next section of the memo, "Plotting a Political Future," seems at first to have the same sort of authority and reliability as Caddell's analysis of existing data. He starts with discrete trends. The public is becoming more independent, and not as strongly affiliated with political parties as it once was. The "tremendous growth in economic prosperity has produced more 'haves' than 'have nots.' " Traditional liberalism, and Franklin Roosevelt's New Deal coalition, have become anachronistic. Then Caddell leaps to this:

> We must devise a context that is neither traditionally liberal nor traditionally conservative, one that cuts across traditional ideology. However, trying to be "liberal" on some issues and conservative on others is not likely to result in a new coalition, but will appear as an attempt to play both sides of the issue . . . What we require is not stew, composed of bits and pieces of old policies, but a fundamentally new ideology. Unfortunately, the clear formulation of such an ideology is beyond the intellectual grasp of your pollster.

The search for a new ideology, a streamlined set of beliefs for Democrats in the Great Affluence of the second half of the twentieth century—a period more amorphous but also much longer, and ultimately more significant, than the Great Depression—would soon become a liberal obsession, and remains so to this day. Caddell, having recognized the limits of his magical powers, retreated onto firmer ground and proposed some anodyne "themes" for the Carter administration: healing, restoring trust, giving a sense of purpose ("goals for the future"). He listed the specific issues that the public was concerned about, and suggested a few initiatives, but without the passion or confidence that marked his other advice. Obviously, Caddell believed that specific policy prescriptions should be left to the experts, but he also warned Carter against getting too wonky: "The old cliché about mistaking style for substance usually works in reverse in politics. **Too many good people have been defeated because they tried to substitute substance for style; they forgot to give the public the kind of visible signals that it needs to understand what is happening**." [Bold mine.]

Caddell wasn't suggesting that Carter substitute style for substance. He was reminding the president-elect that some human elements were necessary if Carter—who tended to be as serious as cancer and as colorful as cement—hoped to sell his programs to the public. And so, Caddell's famous advice on how to govern: "I would suggest cutting back on 'imperial' frills and perks." The public had loved the fact that Carter carried his own garment bag during the campaign. A more humble, casual, candid presidency would suit the times—except now, the humility would be planned, the candor canned. Caddell suggested fireside chats, cardigan sweaters, a frank acknowledgment of the growing public pessimism about the future. "It is sure to excite the public and to give them a sense of both his seriousness and his down-to-earth style."

It certainly excited Jimmy Carter. On the front page of the memo, the president-elect wrote a message to his vice president, Walter "Fritz" Mondale: "Fritz— Excellent. See me on this. J."

Political polling in the mid-1970s may have seemed the next thing to alchemy, but it didn't pay very well. The measly $500 that Gary Hart offered Cambridge Survey Research for its first New Hampshire poll in 1972 became legend. And while Caddell and Gorman had ramped up their fees, "the truth was, it wasn't easy for a full-time political pollster to put food on the table," said Samuel Popkin, who had taught statistics to John Gorman and Danny Porter at Harvard, and later became a part-time guru, number cruncher, and analyst for the firm—and still later, the author of one of the classics of latter-day political science, **The Reasoning Voter**. "Of course, Pat, John, and Danny weren't doing it for the money, at least not at first. They were doing it for the **revolution**"—the Liberal project. "If you had tools, you put them to use for the cause. But for the firm to survive, it needed a cash flow. And to maintain a cash flow, especially in nonelection years, you needed corporate clients. So they created Cambridge Reports. Pat was terrific when it came to selling political clients, but Gorman was the guy to convince the big utilities and oil companies to come aboard for $20,000 a year."

The path from revolution to revelry was slick; Caddell and Gorman slid onto the gravy train. With Jimmy Carter as president, Gorman's pitch couldn't have been very difficult. In the spring of 1977, David Broder of the **Washington Post** listed some of Cambridge Reports' top clients—Westinghouse; Exxon; Citicorp; Merck; Atlantic Richfield; Sears, Roebuck . . . and the government of Saudi Arabia—and wondered about the propriety of the operation. Caddell responded that no one had "come up with a legitimate charge of conflict of interest, and to constantly have the question raised without any grounds is certainly not very helpful. No one likes to have his integrity questioned."

But one gets the sense that Caddell was having too much fun to really care very much. He and Rafshoon shared a fancy office a block from the White House, and an even fancier house in Georgetown, complete with swimming pool, which came to be known as the "R Street Beach." (Rafshoon eventually left the Beach to rejoin adult life and was replaced by Tim Kraft, an entirely raucous Carter operative from New Mexico.) Rafshoon and Caddell were advising the president of the United States . . . and also Francis Ford Coppola, about how to market his new movie, **Apocalypse**

Now. Caddell was showing up around town with movie stars on his arm. He brought Lauren Bacall to the Inaugural Ball.

In some ways, the 1970s were the 1960s for nerds. The Carter years were the last gasp for those who had been too young (or too old) to experience the summer of love and its attendant mind-bending recreational activities a decade earlier. For a time, cocaine replaced marijuana as the drug of choice . . . and the rumors of cocaine use in the Carter White House, and among the president's political advisers, were rampant. (A friend of mine on the White House staff later admitted, "Shit, yeah, there was cocaine all over the place. You'd go to a party and people would be sniffling like crazy, running in and out of the bathroom.") Certainly the administration was divided between certified grown-ups—most notably, Vice President Mondale—and those who thought that the whole thing was just one big hoot.

The president himself was notoriously straitlaced, but he was clearly tickled by his young aides. A few weeks after he took office, I spent a week in the White House, hanging out with Hamilton Jordan and Jody Powell for a **Rolling Stone** cover story. At one point, Jody brought me in to see the president, who was working in the private room, adjacent to the Oval Office, that Bill Clinton and Monica Lewinsky would later make famous. Powell described my story to the president and said, "Mr. President, it's my assessment that Joe represents the first serious threat to this administration."

Carter looked at me with those pale blue eyes and said quietly, "Well then, you're just going to have to lie."

I chuckled, belatedly and uncomfortably. I was thirty years old. This was my first conversation with a president. Carter seemed to grow more serious. "I'm not joking. I can make life difficult for your publication. I have certain powers . . ."

"Well, Mr. President," I said, "I'll certainly try to . . ." and both Carter and Jody cracked up: another Yankee taken to the cleaners.

Caddell had always been prematurely pompous, but there was a mitigating sweetness to him. "You could always say 'Oh Pat!' when he'd go off the deep end in some way," said Dotty Lynch, who joined him in the Washington office. "And he'd laugh with you . . . At one point, he got on an Amtrak train up to Wilmington, Delaware, to meet with [Senator] Joe Biden, but he got on the wrong train. It was an express and it just whizzed through Wilmington with Biden standing on the platform, waiting for him. Pat called me, screaming, when he got to Philadelphia. He wanted to talk to the president of Amtrak. He wanted to sue!" Lynch laughed, and Caddell calmed down. "Eventually 'Oh Pat' stopped working, though," Lynch added. "And he wasn't much fun to be around anymore."

Gorman recalls that Caddell was so absentminded that twice in two years he stepped out of automobiles that he was driving without turning off the engine or putting on the brake. In one case, the car—a classic Mercedes that had been used in the film **The Friends of Eddie Coyle**—continued on its own down a spiral ramp before it crashed into the concrete wall of a parking garage and burst into flames. But Gorman also noticed that Caddell was beginning to bloat with self-importance, his arrogance and impatience and anger migrating from the merely obnoxious to the downright scary. His treatment of the staff was unforgivable. "When he would come up from Washington," Gorman recalled, "most of the staff would figure out a way to have doctors' appointments, sick mothers, or work elsewhere. When Pat was around there would be explosions over the silliest things. For example, we had a company house on Chappaquiddick for a while. The whole staff used it and, at one point, Pat left a sweater there. When he returned two weeks later, it was gone. He came into the office on Monday and went berserk. He said someone had stolen his sweater and no one could leave the office until the culprit confessed. It was way out of control."

Meanwhile, the Carter presidency was a mess. Part of it was the luck of the draw: Carter was paying the inflationary price for the guns-and-butter deficits run up by Lyndon Johnson during the Vietnam War, and for the rise in oil prices after the petroleum exporting countries, especially those in the Middle East, organized themselves into a cartel, OPEC, and began to regulate the flow of oil in the 1970s. But a good part of it, too, was that Jimmy Carter just seemed small for the job. He never quite figured out how to play politics with the big boys—most notably the congressional big boys in his own party, like House Speaker Thomas P. "Tip" O'Neill. After eight years of Republicans in the White House, the congressional Democrats weren't used to taking orders from a Democratic president—especially a self-righteous one who refused to approve spending on the usual local pork projects that kept constituents happy back home. O'Neill complained that Hamilton Jordan wouldn't even return his phone calls.

Moreover, Caddell's initial advice about presidential style had turned out to be wrong. A humble, informal presidency certainly fit Carter's church-deacon personality, but it lacked the heft and authority that the American public, and the world, expected from the president of the United States. Carter seemed decent and trustworthy, but too caught up in the managerial details of his administration—a green-eyeshade sort of president—and emotionally remote. He seemed the sort of person you'd want for a babysitter, but not as a boss (or a friend). He was not the sort to invite Tip O'Neill over for a shmooze and a beer, as his successor, Ronald Reagan, loved to do—and a shmooze and a beer was exactly what Carter needed to get O'Neill to cooperate on pork trimming and other disciplines. Politics is a contact sport, but sometimes the contact involves a good massage. Carter was incapable of that. There was a high-minded, self-improving prissiness to the man. An image lingers: One night Hamilton Jordan was ushering me down a West Wing corridor when we happened upon the president (wearing a tan cardigan sweater, natch), the First Lady, and a few top staff members seated around the big table in, I think, the Roosevelt Room. They were taking an Evelyn Wood speed-reading course.

One imagines Caddell frothing at the mouth over the waning of public approval. One imagines him bristling with polls and ideas and strategies. In April of 1978, Caddell wrote a memo suggesting that Carter was focusing too much on managing the government, that he needed to address broader themes, that he needed to **lead**. Early in 1979, Caddell wrote his own proposed version of Carter's State of the Union address. In it, the president would acknowledge that the state of the union was not terrific—but, according to **The New Yorker**'s Elizabeth Drew, "the President and others thought he was being too alarmist." Indeed, the professionals had pretty much shut the pollster out of the inner circle by then. Hamilton Jordan had learned that the best way to get straight, unspun polling numbers, minus the rant about American alienation, was to go behind Caddell's back and call Gorman in Boston (which led to ever more impossible tantrums when Caddell found out).

But Caddell was convinced that Americans were more alienated, and pessimistic, than ever. They were addled by affluence, and petulant because the bum economy was denying them what seemed their birthright—an ever increasing standard of living. As Carter's approval ratings continued to skid, Caddell continued to fulminate. He was sure the country was going to hell. The crisis, he told one and all, was . . . just . . . so . . . absolutely . . . fucking . . . **historic**. Finally, he decided to bring his case to the Carter Court of Appeals—the First Lady. On April 9, 1979, Caddell and Rosalynn Carter had a two-hour breakfast in the White House. That afternoon, Mrs. Carter summoned Jody Powell to meet with her and Caddell in the Map Room. Powell, undoubtedly hoping that this could be made to go away, asked Caddell to write a memo.

No problem. The memo is dated April 23, 1979. It is called "Of Crisis and Opportunity," and this time it was pure Caddell—unedited by Gorman, who was appalled when he read it. "I said to him, 'Pat, we've got to talk about how I'm going to edit this.' And Pat said, 'We don't have to talk about it. I've **thought** about it.' "

The first paragraph said it all:

America is a nation deep in crisis. Unlike civil war or depression this crisis, nearly invisible, is unique from those that previously engaged Americans in their history. Psychological more than material, it is a crisis of confidence marked by a dwindling faith in the future. It cannot be "seen" in ordinary ways—there are no armies of the night, no street demonstrations, no powerful lobbys. It **can** be read in the polls which monitor the vital signs of the body politic, it **can** be heard in the growing real despair of elites and ordinary citizens alike as they struggle to articulate in concepts the malaise which they themselves feel.

The memo, and Jimmy Carter's presidency, would be remembered in the future by one word in the last sentence of that paragraph: "malaise."

The rest of the memo defined "malaise" and was bizarre, to say the least—by turns, brilliant and unhinged and messianic. The second paragraph, for example, began:

This crisis is not your fault as President. It is the natural result of historical forces and events which have been in motion for twenty years. This crisis threatens the political and social fabric of our nation. **Yet, this crisis, not of your making, also presents the greatest opportunity for you as President to become a great President on the order of a Lincoln, a Wilson, and a Franklin Roosevelt. More interestingly, it presents you the opportunity, so rare in American history, to reshape the structure, nature and purpose of the United States in fundamental ways which your predecessors could only dream.** [Emphasis his.]

To which one can only say: Yikes. But flattery will apparently get you anywhere with a president, perhaps especially with one as garishly humble as Jimmy Carter. It took two months, a second memo, a second oil shock that caused long gasoline lines across the nation, and the total cratering of Carter's approval ratings—he was down to 30 percent by early June—but "malaise" eventually became the defining principle of the Carter presidency, even though the president never actually used the word in public.

Caddell bolstered his memo with some fairly scary polling data. For the first time, more Americans were pessimistic than optimistic: **"One cannot be sanguine when 1 out of every 2 Americans see the country going straight downhill and more significantly when 1 out of every 3 Americans see their own lives going straight downhill . . .** [This] **is a psychological crisis of the first order."** And then he added supporting quotations from books and articles he had been reading, long pages of quotations—from editorials in **US News & World Report** ("The ennui of affluence can overwhelm a nation"), to academic articles by the sociologist James Q. Wilson ("Once politics was only about a few things; today, it is about nearly everything"), to the economists Friedrich Hayek and John Maynard Keynes, to the sociologist Christopher Lasch's book **The Culture of Narcissism**, to the historian James McGregor Burns's book **Leadership**.

It was an intellectual tour de force . . . and a total bummer. It is also an essential document in the recent history of the Democratic Party—an early elaboration of the down-on-America pessimism that became the party's spiritual signature in the television era. There was, first of all, pessimism about America's role in the

world and the use of military force. The war in Vietnam had transformed liberalism from an aggressive an-
ticommunist, internationalist movement into a more
pacifist, anti-imperialist, neo-isolationist cause. After
Vietnam, any and all American military actions—from
the placement of Pershing missiles in Europe in the
1980s, to the removal of Manuel Noriega from power
in Panama in 1989, to the first and second Gulf
Wars—were reflexively opposed by liberals (the more
radical sorts saw them as acts of American imperial-
ism). To be sure, some of these ventures were wrong-
headed, but the Democrats' automatic disdain for the
use of force in a dangerous world would come to seem
not only weak but also unpatriotic.

There was also a growing economic pessimism
among working-class Democrats, which sprouted suddenly during the Carter presidency—although it was
not nearly the force in Democratic Party politics that it
would later become. Manufacturing jobs were starting
to disappear by the late 1970s. Japan was on the rise,
soon to be followed by the rest of Asia, especially
China. The trade unions were no longer an expansive
force pushing for a more equitable society; they had become pinched and reactionary, obsessed with protecting the jobs and privileges they already had.

To the antiwar and economic strands of pessimism,
Caddell now added "malaise," which was more abstract
than the others, but no less dark. It reflected his Harvard education more than his Jacksonville provenance,
and the views of his friends more than the numbers in

his polls: the growing dismay of the 1960s idealists as they slipped away from altruism and hedonism into parenthood and responsibility. Christopher Lasch's theory that affluence had robbed the nation of its sense of community and purpose contained a certain truth— centuries earlier, Machiavelli had written that "**ozio** [indolence] is the greatest enemy of a Republic"—but it was also a form of liberal wishful thinking. It implied that inspired **government** activism could renew the American spirit. But what if most Americans didn't want their spirits renewed? What if—after all the melodrama of the Nixon years—Americans simply wanted the presidency Jimmy Carter had promised: a president who would calm things down, heal the wounds, manage the country? What if they were simply down on Carter because he hadn't delivered?

Jimmy Carter had won the presidency, in part, because he had distanced himself from the mopey left. But he was beginning to feel pretty mopey himself as he returned from an economic summit in Tokyo in late June and found a nation steaming on gas lines— and his job approval rating cratering at 25 percent, a level rivaling Richard Nixon's during the Watergate crisis. "The gas lines were inconvenient for a lot of people," Hamilton Jordan would later recall in a University of Virginia oral history. "But it said something very bad about our country when the rage and panic set in in May and June of 1979 just because people had to wait at a gas pump for 25, 30 minutes, maybe even 45. There was a rage and panic that swept the country out of all proportion to the inconvenience that it caused the average citizen."

It was announced that Carter would give a speech about the energy crisis. But what to say? He had already given four such speeches. Caddell dropped his second memo—a 107-page job—on the president and First Lady on July 1, as the Carters headed to Camp David for a brief respite. "When we read it," Jordan recalled, "we said, 'He's right.'"

In the second memo, Caddell insisted that the American people had stopped listening to Carter. The president needed a "breakthrough" strategy to save his presidency and establish himself as a "transformational" leader. The memo was again full of genius and weirdness. Among other things, Caddell proposed a second constitutional convention, which Vice President Mondale would later call one of the stupidest ideas he'd ever heard.

What followed can only be described as an administration-wide nervous breakdown. Carter canceled the energy speech. He called his top advisers to Camp David for a "domestic policy" summit. A period of mystery ensued. Caddell's memo—and his plan to have Carter directly confront the sour national mood—vied against a more traditionalist agenda, a straight-ahead new energy policy. But the Carters, and the Georgia gang, had grown frustrated with their inability to get legislation through Congress; they agreed with Caddell on the need to do something dramatic to break out of the impasse. Mondale, the administration's lead traditionalist, was appalled by the touchy-feely mumbo-jumbo that suffused the Camp David meetings. The summit continued into a second week, the government on hold as all sorts of "leaders"—intellectuals, preachers, politicians, trade unionists and corporate executives, blacks and Hispanics—trooped up to the Catoctin Mountains to commune with the president. Toward the end, the Carters slipped out and stayed overnight in "average" households in western Pennsylvania to consult with the salt of the earth about the national crisis of spirit.

After ten days, Carter came down from the mountain and gave his famous "malaise" speech—although the word was never used—which turned out to be an awkward amalgam of the Caddell and traditionalist agendas, and one of the stranger presidential addresses in the history of the country. Carter was brutal about his own failures. He quoted a Southern governor: "Mr. President, you are not leading the nation—you are managing the government." And he reported eighteen other comments from Camp David, among them:

"You don't see the people enough anymore."

"Some of your cabinet members don't seem loyal. There's not enough discipline among the disciples."

"When we enter the moral equivalent of war, Mr. President, don't issue us BB guns."

"Be bold, Mr. President. We may make mistakes, but we are ready to experiment."

Then Carter proceeded to make his argument. At

the heart of it was this profoundly Caddellian para-graph:

> In a nation that was proud of hard work, strong families, close-knit communities, and our faith in God, too many of us now tend to worship self-indulgence and consumption. Human identity is no longer defined by what one does but by what one owns. But we've discovered that owning things and consuming things does not satisfy our longing for meaning. We've learned that piling up material goods cannot fill the emptiness of lives which have no confidence or purpose.

Listening to that passage, the Republican pollster Richard Wirthlin figured Jimmy Carter's presidency was over. How would steelworkers, deathly afraid of losing their jobs, respond to this baloney? "President Carter . . . didn't **intend** to insult Americans by blaming them for the woes that many believed his administration had created . . . but how else were voters to feel about a President who spoke about American greatness in the past tense?" Wirthlin would later write. "When I heard it, I about fell out of my chair." And Wirthlin had another realization as well: Carter had perfectly framed the contest that would take place if Wirthlin's client, Ronald Reagan, won the Republican nomination in 1980—a contest between optimism and pessimism that he was now certain Reagan would win.

And yet, for about twenty-four hours, it seemed that Carter had pulled it off. He received standing ovations the next day when he spoke to the National Association of Counties and, more important, to the Communications Workers of America trade union. His job approval ratings soared, according to Caddell. This was, in part, the White House effect—any president's ratings tend to rise, momentarily, when he makes a "major" address to the nation, especially when he gives the appearance of leadership. But the speech also was the closest Jimmy Carter came to having a Turnip Day moment as president, even though it was as far from spontaneous as could be imagined. The message was pure Carter: **You're scarred**. This unflattering and unwelcome assessment was sufficiently different from anything Americans had ever heard from a president before. It had to be real, right?

It would have been interesting to see how long Carter might have sustained this new mood, but two days after the speech his cabinet committed ritual suicide. It is not known whether the president, or perhaps Hamilton Jordan, asked for the members of the cabinet to submit their resignations, or whether, as the Carterites later insisted, Secretary of State Cyrus Vance offered the idea spontaneously. The result was chaos. CABINET RESIGNS was the headline, and the story. Carter ultimately accepted five of the resignations, but the details hardly mattered: the aura of command that he may have gained with the speech vanished. The public's sense that the president was a weakling deepened.

Senator Ted Kennedy decided to run against Carter in 1980, representing the party's traditional liberal base. Carter's malaise might even have emboldened the leadership of the Soviet Union, which invaded Afghanistan five months later; Carter responded, pathetically, by pulling the United States out of the 1980 Moscow Olympics.

"I couldn't handle Jimmy Carter anymore," Dotty Lynch recalled. "All my friends were going to work for Kennedy." In October of 1979, Lynch told Caddell that she was leaving. "How can you be more loyal to Ted Kennedy than to me?" Caddell screamed. It was the scenario he had dreaded all along. In the first malaise memo, he had written of "Edward Kennedy's rising appeal . . . On the issues Kennedy seems not to be in tune with the public. I would argue at the moment that the public doesn't really care. Kennedy, by definition, stands as a symbol of Hope, of a past which was America's high water mark; a period most remembered and cherished."

Caddell was wrong about Kennedy, who proved a dud of a candidate, but he was right that the real threat would come from a politician offering the vision of an America powerful and virtuous and unique among nations. That politician turned out to be Ronald Reagan, who, in the general election of 1980, would be supported by 30 percent of the voters who had backed Kennedy in the primaries—many of whom were the old George Wallace and Robert Kennedy populists of 1968.

Caddell had been prophetic about the importance of working-class populism, but he had over-read history. America was not the South after the Civil War. The nation's "high water mark" was not in the past. Reagan's vision of America as "a city on a hill" wasn't a nostalgic mirage—the mirage was in the poll numbers. It was true that the nation had turned pessimistic after Vietnam and Watergate, but that was a transitory and surface-level condition. The public was blowing off steam when the pollsters called; beneath the anger, most Americans remained exceptionalists—convinced that the United States was a special place, the greatest country in history. It was ironic that Caddell, who **knew** the numbers were only a "crude tool," had fallen for the tyranny of the literal, deluded by his own desire to have the "pessimism" numbers mean what he wanted them to mean.

In the end, Caddell was guilty of malpractice. He had advised Carter to give the wrong speech, a dark and scolding speech—the sort of speech that Lincoln had studiously avoided in the depths of the Civil War and that Franklin Roosevelt would never have delivered during the Great Depression. But the real fault lay with Jimmy Carter, whose emotional austerity—he seemed more a New England puritan than a born-again Baptist—had crippled his presidency. His hilarious mother and redneck brother, Billy, were classic, juicy American eccentrics; his sister was a born-again evangelist. But the president had cauterized his passionate roots. He rarely, if ever, told down-home, corn-pone stories. His oratory was untroubled by gritty expressions or emotions. There was no music to the man. One might even say that **he** was scarred.

Caddell remained a force in the Democratic Party for a time, an increasingly bizarre amalgam of Machiavelli and Don Quixote. He was directly involved in three more presidential campaigns—Gary Hart in 1984, Joe Biden in 1988, and Jerry Brown in 1992—and kibitzed in several others, almost always with the same strategy: the candidate as antiestablishment populist outsider. He won a few battles—he prepared Walter Mondale for his very successful first debate with Ronald Reagan—but he never again won a war. In fact, Caddell seemed increasingly impatient with politicians and disgusted by politics, ever angrier and less reliable over time.

In his 1980 book, **The Permanent Campaign**, Sidney Blumenthal correctly described consultants as the new political bosses, the enduring seat of institutional memory in both parties. Caddell certainly qualified. Indeed, he had become a trophy pollster: he bestowed instant credibility on the politicians he chose to represent in congressional and gubernatorial races. When Caddell "endorsed" a candidate, fund-raising, media buzz, and support from the party's special interests suddenly became easier. His firm—he split, bitterly, with Gorman after the 1980 campaign—was the place to be if you were a young pollster or strategist with ambitions; Paul Maslin, Mike Donilon, and Joe Trippi, all of whom would become major players in the Democratic Party, spent time learning from Caddell. And so did Bob Shrum.

Caddell had become such a name that, for a moment, it seemed possible that he could reverse the natural hierarchy of political consultants. The presiding geniuses of the game, at least in the minds of the politicians, had always been the advertising guys. Tony Schwartz, a brilliant hermit whose studio literally was his home, had pretty much created the myth with a single ad for Lyndon Johnson in 1964. A little girl is pulling petals off a daisy, counting them as they drop. When she reaches ten, an announcer takes over and the count becomes a countdown to a nuclear explosion. As the mushroom cloud billows, the voice of Lyndon Johnson intones: "These are the stakes, to make a world in which all God's children can live, or to go into the darkness. Either we must love each other or we must die."

The ad aired only once. It never mentioned Johnson's opponent, the Republican Barry Goldwater, much less accused him of being a warmonger. But it played to voters' fear of Goldwater's belligerence—and it certainly contributed to the Johnson landslide that year. Over time, the Daisy Ad became the Holy Grail for politicians and political consultants: a single ad that could demolish an opponent. (This might be churlish, but the Daisy Ad also proved to be entirely misleading:

Johnson sank the nation into Vietnam, after implying in the campaign that he wouldn't.)

Few practitioners who followed were as artful as Schwartz. The killer ad would prove a chimera (with, as we'll see, a few notable exceptions). But the ability to destroy an opponent in thirty seconds seemed the most powerful juju imaginable, even more powerful than Mr. Prediction's ability to foretell the future, and media consultants assumed a position of power at the candidate's table. The big names on the Democratic side, people like David Sawyer, Bob Squier, and David Garth, usually chose some Sancho Panza of a pollster, who resided in a cubbyhole counting computer cards, passing the results on to the lead consultant, who would then pass them along to the candidate.

Pat Caddell, for one, felt underappreciated. He was a **strategist**, not merely a number cruncher; he was tired of overly artsy ad guys coming up with fancy, ineffective spots that had no basis in research. He wanted a more active hand in the formulation of campaign strategy and advertising. In the early 1980s, he began a series of conversations with David Doak—a big, taciturn Missourian, who had built a reputation as one of the Democratic Party's best campaign managers. Doak was frustrated with the ad guys, too: they knew nothing about actually running a campaign and they made all the money. They not only produced the ads (the production markups were ungodly) but also charged a percentage fee—as much as 15 percent—of the cost of the advertising time on television. And now, for the first time, big money was really beginning to roll in. In California, for example, Alan Cranston spent $2.5 million to win a U.S. Senate seat in 1980; six years later, he would spend $20 million. "I had spent two years of my life managing two successful statewide campaigns and made a grand total of $60,000," Doak would later say. "It just didn't seem fair."

Together, Doak and Caddell decided to form a full-service consulting firm, which opened for business in 1985. Almost as an afterthought, Caddell suggested that they add Bob Shrum, who had become the party's hottest speechwriter, having composed some of Ted Kennedy's more operatic ventures. The initial split was 40 percent each for Caddell and Doak, 20 percent for Shrum. Doak later decided to donate 10 percent to Shrum, which made him a more equal partner. "I remember when Caddell, Doak and Shrum formed, people were scared shitless," the pollster Ed Reilly said. "People were afraid that they were going to run everyone out of the business."

The firm lasted a year, a melodrama from start to (litigious) finish. There were structural problems: Caddell was the real draw, more equal than the others. His junior partners—people like Paul Maslin and Mike Donilon—had relationships with other media consultants, and they also had clients who wanted Bob Squier or Ray Strother, not Doak and Shrum, to do their advertising. There were also titanic personality problems. "I would get fired every other week," recalls Joe Trippi, a terrific young field organizer who shared Caddell's romantic sensibility and was hired as the firm's vice president, a title more lofty than his position, which he defined as "the kid who got all the shit work."

At one point, during the 1986 Alan Cranston campaign, Trippi and the senior partners were in a van headed to a location shoot in San Diego with the candidate. "Dave said something and Bob replied, 'That's the stupidest idea I ever heard,' " Trippi later told me. "So Dave goes, 'Well your ideas are stupider than mine.' And Caddell rolls his eyes and says, 'Well, who's stupider than who?' And then they're all into it—in front of the candidate: 'You're stupider.' 'No, you are.' 'No, you are.' You could see the candidate going pale, with his three top consultants acting like six-year-olds in a schoolyard, and I blurt out, 'Listen, just nobody escalate to the A-word.' Doak was usually the calm one, but when he went, it was oh man—and this was his turn to go. He screams at me at the top of his lungs, 'You're fired!' We had pulled up to a stoplight and I got out, hailed a cab, and took the next flight back to Washington. Just left them there—and I was the only one who knew where the location was. I think they spent the next two days wandering in the desert."

Well, maybe not the next two days—and Trippi was quickly rehired, only to be fired and rehired again. But the Cranston campaign did prove to be a turning point for Caddell, at least in retrospect.

It was a difficult race. Cranston had run an embarrassing campaign for president in 1984, a campaign memorable mostly for the fact that he had dyed his steel-gray hair a color not found in nature. Now he had to prove that he wasn't a desperate old man, a loser, a has-been; the problem was compounded by the fact that he was running against an attractive young moderate Republican, a successful Silicon Valley businessman named Ed Zschau. California was, and is, a gold-rush state for political consultants—too large for door-to-door campaigning, the entire campaign is run on television, mostly through paid advertising. The initial Caddell-Doak-Shrum strategy was a traditional one: ignore the unknown challenger, remind the voters of Cranston's credentials and accomplishments, and try to convince people that he wasn't just a foolish old coot with dyed hair. An early ad showed Cranston jogging around a track, as an announcer touted his record. The trouble was, Cranston was balding and thin—he looked like a skeleton waiting to happen, death jogging. It just wasn't working. The race was going to be decided by younger, moderate voters and they weren't buying the old guy. The race was getting tighter.

There were, at this point, certain rules of the road about the use of negative TV ads. It was believed that negative ads worked best against incumbents, especially well-known candidates with established voting records. In 1978, an independent organization—the National Conservative Political Action Committee (NCPAC)—had targeted Iowa's liberal senator John Culver, and beaten him with a spew of negative ads; in 1980, NCPAC had targeted five more liberal senators and defeated four of them (with a total budget of only $1 million—ah, those were the good old days!). But it was conventionally believed that negative ads worked less well for an incumbent running against an un-known challenger—going negative against an unknown would only give the challenger name recognition.

Caddell, however, had a brainstorm during a long, panicked conference call to the Cranston campaign. "It was dark," he later told me. "My office looked out over the river, and there were no lights on, and I'm on the phone, and I'm explaining very carefully that the only way we can win is if we drive the vote down." The young moderates were marginal voters, turned off by negative campaigning. "By turning the campaign so ugly and dirty and vicious beyond belief, we could drive them out of the fucking premises." The break-through wasn't merely the idea that an incumbent could negatively "define" a less well-known challenger—Caddell had proposed a similar strategy to Carter in 1980, and H. R. Haldeman had suggested the same to Nixon in 1972. Caddell's real insight was the perverse realization that he could make the race so obnoxious that he would actively discourage people from voting.

It was a diabolical thought. And it worked. Trippi came up with a hilarious idea for an ad, a takeoff on the cheesy K-tel music compilations—**Greatest Hits of the '60s**, for example—that would be breathlessly pro-moted in non–prime time on nonnetwork television: Ed Zschau's Greatest Hits. He wrote some lyrics ridi-culing Zschau—"Do the Zschau Flip-Flop" and "How

Many Times Can a Man Change His Mind"—hired a band, an announcer who sounded like the famed Los Angeles disc jockey Wolfman Jack (Trippi called him Jackman Wolf). The ad proved to be a surgical strike, nuking the young moderate voters—they still weren't going to vote for the old guy, but maybe this guy Zschau was kind of stupid, too. The ad was so effective that **Nightline**, the highly respected late-night ABC news program, did a whole show about it.

Caddell was stunned. Don Quixote was appalled by Machiavelli. "I was sitting there in my office in the dark, and I put down the phone, and I realized this is not what I got into politics to do. I'm now sitting here trying to drive people out of the fucking process. And that was it. I decided to quit."

Just before election day, Caddell spoke with reporters at a Sperling Breakfast in Washington and announced he was leaving the business.

But there was one race left to run: Senator Joe Biden's campaign for president. Biden had been a Caddell client since 1972, and was an early favorite to win the nomination in 1988. He was an old-fashioned, tub-thumping speaker with an inspiring personal story, a big smile, and an easy, charming manner. But he started slowly in Iowa and, by most accounts, Caddell was totally out of control, screaming at staffers, screaming at the press. Biden tanked late in the summer of 1987, when he was found to be lifting some of his rhetoric on the stump directly from a speech given by Neil Kinnock. Caddell publicly accused his former partners

Doak and Shrum, who were working for Congressman Dick Gephardt's presidential campaign, of slipping copies of the Kinnock speech to the press. (They hadn't; the culprits were John Sasso and Paul Tully of the Michael Dukakis campaign.) The Kinnock story blew a hole in Biden's candidacy, and other stories followed: Biden was accused of plagiarizing Robert Kennedy (in fact, Caddell had inserted the language into a Biden speech without attribution) and of puffing up his records at Syracuse Law School. It was clear the campaign was over, but Caddell wanted to keep fighting. On the day before Biden dropped out, Caddell stormed into a staff meeting and screamed, "You're a lynch mob, trying to kill my candidate. Fuck you." And stormed out.

Two months later, Lois Romano of the **Washington Post** wrote Caddell's obituary, full of juicy quotes from Democratic operatives celebrating the pollster's demise. "People," said his old friend, Gerald Rafshoon, "are hanging garlic from their windows."

"I read that 'Democratic insiders say Pat Caddell is dead as a consultant,' " Caddell told the **Post**. Then, no doubt thinking about the decision he made during the Cranston campaign, he added, "But I died already. I killed myself."

2

He Looks Me in the Tie

★ ★ ★ ★

In late May of 1976, Ronald Reagan had Gerald Ford on the ropes in the Republican race for the presidential nomination. It was a development every bit as stunning as Jimmy Carter's surge from nowhere on the Democratic side: no incumbent president had ever been defeated in a primary campaign.* After some critical early losses—in New Hampshire, Florida, and Illinois, among others—Reagan won in North Carolina and Texas, and then clobbered Ford in Georgia, Alabama, Indiana, and Nebraska. An unsigned White House memo distributed after the Texas loss concluded, "We are in real danger of being out-organized by a small number of highly motivated right-wing nuts."

Ford won his home state, Michigan, on May 18, but that was to be expected. His campaign badly needed a

---

*Lyndon Johnson withdrew from the 1968 race after Eugene McCarthy nearly beat him in the New Hampshire primary.

meaningful victory. There would be four primaries on May 25, and the most significant of these was Tennessee—a state whose moderate Republican tradition, which dated back to the Civil War, was rapidly being overtaken by New South conservatism. Reagan was on a roll in the South. Tennessee, it seemed, was his to lose . . .

He lost it. And with it, he probably lost the Republican nomination—all on a matter of principle.

The Tennessee Valley Authority (TVA) is a famed, government-owned, rural electrification project, a signature program of Franklin Roosevelt's New Deal. It had been a godsend during the Great Depression, delivering construction jobs to the region and then electricity at lower-than-market rates. It remained a beloved institution, untouchable even by local conservatives. To conservatives residing outside the Tennessee River valley, however, the TVA seemed an anachronistic bastion of state socialism that was ripe for privatization.

And so the inevitable question, asked in a press conference on the weekend before the Tennessee primary: Governor Reagan, would you privatize the TVA?

"I still believe in free enterprise," Reagan replied, trying to avoid a straight yes or no answer, "and I don't believe government has any place in it."

But would he sell the TVA?

"We'd have to look at it," Reagan said.

And, kaboom. The statement quickly splashed out of Tennessee, across the border into Kentucky—which also benefited from TVA power and also was voting on May 25—and then across the nation, pounced upon by the Ford campaign as confirmation that the former governor of California was an off-the-deep-end, free-market extremist. Reagan tried to leaven his remarks, but he couldn't quite bring himself to step away from his position. He said that while he was "philosophically opposed" to big-government power programs, he had no plans to sell the TVA.

Reagan lost Tennessee by two thousand votes. He also lost Kentucky, Oregon, and New Jersey that day. He would continue to battle Ford for the nomination, but the race was over.

In retrospect—and seen from the point of view of "political experts" (that is, the reporters and consultants who cast judgment on such things)—Reagan's TVA gaffe seems a monumental political mistake. No doubt his handlers were tearing their hair out; perhaps the governor was, too. If Reagan had finessed the issue—"Now, boys, you know what a free-market guy I am, but TVA is one of the great monuments created by my political hero, FDR, and someone's going to have to make a darn good argument for me to think about messing with it"—he would probably have won Tennessee, and maybe Kentucky, and perhaps gone on to win the Republican nomination. If he had won the nomination, he might well have beaten Jimmy Carter, who nearly squandered his early thirty-two-point lead over Gerald Ford.

But if Ronald Reagan had finessed the TVA, he

wouldn't have been Ronald Reagan. It was an ideological Turnip Day, an unplanned signal sent to supporters and detractors alike about who he was and what he
really believed. Indeed, "mistakes" were among Reagan's most reliable means of communication with his
hard-core supporters. When left to his own devices—
when he told an impolitic truth (or, as was often the
case, indulged in anecdotal fantasies)—Reagan was a
knee-jerk conservative. It may have cost him dearly in
1976, but his inability to fudge his philosophical position on the TVA, and all the other moments like it,
helped to define him in the long run. A deep bond developed between Reagan and his supporters, unlike any
other between a successful politician and the public in
the television era. That loyalty made his second, successful run for the presidency possible in 1980.

Which is not to say that Ronald Reagan didn't finesse other issues, or that he never acted pragmatically.
For one thing, he never did privatize the TVA. He defined his presidency by enacting the largest tax cuts in
American history in 1981, then turned around and imposed two of the largest tax increases in history, in
1982 and 1983, after his tax cuts sent the federal
budget deficit into the ionosphere. He said that "government was the problem, not the solution," and yet
he spent little political capital cutting or reforming the
federal morass (that would be left to Bill Clinton, who
cut more than 250,000 federal jobs and balanced the
budget). Reagan styled himself as the ultimate hawk,
and yet he violated one of the core principles of U.S.

national security policy: he negotiated with terrorists during the Iran-Contra debacle, trading arms for the release of hostages. But no matter how egregious the inconsistency, Reagan never lost the support of the faithful because they were absolutely convinced that they knew who he was and what he believed. They were convinced that he acted pragmatically only when his arm was twisted, only when he had no other choice (or when his consultants led him astray). Which, when you think about it, was refreshingly strange, given the prevailing cynicism about politicians. But then, leaders of ideological movements rarely get themselves elected president—Abraham Lincoln and Andrew Jackson were, arguably, the only other two. Reagan did, and like Lincoln and Jackson, he pretty much had to create a new political party to get there.

In 1974, the Republican Party seemed as comatose as the Democrats would in 2004. It was in desperate need of a core philosophy, a new direction, something true. It was the party of pragmatism, of Buick owners, of businessmen from Wall Street to Main Street. It had never quite responded intellectually to Franklin Roosevelt's New Deal; its congressional minority aquiesced, grudgingly, in what seemed the endless and inevitable expansion of government power. In some ways, Richard Nixon's presidency was the final capitulation to what seemed a permanent liberal tide: he imposed all sorts of new government regulations, creating the Environmental Protection Agency and the Occupational Safety and Health Administration; he imposed wage and price controls, and proposed a mandatory employer-provided universal health insurance plan (which was defeated by Ted Kennedy, who wanted a state-run plan); he negotiated with the Russians, opened the door to Communist China, and cut military spending. Conservatives—a tiny band, at that point—were so distraught by these heresies that they talked about forming a third party (Reagan, by the way, was among the first Republicans to call for Nixon's resignation). The GOP was nearly obliterated in the first post-Watergate election, losing forty-three seats in the House and four in the Senate. They were now outnumbered two to one in the House and, with only thirty-eight seats in the Senate, didn't have the numbers necessary to mount a filibuster. "It was no wonder that many thought the GOP would go the way of the Whigs," wrote the Republican political consultant Craig Shirley in **Reagan's Revolution**, his account of the 1976 campaign. "Republicans, it seemed, could only win the Presidency when Democrats screwed up, as in 1968 and 1972, or when they nominated a popular war hero like Eisenhower."

In January of 1975, the pollster Robert Teeter found that only 18 percent of the voters he surveyed identified themselves as Republicans. That same month, Ford offered a premonition of malaise to come in his State of the Union address: "The State of the Union is not good."

That must have appalled the congenitally optimistic Ronald Reagan, who recently had completed two successful terms as governor of California. Reagan was an enigma to those who didn't agree with him and to many who did (including his chosen biographer, the distinguished historian Edmund Morris, who was so boggled by Reagan's opacity that he lapsed into fiction writing to convey what he guessed was the essence of the man). Most liberals outside California simply didn't take Reagan seriously. He was, they figured, a pleasant fellow—an "amiable dunce" according to the Democratic grandee Clark Clifford—a B-movie actor playing a politician, mouthing a script about an America that resembled nothing so much as the cheery, white-picket-fence fantasies peddled by Hollywood in the depths of the Depression. He seemed entirely synthetic, an animatronic figure traveling around the country for the General Electric Corporation and then for the Republican Party, armed with a saccharine confection of platitudes—"The Speech," his aides called it—about the glories of the free market, the perils of big government, and the need for an all-out crusade against the Soviet threat. He looked and sounded like a visitor from a more innocent time, defiantly resisting the styles and fashions of the 1960s—he still used **Brylcreem**, for God's sake, on his impossibly retro pompadour. (The goo had the additional benefit of darkening his few gray hairs.)

But Reagan was nobody's fool. The clarity of his thinking became apparent even to his detractors with the release in the 1990s of thousands of letters and radio scripts that he had written in longhand. He had come to his philosophy honestly, and presciently. He had been the president of a union, the Screen Actors Guild, at a time when communists had considerable support in the labor movement, especially among Hollywood's dilettante fellow travelers, and he had reacted viscerally—and appropriately—against the left's arrogance and reflexive anti-Americanism. Gradually, his anticommunism morphed into antiliberalism and here, too, there was a strong element of validity to his concerns about the corrosive slovenliness of the bureaucratic welfare state. In fact, Reagan was absolutely right about some very important things: the moral superiority of free enterprise over socialism; the need for unwavering strength in the face of totalitarianism; the importance of tradition and civility at a moment when both were being called into question.

And yet Reagan's reaction to liberalism ultimately proved an overreaction. He opposed the civil rights laws of the 1960s; he opposed Medicare, Medicaid, and the Environmental Protection Agency. Indeed, he seemed to believe there were few common **societal** interests for government to address beyond law enforcement and national defense.

But unlike his friend, the British prime minister Margaret Thatcher, who was a perfect profile in titanium zealotry, Reagan was a languorous extremist. He was not an angry man, and his innate graciousness was an absolute political necessity. It smoothed the rough edges of a philosophy that could seem harsh, to the point of heartlessness, in lesser hands and sometimes even in Reagan's. His stories on the stump about welfare queens riding around in Cadillacs seemed egregious, and his flamboyant "evil empire" anticommunism could easily pass for warmongering—but his creamy baritone, the aw-shucks nod of the head, made it difficult for most Americans to believe that Reagan would ever actually do anything unreasonable or cruel. (As it happened, he was right about the need for welfare reform and about the evilness of the empire.)

Indeed, Reagan's conservatism seemed to flow naturally from his demeanor, which was pleasant, rectitudinous, and formal, in an old-fashioned way. He insisted on wearing a jacket and tie when he entered the Oval Office. His equanimity was so intense as to seem downright eerie. It was easily mistaken for emotional distance, even by his children (but never by his wife, Nancy, whom he fastidiously adored). One of his closest political friends, the Nevada senator Paul Laxalt, once told the Reagan operative Ed Rollins, "He never calls me, and if he does, I'm on a call list that [chiefs of staff James] Baker or [Ken] Duberstein put together."

As Rollins would note in his memoir, **Bare Knuckles and Back Rooms**, "You could walk away from a dinner with Ronald Reagan believing he was your new friend for life—and you'd never hear from him again." Nevertheless, Rollins believed "He was the most unpretentious politician I've ever known, and certainly the best human being. He had a big heart and a kind soul, and he preferred to believe the best about everyone."

Reagan's closest aides, the tight inner circle that

served him from California to the White House, wor-
shipped the man. The memoirs of his two most important image consultants—the "visuals" expert Michael
Deaver and the pollster Richard Wirthlin—are hagio-
graphic. According to Deaver, Reagan abhorred political phoniness. Early on, when Deaver handed Reagan
some questions he had planted with a friendly chamber
of commerce audience, Reagan tossed the questions
into the wastebasket. "Mike, this won't work," he said.
"You can't hit a home run with a softball."

Deaver also tried to stage-manage a "day with the
governor" that had been granted Tom Brokaw, then
a young Los Angeles correspondent for NBC news.
"Knowing that [Reagan] was an ex-actor, I thought he'd
appreciate a well-scripted event, so I choreographed the
day down to the last minute," Deaver writes. But Reagan refused to go along. "You're asking me to do things
that I'm not comfortable doing," he tells Deaver. "If
I'm not comfortable, the people at home watching this
aren't going to be comfortable, either."

Deaver, suitably chastened, writes: "Professor Reagan had given me my second lesson in as many
weeks . . . I was grateful he never talked down to me in
those early years . . . As a boss there was just something
about him that made you want to please him and do
your best . . . All of us on his professional staff—in
Sacramento and later in Washington—responded to
him almost as if we were seeking a father's respect and
judgment."

It is difficult to imagine any Democratic image

maker of the past twenty-five years writing with similar affection, and respect, about a politician. It is also difficult to believe that Deaver—who remains the gold standard as a political choreographer—is telling the unvarnished truth here. Leslie Stahl remembers the obsession that the Reaganites had with the staging of events, down to the careful placement of camera platforms at photo ops. Late in the 1984 campaign, Stahl did a tough piece for the **CBS Evening News** about the impact of Reagan's budget cuts on the poor, the handicapped, and the elderly. As she laid out the facts of the case, there were images of Reagan in nursing homes and with the handicapped, and then pictures of Reagan on the stump, with balloons and brass bands and American flags. "When you turned the sound off, he just looked great—and even if you left the sound on, he looked great," Stahl said. "The next day I get a phone call from the White House **thanking** me for the piece that I had thought was devastating. A bunch of them were in Jim Baker's office laughing. Dick Darman, who was then Baker's assistant, says, 'You guys really haven't figured it out yet, have you?' The pictures were the only thing that mattered."

It seems clear, in retrospect, that Deaver and the others were molded by Reagan's own sense of performance, by his innate feel for what seemed authentic and what didn't (even if some of the things that seemed authentic weren't quite—as with Reagan's occasional tendency to mistake scenes he had seen or played in movies, especially war movies, for the real thing). And yet despite Reagan's sophisticated understanding of what the audience wanted, he remained—reflexively—an actor, an oddly passive performer in his own political career, very much at the mercy of his directors. Indeed, his career was almost waylaid by a disastrous relationship with a political consultant—John Sears, an elegant easterner whom Reagan hired as his lead strategist in 1975.

The Reagan-Sears story is often overlooked, or seen as a slightly embarrassing detour in a career that has been mythologized as a triumph of conviction. But it is an early case study in the perils of political consultancy, an avatar of many horror stories to come, especially—ironically—on the Democratic side.

The first act of the disaster is always the same: the trophy hiring of a big-name professional who doesn't know the candidate very well. Sears had worked for the Nixon presidential campaign in 1968, and he offered instant credibility with the Washington establishment, especially the media—which, Reagan's California group would soon learn, meant that he confided in a favored circle of reporters, usually to the detriment of his bureaucratic opponents within the Reagan campaign. It is odd that Reagan's Kitchen Cabinet—true believers all—thought their hero **needed** the sort of credibility and expertise that Sears would bring. But the hired gun's opening move usually is to make the yokel candidate and his staff feel inferior, to impress them with flashy insights and inside information. (Reagan biographer Lou Cannon reports that Sears snowed the California gang with Washington gossip and analysis about Watergate—he predicted Nixon was a goner—in an initial meeting at Reagan's Santa Barbara ranch in the spring of 1974.)

The next thing that happens in a bad-consultant scenario is a power struggle: hired gun versus loyal old-timers. If the candidate is strong and his insiders able, as Reagan's team was, the hired gun is eventually rejected like a mismatched liver transplant. Which is what happened to Sears, although the road to oblivion proved exceptionally long and torturous. (If the candidate is weak, and allows his close advisers to be paved over, or fired, by the newcomer, the results are almost always disastrous.) Ed Rollins, never one to pull a punch, writes that Sears "alienated just about everyone with his attitude, which was: I'm so smart I can even get that dumbshit Reagan elected president." Indeed, the Reaganauts' favorite mantra—"Let Reagan Be Reagan"—was initially concocted because Sears wouldn't.

Richard Wirthlin blames Sears for Reagan's loss to Ford in the 1976 New Hampshire primary. In his memoir, **The Greatest Communicator**, Wirthlin writes that he was stunned when Reagan left the state two days before what promised to be a very close election and went off campaigning in Illinois. "But the problem with my logic was that it was based on the assumption that John Sears had actually **shown** the candidate my polling data and **discussed** my strategy memorandum," Wirthlin writes. Not only did Sears neglect to tell Reagan about Wirthlin's numbers, he also waited until the last minute before asking the pollster himself to deliver the bad news to the candidate. Reagan responds with—surprise!—equanimity as Wirthlin lays the latest numbers on him in the plane returning to New Hampshire on the evening of election day. "With his eyes fixed on the shimmering lights of the town below, Reagan said, 'Well, Dick, I sure hope someone down there lights a candle for me.' "

Later, Wirthlin confronts Sears:

"Why didn't you apprise the governor of what was happening?"

"The presence of the candidate would have taken away from the manpower of the campaign volunteers and the get-out-the-vote efforts on the ground," he said.

"How could you **possibly** reach that conclusion?" I pressed.

"Because that's been my experience, Dick," Sears said.

An honest mistake, perhaps—and perhaps not even a Sears mistake: Lou Cannon lays it on former New Hampshire governor Hugh Gregg, who was managing the local campaign. But the tendency to apply a universal cookie-cutter theory of political practice to every race is one of the most common errors made by hired guns. Sears and Gregg were fighting past wars—local wars, in Gregg's case; the 1968 Nixon campaign for Sears. But Reagan was sui generis and usually at the top of his game in the last days of a close contest. "His enthusiasm would soar, his sights would focus and his passion would stir," Wirthlin writes. "He was one of the few leaders I've ever known who actually derived **pleasure** from confrontation."

Victory in New Hampshire had been the lynchpin of Sears's strategy; defeat led to a string of losses, culminating in Florida. The campaign was out of money. Various great and powerful Republicans were calling for Reagan to withdraw, but he pushed on to North Carolina and Sears was shoved, for a time, to the periphery of the campaign. Senator Jesse Helms and his chief political strategist, Tom Ellis, insisted on running the show themselves—even to the point of conducting their own fund-raising operation and hiring their own consultant, the exceedingly secretive Arthur Finkelstein, who, unlike Sears, was a movement conservative. (Over the next twenty years, Finkelstein would almost single-handedly turn the word "liberal" into an epithet: his ads usually branded Democrats as "hopelessly liberal" or "liberal, liberal, liberal." Ultimately, Finkelstein turned out to be more of a libertarian than a classic conservative: after being "outed" as a homosexual, he married his longtime partner in a Provincetown, Massachusetts, ceremony. Jesse Helms did not attend.)

The Helms-Ellis-Finkelstein strategy changed Reagan's basic pitch from Searsian statesmanlike moderation—the fuzzy and rather questionable notion that Reagan was a "more experienced" leader than Ford—to carnivorous conservatism. There were all sorts of fat targets available: Ford's secretary of state Henry Kissinger was considered a secret socialist by the right because he favored détente with the Soviet Union and had opened informal diplomatic ties with the Chinese communists. The proposed Panama Canal treaty was seen as near traitorous. Reagan started hammering these themes on the stump. He ditched his careful speech notes, written out on four-by-six cards, and began to speak extemporaneously. "He was like a little kid when he got rid of those cards," Paul Laxalt would later say. Reagan's Panama line was as terrific as it was demagogic: "We bought it. We paid for it. It's ours and we're gonna keep it." He slammed Ford on the local pork-barrel spending that materialized suspiciously in each primary state: "When the President comes to North Carolina," Reagan is quoted in Craig Shirley's book about the 1976 campaign, "the band won't know whether to play 'Hail to the Chief' or 'Santa Claus Is Coming to Town.' "

Sears apparently had overthought Reagan's biography as well, playing down the Hollywood angle, assuming that the general public would share the elite's misgivings about a former actor running for president. But now Reagan's old pals—John Wayne, James Stewart, the singer Pat Boone, the television actors Efrem Zimbalist Jr. and Jack Webb—popped up on the campaign trail, apparently at Nancy Reagan's suggestion, and they brought new energy and star power to a victorious North Carolina campaign.

Reagan, safely Reagan again, rolled all the way through to Tennessee and his TVA armageddon . . . and then, with his candidacy stalled just short of the number of delegates needed for the nomination, Sears resurfaced with another of the chronic mistakes in the hired gun's playbook: the inappropriate tactical masterstroke. Sears proposed that Reagan announce, just before the Republican National Convention began, that he had chosen Senator Richard Schweiker of Pennsylvania as his running mate. Schweiker was a moderate Republican, with a pro-union voting record—anathema to the red-meat crowd—but Pennsylvania was one of the states with a prime cache of still-uncommitted delegates. It is curious that none of Reagan's California loyalists seems to have objected to this garish ploy. Sears apparently made a strong case for Schweiker; the wooing of moderates was, after all, his specialty. A secret meeting between the Reagans and the Schweikers was arranged. Reagan, as was his wont, decided the Schweikers were good folks, conservatively raised in Pennsylvania Dutch communities. The ticket was announced . . . and almost immediately dismissed by the press and, more important, by Republicans as transparent and ridiculous. The Pennsylvania delegates went to Ford; worse, Reagan suffered losses among his conservative Southern supporters. Deaver remembers a meeting with the Mississippi delegation where, with the Schweikers present, a delegate berated Reagan about his vice presidential selection: "I don't know how you could have picked this fella . . . I would rather my doctor had told me my wife had a dose of clap."

And yet Sears somehow survived to fight another campaign, Reagan's second try for the nomination in 1980. "We had a western inferiority complex," Michael Deaver later explained to Lou Cannon. In other words, Sears was still assumed to be the key to winning moderate northeastern support—and northeastern support was, among other things, a euphemism for money. The 1976 campaign had been nearly broke throughout, and 1980 wasn't looking much better. The party's biggest fund-raisers—the Wall Street and corporate elites—were assumed to be concentrated in New York, although that was something of a mirage. The big donors were moving south and west with the demographic base of the party—in any case, given the post-Watergate limitations on political contributions, big donors weren't as big as they used to be, which led to another major change in political consultancy.

In the 1980 campaign, Republicans began to emphasize one of the few successful tactics that emerged from George McGovern's 1972 disaster—sending letters to targeted supporters asking for contributions, also known as direct-mail fund-raising.* Conservative pioneers in the field like Richard Viguerie used polling

---

*"Direct mail was seen by our party as a McGovern thing," the Democratic consultant Joe Trippi would later tell me, "and anything McGovern had to be avoided. It took us a long time to catch up."

to help compose letters that scratched every right-wing populist itch, and the results were spectacular: not only did Republicans outraise Democrats by $44 million to $12 million but the average per-person contribution to the GOP was $38, compared with $118 for the Democrats. This was a reflection of the monumental tectonic shift that Reagan had incited: the Republicans were moving downscale toward the masses; the Democrats were losing their working-class base. Direct-mail experts soon became a major new consultant power center in the Republican Party; those with the best mailing lists had the hottest client lists. (It is no accident that Karl Rove, who began his consulting career in the early 1980s, started out as a direct-mail expert.)

But it was impossible to forecast these changes in 1978, as Reagan geared up for another presidential run. John Sears was seen as necessary, if not entirely dependable. He would manage the campaign, but this time he would share power with Reagan's ideological consigliere Edwin Meese. There was no way this could work, of course. Collective leadership requires deliberation—and deliberation is impossible in the warp-speed world of presidential politics. (It is simply amazing how often Democrats would make this mistake in the future; Republicans carefully studied Reagan's early blunders, and almost always created campaigns with clear lines of authority.)

Sears moved gradually, and then more aggressively, to consolidate his power. Finally, he reached into the bad consultant's trick bag for a last desperate tactic: the coup attempt. The precipitating excuse was fund-raising problems. The target was Lyn Nofziger, who had been Reagan's combative and fabulously unkempt gubernatorial press specialist, now nominally in charge of fund-raising but spiritually incapable of the oiliness necessary for greasing contributors. Sears convinced Michael Deaver that Nofziger had to go—a big deal, since Deaver was universally assumed to be the voice of Nancy Reagan in the campaign. When Nofziger was duly fired on October 26, 1979, the red-meat conservatives were infuriated. The magazine **Human Events** attacked Sears as a graduate of the "Richard Nixon school of politics . . . a devout pragmatist who has little affinity for issues in general, and even less affinity for conservatives." On the way out the door, Nofziger predicted to Deaver: "You'll be next."

He was right. Deaver was now the odd man out, consigned to Nofziger's old spot in the fund-raising operation and doing no better than Nofziger had. Sears—intent on running the campaign exclusively with his two top deputies, strategist Charlie Black and press secretary Jim Lake—was threatened by Deaver's closeness to the Reagans, especially his closeness to The Spouse, a woman who terrified just about every staff member who ever worked for her husband. The Sears gang began to pressure Deaver. The sniping became so intense that on November 26, 1979, Reagan summoned Deaver, Sears, Black, and Lake to his Pacific Palisades home to settle the dispute. Lou Cannon's account of the meeting is a classic of the staff-shake-up genre:

What followed was not reconciliation but a show-down. With Deaver and Nancy alongside him, Reagan found himself faced with a united front of Sears, Lake and Black demanding that he make a decision between keeping Deaver or the three of them . . . Reagan wanted a compromise, but Sears and his allies remained adamant, unwilling to accept any arrangement that would keep Deaver in the campaign. Seeing what was happening, Nancy Reagan said to her husband: "Yes honey, you're going to have to make a choice." Before Reagan could respond, Deaver spoke up and said, "No, governor, you don't have to make that choice. I'll resign." And with that he walked to the front door. Reagan followed him, agitated, and insisted that he didn't want Deaver to leave.

Reagan returned to the living room in a fury. "The biggest man here just left the room," he said. "He was willing to accommodate and compromise and you bastards wouldn't."

Reagan never quite trusted Sears again. "I look him in the eye, he looks me in the tie," the Gipper would later tell Deaver. Meanwhile, Sears continued to overmanage the campaign. He kept Reagan—who was considered the prohibitive front-runner for the nomination—out of a big debate just before the Iowa caucuses. Reagan's Republican opponents made the most of this, spreading the word that the old guy was too slow for the rough-and-tumble. The beneficiary turned out to be George H. W. Bush, who narrowly won Iowa and goofily announced that he now had the "Big Mo," which was Connecticut for "momentum." Bush, who had held a series of appointed positions (UN ambassador, CIA director, Republican Party chair), never had been all that successful in elective politics and it was fairly easy to see why. He seemed likable and energetic, but terminally preppy in a way that came off as puerile and condescending on the stump. I remember watching Bush dash about the early primary states, chirping like a magpie on methedrine: "I'm up . . . I'm up . . . I'm up for the '80s! We've had enough of Jimmy Carter's malaise days!" (Indeed, Bush—who was solid and intelligent in private, a war hero and a man who had experienced a deep personal tragedy, the death of a daughter—suffered from the same affliction as Al Gore and more than a few other private men I've watched run for president: he was never quite sure of himself in the presence of strangers. He was the sort of man who might have reached the presidency through a backroom deal in the old days, but was fundamentally unsuited to campaign in the age of television.)

Bush's public awkwardness was all too apparent on the Saturday before the New Hampshire primary, when he was sandbagged by Reagan at what was supposed to be a one-on-one debate at Nashua High School. I was sitting somewhere in the rafters of the gymnasium as Reagan trooped in with the other Republican candidates—Bob Dole, John Connally, John Anderson, and Philip Crane—who were clearly enjoying the moment, as was the audience, which whooped and hollered. Bush wasn't. Reagan insisted the other candidates be allowed to debate; Bush stared straight ahead, red-faced and silent—unable to come up with a Turnip Day line in a spontaneous moment. Jon Breen, the publisher of the **Nashua Telegraph**, which was sponsoring the debate (although the Reagan campaign had agreed to pay for it), insisted that the rules remain as stipulated: one-on-one. Reagan, it seemed to me, was very much onstage at that point—feigning anger, defending the rights of the other candidates. Breen was playing a role, too, only he didn't know it. He tossed Reagan the ultimate straight line: "Turn Mr. Reagan's microphone off," he said.

"I paid for this microphone, Mr. Green!" Reagan thundered, inaccurately but effectively, bringing down the house and winning the primary right then and there. (The line may have been an homage to Spencer Tracy in the 1948 film **State of the Union**: "Don't you shut me off! I'm paying for this broadcast!")

The Nashua sandbagging had been planned by John Sears, and it was the rare cutesy tactical move that actually worked. It was also his last. Reagan had decided the night of the Iowa loss that Sears had to go, at the first available opportunity. Even though Sears played the New Hampshire primary perfectly—he finally let Reagan be Reagan—Nancy was secretly back in touch with Deaver, Nofziger was lurking about, Wirthlin and Meese were lobbying for the change. So Reagan fired

Sears, Jim Lake, and Charlie Black on the day of the New Hampshire primary, an elegant move: the big news was the Reagan victory, the Bush "Mo" crushed. The massacre of the Reagan consultants was barely an afterthought.

How on earth did Reagan survive Sears?

Over the next twenty-five years, there would be many similar relationships between politicians and consultants. Almost all of them ended disastrously for the politician in question. My guess is Reagan was different because Reagan was different. His supporters, who were now a critical mass in the Republican Party, were absolutely certain that he was not a standard-issue politician. They assumed that all the stupid consultant tricks—the efforts to sand down the candidate's conservatism and make him safe for general-public consumption (that is, a standard-issue politician)—were window dressing. After all, Reagan had a long paper trail of speeches and weekly radio broadcasts, and these were big speeches with big ideas, "bold colors, not pastels," as he liked to say. Left to his own devices, speaking spontaneously at the Republican National Convention in 1976—a speech that is as important to conservatives as John Kennedy's "Ask Not" inaugural is to liberals—Reagan railed against "the erosion of freedom that has taken place under Democrat rule in this country." That sort of untrammeled language has now become common for Republicans, but it seemed remarkably fresh in 1976—and especially fresh because the language was Reagan's own, unmitigated by his campaign staff. Such moments were rare, even after the departure of Sears: the staff was continually trying, and failing, to keep the Old Man on message. Reagan kept the faith with his troops through gaffes—ideological "mistakes" like his desire to privatize the TVA; made-up stories about people buying orange juice with food stamps and using the change to buy vodka—and the troops were convinced that these Turnip Day moments were windows into their hero's true character.

Character is one of the most overused and under-analyzed words in American politics. Let's attempt a simple definition: character is the intersection of beliefs and humanity. Beliefs are not policies; they are more fundamental than that—a coherent and accessible worldview. And a convincing demonstration of humanity involves more than photo ops at the state fair; it always involves some form of spontaneity. Usually a convincing humanity is the most important quality that a politician can bring to the table: in every election of the television era—with the exception of the Nixon elections—the "warmer" candidate has beaten the "colder" one. But in Reagan's case there was an odd inversion: the strength and clarity of his beliefs was the key to his success. His Turnip Day moments were about his beliefs, not his humanity.

Oh, the likability was surely there—but for Reagan, that aspect of his character was . . . his "character." That is, the character he played: his brilliant interpretation of what a president of the United States should look and sound like. Even his spontaneous moments sounded scripted: "I paid for this microphone," and, most famous, "Honey, I forgot to duck" when he was being wheeled into the operating room with a bullet less than an inch from his heart. Reagan thought like an actor. There were certain moments that required a great line (and he usually retrieved those lines from the Rolodex of scripts rattling around in his brain). This "character" was essential to his success because it enabled him to sell a belief system that represented a radical departure from the path of governance that had been in place for fifty years.

Reagan may or may not have had a good political gut. One senses that he would have campaigned on what he believed whether the American people were ready for his revolution or not. As it happened, they were ready.

As early as 1970, the pollster Richard Scammon and his strategist partner Ben Wattenberg had identified the most important person in America in their book **The Real Majority**: a "forty-seven-year-old wife of a machinist living in Dayton, Ohio," who was "unyoung, unpoor and unblack," whose "brother-in-law is a police officer and she does not have enough money to move if her suburban neighborhood deteriorates." Scammon and Wattenberg believed she was up for grabs, and the party that won her loyalty would domi-

nate American politics for the next generation. Pat
Caddell, as we've seen, was privately worried about the
erosion of loyalty among working-class whites, especially Roman Catholics. In the 1980 campaign, Reagan's pollster Richard Wirthlin specifically targeted
those people, whom he called "Reagan Democrats."

"I think Wirthlin was way ahead of us in the sophistication of his targeting," said the Democratic pollster
Peter Hart. "But then the Republicans always had a lot
more money than we did." Wirthlin was a former economics professor and devout Mormon with a passion
for complex computer models and a distressing tendency to create mind-numbing acronyms for all of
his innovations. He called his 1980 computer system
PINS (Public Information System).

In the first poll that Wirthlin conducted for Reagan,
back in 1968, he had noticed that the governor ran five
to seven points stronger with blue-collar Catholics
than with other Democratic constituencies—and now
PINS allowed him to pinpoint exactly where such people lived, what they read and watched on TV, and to
develop a media strategy to target them. In 1984,
Wirthlin was able to augment PINS with HVM (Hier-
archical Values Map), "a theoretical model capable of
mapping voters' decisions based on three factors: issues, policy program traits and values," Wirthlin later
wrote. The HVM itself looked like a spiderweb with
rectangles sprinkled throughout. "It allowed me to
monitor which candidate 'owned' which issues and values, and to understand the linkages between them."

One can only imagine.

Wirthlin was the most dangerous political commodity out there, a compulsive and hyper-literal pollster: "Engaging in excessive preparation is a charge of which I am almost always found guilty," he would write. Ed Rollins, Reagan's 1984 campaign manager, writes of having to "hose down" Wirthlin: "When I saw his budget, two words leaped to mind: 'ridiculous' and 'profiteering.' For a President running unopposed in his own party, the volume of polling Wirthlin proposed to do in the primaries was absurd . . . It made no sense—except that the data he'd be collecting would be very useful to some of his other clients." It is impossible to know if Rollins's accusation was true, but doubling-down on polling—charging multiple clients for the same poll—became a common trick used by political pollsters to get more bucks for their bang.

Wirthlin's strategic memos eclipsed Caddell's in detail, if not in high-flown theory. His "Black Book" strategic plan for the 1980 campaign was 176 pages long; the 1984 plan was 180 pages long. The sheer detail of Wirthlin's data might have proven paralytic if his client had been at all interested in what he was doing—the over-reading of polls was becoming a statistical plague that afflicted legions of lesser American politicians. But Ronald Reagan was only vaguely interested in the broadest interpretation of the numbers: was he up or was he down, did people like his ideas or not—and if they didn't, his reaction was a shrug of the shoulders and a request to Wirthlin for some better ways to sell the ideas in question. In other words, Wirthlin was essential to the operation, but **peripheral**. The only thing that really mattered was Reagan himself.

In his memoir, Wirthlin hilariously tries to analyze why Reagan was so good: "Over a lifetime spent communicating to the public, he had developed a rhetorical method best summed up in six simple words: **Persuade through reason. Motivate through emotion**." Aha! "Reagan understood that mindlessly saying the words 'family values' or telling people to 'be patriotic,' as so many politicians do, accomplishes nothing . . . Communicators must tap into an audience's emotions if they want to propel people toward action." Aha again! Another secret was "his integration of stories in his communications. Stories work because they don't raise the red flag of 'hard sell.' "

The truth was, **nothing** raised the red flag of hard sell when Reagan was speaking—even when he was saying bellicose things like "Mr. Gorbachev, tear down this wall"—because of his rosy cheeks, his easy smile, his slightly befogged avuncularity, his utter serenity. Reagan's ability to say tough things in an unthreatening way, his ability to get away with almost anything, was called "Teflon" by the press and drove his opponents to distraction. In 1980, Jimmy Carter—an ex–peanut farmer who didn't believe that an ex-actor could be a serious candidate for president—destroyed his nice-guy image by running a far more negative campaign than Reagan did. In their only debate, which was held very late in the campaign, Carter was constantly on the attack. Reagan airily dismissed his assaults with a wink and a nod, saying, "There you go again." (Deaver would later claim that the line was unscripted, pure Reagan, invented on the spot.) In 1984, Reagan's advertising spots were the preternaturally benign "Morning in America" campaign, featuring the oatmeal-and-honey voice of Reagan's old buddy Hal Riney, and scenes of a placid, rural, flag-waving America.

In retrospect, one of the most remarkable things about Ronald Reagan's two successful campaigns for president was how un-negative they were. He could be withering in his criticism of those who opposed him—that vague mob of academics and socialized health-care aficionados who hung out in faculty lounges across America—but he was unfailingly polite to his opponent.

It is also rather amazing how simple Reagan made it seem. His platform was elegant and nearly unassailable: Strong military. Low taxes. Traditional values. He was optimistic about the future. He believed in God (but rarely went to church and tried to lowball the social issues—abortion, homosexuality—that obsessed God's legions). He disdained freedom's enemies. His patriotism was flamboyant, nostalgic, emotional.

And yet, there was something missing. Reagan never asked anything of the American people. The habits of citizenship—the service, sacrifice, and discipline that had distinguished his own "Greatest" generation—

were allowed to fade amidst the narcotic haze of the Great Affluence. Worse, civic irresponsibility was encouraged: Reagan's belated embrace of supply-side tax cuts—just in time for the 1980 election season!—made a mockery of his stated belief in fiscal conservatism. He had intellectual arguments for all these positions. Conservatives believed that it was important for government to recede from its central position in American life, and allow free enterprise to flourish; conservatives believed that the huge budget deficits caused by the Reagan tax cuts would prevent the further expansion of the government.

But those arguments were short-sighted and insidious, and the Reagan style of leadership would contribute mightily to the trivialization of American politics. After Reagan, it became practically impossible for a candidate to propose any sort of long-term program involving short-term sacrifice (unless it involved a very narrow definition of national security). Any talk of energy independence, global warming, or even free-market reforms of the health-care system or old-age entitlements came to seem airy and unrealistic. Government was no longer a common public enterprise; it was the enemy of freedom. The nation's capital was an utterly corrupt foreign land.

Years later, I found myself trapped on an escalator in Des Moines with Bob Dornan, a militantly conservative congressman from California who was running for president, or so he thought. I asked him how things were going. "It's really amazing," Dornan said. "They just hate politicians. They don't believe anything we say. How did that happen?"

"Well, Congressman," I replied. "What have **you** been saying about politicians—and about Washington—for the past twenty years?"

That, too, was part of Reagan's legacy, as was an antiseptic, carefully programmed political style that was about performances and appearances, photo ops and platitudes—but was entirely bereft of Reagan's most compelling quality: his insistence on blurting out his politically inconvenient beliefs.

There was one tough moment in Reagan's last campaign against Walter Mondale in 1984. Reagan seemed flustered in the first debate. Wirthlin believes the problem was that Reagan was over-crammed with facts and figures in a last-minute, policy-oriented debate prep supervised by chief of staff Jim Baker and his assistant Richard Darman. Mondale—prepped by Pat Caddell—had proven an elusive target, never attacking Reagan directly, working hard to maintain his low-key Minnesota cool. And the Old Man **was** getting older (it is an open question whether he was already suffering some mild effects of the Alzheimer's disease that would kill him). Ed Rollins had been worried about the age issue for weeks, and would later maintain that Reagan's poor performance was attributable, at least in part, to the late hour of the debate—9:00 PM central standard time (which was the president's normal bedtime,

10:00 PM eastern time). Reagan certainly seemed to lose steam as the debate wore on, and in the end he seemed to lose everything—forgetting his closing statement and attempting to retrieve a poetic portion of his speech to the 1976 Republican National Convention in which he is "riding down the coast in an automobile, looking at the blue Pacific out on one side and the Santa Inez mountains on the other, and I couldn't help but wonder if it was going to be that beautiful a hundred years from now . . ." **That** Pacific coast drive had launched a powerful speech about the challenges America had to confront. The 1984 debate version was muddled and led nowhere. "There's no question our morale went into the toilet temporarily," Rollins wrote. "It was obvious as hell that Reagan had lost the debate."

The campaign team was so worried that it brought in an outsider, Roger Ailes, to prep their candidate for the second debate with Mondale. "I drove over to the White House," Ailes later told me, "in a limo surrounded by Reagan guys who were saying, 'Whatever you do, don't mention the age thing. Don't mention the age thing. Don't mention the age thing.' They must have said that a hundred times—and I tried, I really tried . . ."

In his memoir, Wirthlin gives Ailes credit for conducting a brilliant session:

Roger said, "Mr. President, we are going to do a little batting practice. When we throw a question your way, all we want you to do is follow your first instinct." We told him to "swing" naturally, stay on the offensive and, whatever he did, not to over-think his response . . . Initially, he was still being too cautious in his responses . . . But then something wonderful happened. As we pelted him with all kinds of pitches, the Reagan we had all been accustomed to began breaking through the surface. We kept hurling harder and harder questions. And, one right after the other, he made contact, often cracking them out of the park.

There is some dispute about what happened next. Wirthlin remembers asking Reagan how he would handle the age question and Reagan saying, "Don't you fellas worry about that. I'll handle that one."

Ailes told me a different story. "So I was trying really hard to do what they had said—not ask him about the age question. But that's just not me. I was biting my tongue. I had to ask the damn question. It would have been malpractice if I hadn't. So, on the way to the elevator, I asked him and he said, 'Roger, I once was part of an act in Vegas, and there was this great line.' He told me the line. We worked on it—and you know the rest."

The rest was this. In the second debate, Henry Trewhitt of the Baltimore **Sun** asked the age question in a clever, oblique way: "President Kennedy had to go for days on end with very little sleep during the Cuban missile crisis. Is there any doubt in your mind that you would be able to function in such circumstances?"

"Not at all, Mr. Trewhitt," Reagan replied. "And I want you to know that . . . I will not make age an issue of this campaign. I am not going to exploit, for political purposes, my opponent's youth and inexperience."

Even Mondale was laughing. The election was over. Reagan's second term was assured.

3

Banana-Peel Words

★ ★ ★ ★

In early June of 1981, some sixty million years after the last dinosaurs, chilled by the cooling air and addled by the heaving earth, stumbled toward extinction in the Colorado highlands, the leaders of the Democratic Party arrived in Denver for a meeting.

The Democrats, as always, divided themselves into caucuses: Women (concerned exclusively with the Equal Rights Amendment, a futile and symbolic gesture and therefore favored ground for Democrats), blacks, Hispanics, homosexuals (a lonely caucus of one), progressive-liberals and ethnics (a caucus for Caucasians?). They argued over rules and procedures, though less vehemently than in the past. They passed resolutions, none of which showed the slightest spark of ingenuity or the faintest glimmer of a new idea. They railed against Reagan and wallowed like happy brontosauruses in a turgid pool of self-congratulatory idealism. In the strictest sense of the word, they had become conservatives—defending the past, the troubled social programs of New Deal and Great Society vintage, with a vengeance.

I wrote that in the September 17, 1981, issue of **Rolling Stone**. It was my formal declaration of apostasy—to paraphrase Ronald Reagan's cliché: I had left the liberal wing of the Democratic Party because the liberal wing of the Democratic Party had gone off the deep end. The multifarious "progressive" tribes had lost track of the American public just as "progressive" jazz musicians had wandered off into melodic abstraction in the 1950s; in both cases, the adjective "progressive" was the antonym of "popular." The musicians and the Democrats had progressed well beyond their audience. Reading through the rest of the **Rolling Stone** piece now, I am stunned by how little has changed—and how often, over the years, I have rewritten that same story. Inevitably, various Democrats predict that the Republican project is too extreme to be sustained: "It could be a tidal wave," said Congressman Les Aspin of Wisconsin in 1981, predicting a Democratic renaissance, "especially if Reagan insists on following the right-wing line on issues like abortion." Inevitably, other Democrats are convinced that the problem is merely technical, that the party has to catch up in field organization or fund-raising or in developing its own think tanks, or whatever, and then all will be well.

"We're focusing on modernization, computerization, direct mail," Democratic National Committee chairman Charles Manatt told me in 1981. Inevitably, I consult with various academic sages who put a frame around the larger picture, announcing the transition from the industrial to the information age—and decry the Democrats' tendency to confuse bureaucracy with the liberal ideal. (In 1981, it was John Naisbitt, who would soon become famous for his book **Megatrends**, who told me that he had just met with a group of Democrats trying to rethink their party: "Close to hopeless," he sniffed.)

Inevitably, there are "New" Democrats hoping to steer the party away from the thrall of the various liberal interest groups. "They need a real maverick to shake them up," the direct-mail expert Tom Mathews told me in 1981, "a candidate of the radical middle, someone who isn't afraid to say goodbye to the past." (A tip of the cap to the late Tom Mathews: "radical middle" would become my own overused personal mantra; in 1995, I would even write a cover story for **Newsweek** called "The Search for the Radical Middle." It didn't sell very well.) And inevitably, I would check in with Ted Kennedy—ground zero of the party's liberal establishment—who would express mystification and vague disappointment with all this radical-middle, neoliberal, New Democrat stuff: "I still believe in the commitments we've made to the poor, the elderly, the working people who want to send their children to college, the sick and the handicapped," he told me in

1981. "There can be **no retreat** from these basic principles." Which would give me pause—until I remembered that the Democrats' solutions to all those problems were tailored to appease their various interest groups, to ignore the welfare-dependent culture of poverty, to maintain the stone-stupid bureaucracies of the past, to underestimate the importance of entrepreneurship at home and the projection of strength abroad.

Well, I still believe in a place called the radical middle . . . but I'll not rehearse that argument here. What's most interesting now about my 1981 version of **Democrats in Disarray** is what's missing: any specific mention of **race**, the transcendent American social and political dilemma—although the fact that the Democrats had already splintered themselves into caucuses does hint at the problem. While Reagan's Republicans were offering a unified, national message, the Democrats presented a fractured image that emphasized the primacy of their interest groups and, bizarrely, divided people according to racial identity a mere decade after liberals had made it a point of honor to oppose racial segregation. No doubt it would have been near impossible for the leaders of the party to tell the newly elected African American members of Congress that separating themselves into a black caucus was a bad idea—but it was a bad idea, which led to the creation of all those other caucuses, and to a public role for liberal interest groups that the Republicans never granted their own powerful special pleaders. This was especially true in the presidential election process. Inevitably, each of the various liberal sects would stage debates in which the Democratic candidates for president would be expected to endorse every last extreme item on the wish list.

In retrospect, it seems clear that a primary cause of the Democratic Party's decline was its refusal to acknowledge legitimate public concerns about crime, welfare dependency, affirmative action, and forced busing to achieve integration—all of which, obviously, had a racial dimension. Most Democrats running for office understood what a pickle they were in on what came to be known as the "social" issues . . . and they asked their consultants to solve it for them, to figure out ways to finesse the worthy but implausible positions favored by their party. Running for president in 1968, Hubert Humphrey stumbled through an elaborate tap dance on school busing. He said he opposed "massive compulsory busing that has as its sole objective racial balance based on a mathematical formula." But he also said that it was "fit, right and proper that you bus a child from an inferior school to a good school."

Humphrey was a harbinger. The tap dance became the template for Democratic inanity. Liberals were against "racial quotas" but they were in favor of "racial preferences." They said they favored "a hand up, not a handout," but they supported a welfare system that delivered handouts and asked for absolutely nothing in return. Their speech became gerundial, evasive—it reflected the sensibility of the teachers and social workers, the "helping professions" that became the party's most loyal voters. They seemed more concerned with understanding bad actions than with punishing them. I once asked David Dinkins, the mayor of New York, if he thought **evil** had any role in criminality, and he responded, testily and no doubt unconsciously, with examples of how the evil subjugation of the poor had produced the conditions that induced people to commit crimes. Yes, poverty and discrimination induced criminality to a certain extent. But Dinkins was simply incapable of saying, as were most liberals of his era, that there were some bad people out there—in the city and in the world—who needed to be taken out of public circulation. Indeed, liberals tended to cringe when Ronald Reagan called the Soviet Union an "Evil Empire" or when George W. Bush later called terrorists "evildoers." To paraphrase the old line about puritans, a liberal became a person who worried that someone, somewhere might be offended.

The failure to speak plainly would haunt the Democrats for a generation and infect their positions on non-race issues as well (John Kerry speaking about the Iraq war in 2004 sounded an awful lot like Hubert Humphrey talking about busing in 1968). In early 2005, the Democratic pollster Diane Feldman realized the extent of the damage while conducting a focus group in a midwestern state. "I showed them a fairly typical [Democratic] policy statement and an old guy said, 'That's awful.' I asked him why and he said, 'It's filled with banana-peel words.' I asked what that meant and he said, 'Those slippery words you politicians always use.' "

The descent from turnips to banana peels, which gathered tremendous speed in the 1980s, was, to be sure, a universal political phenomenon—Republicans have their banana-peel words, too—but I suspect that Democrats suffered from the affliction worse than Republicans did, and their suffering had everything to do with their labyrinthine contortions on racial issues. It is impossible to understand the dynamics of American politics in the television era without a clear-eyed look at how the Democrats managed to get themselves so hopelessly boggled.

They came by their dilemma honorably. They opposed racial segregation. They chose to support the civil rights movement. A great many Republicans, especially conservatives, did not—a historic moral disgrace that the party has yet to overcome. Even otherwise honorable men like Barry Goldwater, who paid lip service to integration, opposed the legislation that would make it real (on the flimsy grounds that it violated states rights). After Lyndon Johnson—who was intimately acquainted with the darker side of his home region—passed the Civil Rights Act of 1964, he accurately predicted that the South would be lost to the Democrats for a generation. South Carolina's segregationist U.S. senator Strom Thurmond started the ball rolling by jumping from the Democrats to the Republicans soon after the act was passed. In 1968, Richard Nixon made a blatant pitch to what his young strategist Kevin Phillips called the "Emerging Republican Majority," which was to say: white Southerners. There was a fair amount of racist crudeness to this on the grassroots level; more prominent Republicans communicated through winks and nods. The Republican appeal to white Southerners was not entirely racial—it was also religious and patriotic. It played to cultural fears about sexual permissiveness and moral relativism, and appealed to the regional tradition of military service. In any case, it was wildly successful: by 2005, Louisiana's Mary Landrieu was the only Democrat in the U.S. Senate who hailed from the Deep South.

There was probably no way the Democrats could have held on to the South, but they also began to lose traction with the white middle class in the rest of the country as well—and this was directly attributable to the intellectual cowardice and political correctness that prevented liberal Democrats from looking clearly at the dramatic pathologies that had begun to affect poor black communities. In 1965, Daniel Patrick Moynihan published a paper called "The Black Family," which argued that increasing out-of-wedlock birth rates were causing serious social problems. In a later paper, he was able to show that the welfare caseload—which in the past rose and fell with the unemployment rate—had exploded in the 1960s even as the unemployment rate was falling (the welfare caseload in New York City **tripled** during those years). This was something new under the sun, a "culture of poverty" caused by individual behavior rather than by economics, and marked by intergenerational dependence on the welfare system. At the heart of this phenomenon was the refusal of many men to take responsibility for the children they sired.

Moynihan was immediately and viciously attacked as a racist. It was considered racist to even **discuss** the possibility that a new set of destructive mores had taken hold in the urban ghettos. The truth of Moynihan's theory would not be accepted by liberals for twenty years, when the black sociologist William Julius Wilson finally acknowledged—in a 1987 book called **The Truly Disadvantaged**—the horrific sociological findings that had been piling up: poor children raised by single mothers were far more likely to drop out of school, become drug addicts, commit crimes, and produce out-of-wedlock babies of their own. The rise in out-of-wedlock births had soared in the intervening years from 26 percent, when Moynihan wrote his initial report, to nearly 80 percent in some poor black communities by the late 1980s. The rise in crime was unimaginable. In New York City, for example, robbery rates—the most accurate index of criminal activity—had remained stable through much of the twentieth century (even during the Great Depression). But robberies quintupled between 1962 and 1967—from 6,634 to 35,934 per year—and then doubled again from 1967 to 1972 (to 78,202), and kept rising.

And the Democratic Party's response to this? Utter denial. The party line on the culture of poverty came from the lyrics of **West Side Story**: the poor were victims, depraved on account of being deprived. Any attempt to modify the perverse incentives of the welfare system was derided by liberals as "blaming the victim." The refusal to work was justified: poor blacks were being asked to perform "dead-end jobs" (which, of course, were eagerly snapped up by immigrants, many of whom used them as a springboard into the middle class). Any discussion of "law and order" was considered a coded attempt to appeal to racial bigotry. Any attempt to raise the responsibilities inherent in parenthood was dismissed as hopelessly old-fashioned and racist to boot. More money—to the poor, to the schools, to the corrupt urban machines that were now run by some fairly flagrant, and gratuitously incendiary, minority politicians—was the only permissible response to the devastation taking place in the cities.

If the Democratic Party's support for racial equality in the 1960s was among the most honorable and politically costly stands taken by a political party in American history, its condescending failure to confront the social pathologies of the poor in the 1970s and 1980s was among the most careless and squalid. But the fecklessness was understandable, in an extremely sad way. The upper reaches of the party were now populated by the rebels of the 1960s, people who had experimented with drugs and celebrated sexual freedom—and who now thought it hypocritical to tsk-tsk poor blacks who were indulging in the same indulgences.

But the indulgences weren't the same. The poor didn't experiment with drugs; they **used** them. And sexual freedom all too often meant unwed motherhood. It was a phenomenon that the economist Adam Smith had warned against two hundred years earlier when he noted that "wanton and even disorderly mirth, the pursuit of pleasure to some degree of intemperance [and] the breach of chastity" did not necessarily hurt a nobleman, who could sleep late after a night on the town, but "the vices of levity are almost always ruinous to the common people, and a single week's . . . dissipation is often sufficient to undo a poor workman for ever."

The "vices of levity" had become something of an ideology in the 1960s—among not just the fun-loving collegiate counterculture but also the business executives who marketed feral consumerism, which reached the poorest and least sophisticated Americans through their television sets. Throughout most of the nineteenth and twentieth centuries reformers had been puritanical sorts, rooting out immorality in the slums. Now liberals not only tended to absolve antisocial behavior, they also identified with it as a revolt against shallow and restrictive "bourgeois" values. There was a tacit alliance between the intelligentsia and the outlaw poor—announced and promoted by writers like Norman Mailer—that romanticized alienation. Later, as the body count in the inner cities ballooned, the alliance metastasized into a sloppy, undifferentiated empathy. Crime had "root causes" that needed to be understood. Evil was not one of them.

The courts certainly seemed to understand—and the Democrats began to develop an unnatural dependence on the judiciary. Again, this was a tendency that had started honorably: the federal courts enforced Lyndon Johnson's civil rights legislation, and compelled Southern states to desegregate. But the Democrats changed the racial bargain in the late 1960s: they moved from equal rights to favoring special privileges—racial preferences—for those who had been discriminated against in the past, and the courts followed the prevailing liberal sentiments (while also issuing a series of rulings that seemed to make life easier for criminals). Needless to say, these were exceedingly unpopular positions among white middle-class voters—and Democrats found them nearly impossible to explain. Worse, there was a slightly rancid racial condescension that attended all this. Until Bill Clinton criticized the rap singer Sister Souljah for her racist lyrics in 1992—a classic consultant gimmick that worked—no Democratic politician was willing to say anything critical of even the most hateful and extreme blacks (and precious few have been willing to do so since). Even Robert Kennedy had succumbed in 1968, taking a rhetorical beating from a group of Black Panthers in Oakland without offering a word in his own defense. Afterward, one of his aides had asked why he'd listened to all that crap. "Someone has to," he replied.

Most Americans disagreed. Most Americans believed that liberal Democrats were either terminally weak or transparently phony for not standing up to black extremists. As early as 1976, a CBS poll found that 50 percent of white Democrats thought the party was paying too much attention to blacks and other minorities (only 18 percent supported busing).

Life was much easier for Republicans. Ronald Reagan had given his party the gifts of simplicity and clarity and, as we have seen, a coherent belief system that could be explained in sentence fragments: Military Strength. Low Taxes. Traditional Values. The Democrats, by contrast, were the party of the complex, clause-draped sentence: "We need to spend money on Head Start programs in order to . . ."

There was an essential political conundrum that shaped the futility of liberalism in the television era. Democrats slouched toward public pessimism—the middle class was always suffering silently, the poor neglected, the environment degraded—but they were philosophically optimistic: humankind was improvable, reform possible, government could help make things better. Republicans, by contrast, were publicly optimistic—the United States was exceptional, the greatest country in the world, and anyone who said otherwise was unpatriotic—but privately realistic and often pessimistic: people were who they were, the poor would always be with us and there was no sense trying to change them. These fundamental beliefs had significant implications when it came to running political campaigns.

In public, Reagan's 1984 "Morning in America" was countered by Congressman Richard Gephardt's 1988 "it's close to midnight and getting darker all the time." In private, Democrats were perennially trying to hatch new high-minded schemes—new government programs—to lure the public to their side, while all too often the Republicans were hatching cynical ways to appeal to the basest instincts of the voters. In 1968, for example, an academic named William Gavin, who would later become a White House speechwriter, sent Richard Nixon a memo about communications strategy: "Voters are basically lazy, basically uninterested in making an **effort** to understand what we are talking about." He went on to discuss the difference between intellectual and emotional appeals: "Reason requires a high degree of discipline, of concentration; impression is easier. Reason pushes the viewer back, it assaults him, it demands that he agree or disagree; impression can envelop him, invite him in, without making an intellectual demand."

Even earlier, in the 1930s, the husband-and-wife public relations team of Clem Whitaker and Leone Baxter had established Campaigns, Inc., probably the first independent political consulting firm, to give advice to California Republicans. None of the advice was high-minded. "The average American doesn't want to be educated," Whitaker proclaimed. "He doesn't . . . even want to work, consciously, at being a good citizen. But there are two ways you can interest him in a campaign, and only two that we have ever found successful. Most every American likes a contest. He likes a good hot battle, with no punches pulled. So you can interest him if you put on a fight! Then, too, most every American likes to be entertained . . . he likes fireworks and parades. So if you can't fight, put on a show!"

Whitaker and Baxter's idea of a good show was to put up two thousand billboards in the 1934 gubernatorial campaign against the Democratic socialist Upton Sinclair, which read: "If I am elected governor, half the unemployed in the country will hop the first freight to California—Upton Sinclair."

Lee Atwater liked a good show, too. Certainly, he had strong feelings about what motivated voters. "The average voter could absorb only a limited amount of information about his candidate . . . and should never be bewildered with specifics," John Brady writes in **Bad Boy**, a balanced but not unsympathetic biography of Atwater. "It was Lee's job to find the specific example, the outrageous abuse, the easy-to-digest tale that made listeners **feel**—usually repulsion—rather than **think**. Like the old carnival barker, he needed a hook to get them into the tent. And so began the search for wedge issues for George H. W. Bush—simple, impressionistic issues that appealed to attitudes, created a reaction, not a thought."

Atwater, then, stood at ground zero in the not-so-grand Republican tradition of assuming the worst about voters—and he stood there at the moment when the press became transfixed by the process rather than the substance of politics. With two weak candidates—Bush and Dukakis—peace and prosperity in the land, and not much of substance on the table, there was little else to write about in 1988. It was the year that political consultants became celebrities. They were featured on television almost as frequently as their candidates were (and they certainly were a lot more fun to watch than the politicians). Their version of reality, which was called "spin" for its transparently preposterous torque, became the prevailing language of politics and punditry. After a major debate, thunder squalls of spinners would congregate in the press room—later they would be given their own room, "Spin Alley"—to shamelessly attempt to alter reporters' impressions of what they had just seen (you could always tell the losers in Spin Alley: they worked harder and stayed longer). In late September, **Time** magazine ran a cover story by Walter Shapiro that made it official: 1988 was the Year of the Handlers. "Something has truly gone awry in 1988, as the election becomes transformed into a handlers' handicap," Shapiro wrote. "More than any other race in history, this has become a narrow-gauge contest between two disciplined teams of political professionals."

Okay, maybe it was only one disciplined, professional team. There was a gleeful bloodlust on the Republican side. There were colorful characters like Atwater and Roger Ailes who thrived on the hugger-mugger of politics. And worst of all for Democrats, there was a plan: "Every single thing I did," Ailes later

said, "from debates to rhetoric to speeches to media was
to define the two [candidates] and push them farther
apart." All of which caused a new excuse to be added
to the Democratic Party's litany of reasons why it remained out of power: the Republicans didn't fight fair.

Atwater, who was ringmaster for this circus, was an
entirely feral human being, a backstabber and flamboyant self-promoter—and yet he was irresistible, especially to political reporters, because he was so blatantly
and unapologetically what he was, a perfect rogue. He
had the attention span of a paramecium; he was always
jiggling, speed-rapping, spinning. The only way to get
him to slow down—for me, at least—was to talk music, the funkier the rhythm and blues the better. So I
would leave messages with his assistant: "Tell him I saw
Little Milton the other night." And sure enough, a day
or a week later, usually in the early evening, I'd get a
phone call, which would begin unceremoniously, without so much as a hello, "Did they back him with
horns?" Over time, Atwater came to trust me some—
although he always figured that I was on the other side
politically, more or less—and, ultimately, did me the
enormous favor of introducing me to his chief researcher and designated brainiac Jim Pinkerton, who
became a great friend.

Atwater came from a middle-class family in South
Carolina and learned his trade through the Strom
Thurmond organization. He worked the South for the
Reagan campaign in 1980 and landed a job in the
White House political office with a strong recommen-

dation from Thurmond. He immediately began squirm-
ing upward. "Lee loved to impress people with his
smarts," Ed Rollins, Atwater's boss in the political office, later wrote. "His staff would summarize best-
sellers and political tomes so Lee could throw out
quotes at meetings and parties of books he had never
read. He was always bringing me 30-page memoranda
he'd just whipped up, but he couldn't write a sentence.
Most of the memos were written by his in-house guru,
Jim Pinkerton."

One thing Atwater did know was politics, especially
Southern politics. In a 1983 memo that Lee may actually have written himself, he proposed a Southern strategy for the Reagan reelection campaign. There were
three main voting blocs, he wrote: the country clubbers, who were reliably Republican; the blacks, who
were militantly Democratic; and the populists, who
were up for grabs. Democrats would try to woo the
populists by appealing to their economic interests;
but populism, as Atwater understood it, was more an
attitude—a quality of resentment—than anything else.
"Republicans in the South could not win elections by
talking about issues," he said. "You had to make the
case that the other candidate was a bad guy." He was
very good at that.

Atwater spent most of the first Reagan term fi-
nagling a place for himself on the George H. W. Bush
campaign team. His goal was to manage Bush's 1988
presidential campaign—which seemed an unlikely
prospect, given the vice president's upper-class play-

fair sensibility. Atwater figured he had to do a high-tone sales job in order to win the gig, and so he had Pinkerton—undoubtedly, it was Pinkerton this time—write a memo, dated December 19, 1984, laying out a political strategy for the campaign: "A cosmology that no politician to my knowledge has yet appropriated comes from Alvin Toffler," the memo—as quoted in the Brady biography—actually proposed, and then proceeded to cite, Toffler's Third Wave theory. (Toffler was one of Pinkerton's absolute favorites.) The first wave of human development had been agriculture, the second had been industry. "The Third Wave is more than just computers and high tech," the memo argued. "The Third Wave is decentralization, de-massification, and the entropy of giant institutions. It is entrepreneurialism. It offers new freedom and independence to the individual . . . It is the Third Wave, Toffler would say, that had been disrupting American politics in the '60s and '70s." This development was particularly threatening "to those whose livelihoods and outlooks are firmly wedded to the much different values of the second wave, e.g., unionized workers, government bureaucrats, family traditionalists and TV network executives."

This was very smart, but it didn't have much to do with the campaign that Bush would actually run, which was a national version of Atwater's Southern strategy: an alliance between the country clubbers and the populists (indeed, the relationship between Atwater and Bush writ large). "Populists—generally middle and lower middle class—across the country are 'anti' in outlook," the memo continued, in a more Atwaterian vein. "They are anti–Big Government, anti–Big Business, anti–Big Labor. They are also hostile to the media, to the rich and to the poor. They are often called 'Middle American Radicals.' Because populists are opposed to a lot more things than they are for, it is difficult to mobilize them." Finding new ways to rev up the resentful would become the defining characteristic of the vice president's 1988 campaign.

Bush loved it. "Christmas might seem like a peculiar time to read a brilliant somewhat provocative paper on a possible future for the V.P.," he responded, in one of his famously gracious notes, "but I did read it today and I am staggered by its thoughtfulness, its clarity of thought and its brilliance."

But it still required a command performance at a Bush family murder board at Camp David in the spring of 1985 for Atwater to win the job. ("If there's a hand grenade rolling around George Bush, we want you diving on it first," Jeb Bush reportedly said.) The family was mystified by Atwater, who must have seemed the sort of person you hired to clean out the septic system (then again, given the vice president's disdain for the rough-and-tumble, politics did seem a form of sewer work). Yes, Atwater's warp-speed pitch sounded smart—the Bushes were into fast; they even played speed golf—but could he be trusted? He was rumored to be overly ambitious, a publicity hound, a married man who was flagrantly unfaithful to his

wife—all of which was true. And so, at Atwater's behest, the Bush family decided to send its own designated screwup, the vice president's oldest son, George
W. Bush, to keep tabs on the consultant. It was an inspired casting call: George W. totally enjoyed Atwater's
outlaw sensibility and he learned a fair amount of political tradecraft that he would later apply to his own
campaigns.

Atwater's job was not easy in 1988. People simply
didn't like Bush the Elder very much. A famous **Newsweek** cover portrayed the vice president pushing his
speedboat into what seemed a stiff headwind, with the
headline FIGHTING THE WIMP FACTOR. Bush, a World
War II bomber pilot, certainly was no wimp—but he
wasn't even remotely a populist, either, and Atwater's
Southern strategy was going to require a candidate who
could pass as a standard-issue American human being.
At the beginning of the campaign, Bush was still very
much Connecticut. He complained that he didn't do
well in an early Iowa straw poll because his supporters
were off taking their daughters to debutante balls
at their local country clubs. After Bush finished
third in Iowa, behind Bob Dole and the Reverend
Pat Robertson, Atwater sent Bush hurtling across
New Hampshire using various populist means of
conveyance—trucks, earthmovers, snowmobiles—
images that seemed quite incredible, especially after the
vice president asked for a "splash" of coffee at a New
Hampshire truck stop. But Bush survived New Hampshire, mostly because Dole was reluctant to sign a "no

tax" pledge in that virulently antitax state. Eventually, Atwater pounded his candidate into populist fighting trim. In the general election, Bush suddenly discovered a taste for pork rinds and country music, and admitted to being one of the world's least likely born-again Christians.

All of which might have proven disastrously risible if Bush hadn't lucked into an opponent who seemed even more effete than he did, a man who embodied all the wrong turns the Democratic Party had taken since the 1960s. Michael Dukakis, the governor of Massachusetts, hailed from the National Public Radio wing of his party. He was stratospherically high-minded, a man of preternatural calm and utter rationality, a man who seemed to believe that emotions were a form of human frailty badly in need of legislative reform. In the most embarrassing moment of the campaign, Dukakis was asked, during a debate with Bush, whether he would favor the death penalty if his wife—the vivacious and eminently human Kitty Dukakis—were raped and murdered. Needless to say, Dukakis did not respond with a surge of testosterone. He didn't even wince when the questioner, Bernard Shaw of CNN, raised the image of Kitty savaged by a thug. He serenely reiterated his opposition to the death penalty, and committed political suicide.

Actually, thanks to Atwater—and Pinkerton, who led the opposition research team—rapists and murderers had already played a prominent role in the 1988 campaign. With the well-known Bush trailing the largely unknown Dukakis by ten to twenty points in the spring horse-race polls, Atwater decided to run a campaign very similar to Caddell's scorched-earth strategy against Ed Zschau in California two years earlier—it would be the very opposite of Reagan's sunny jaunts across the political landscape. It would be the darkest, emptiest presidential campaign in history (at least, to that point).

Pinkerton was given a $1.2 million budget and a hundred researchers working around the clock on opposition research; they quickly produced a 312-page compendium of liberal excesses called **The Hazards of Duke**. The most important discoveries involved crime and race, of course. In a classic what-was-he-thinking? moment during his first term as governor, Dukakis vetoed a bill that would have banned weekend furloughs from prison for murderers. In his third term, a gentleman named William R. Horton Jr., who was serving a life sentence for stabbing a gas-station attendant to death (nineteen times, with a six-inch blade), was released on a weekend pass from the Massachusetts State Correctional Facility at Concord. Horton decided to wander down to Baltimore, where he proceeded to terrorize a young couple for twelve hours—slashing the man twenty-two times across the midsection, then raping the woman twice—before the police captured him. Horton was black; the couple was white. Willie Horton would soon take his place in American political history. "The only question," the Republican media consultant Roger Ailes told **Time** magazine in a moment of irrational exuberance, "is whether we portray Willie Horton with a knife."

There were other wonders to behold in the Dukakis portfolio and I, inadvertantly, had a role in one. On an early campaign swing through Iowa, I heard Dukakis proudly announce that he was "a card-carrying member of the ACLU." This seemed gratuitously lunkheaded at the time, a liberal act of irrational exuberance. For one thing, Dukakis's formulation inferred, and subconsciously linked him to, the alliterative McCarthy-era canard "a card-carrying member of the Communist Party." For another, the American Civil Liberties Union was associated in the public mind—if it was known for much of anything at all—with protecting the rights of criminals. (Around that time, the ACLU tried to prevent the Chicago Housing Authority from putting metal detectors in the free-fire zones that passed for housing projects, a point of principle incomprehensible to almost everyone.) So I reported the ACLU line in **New York** magazine and, sure enough, George Bush was soon traveling about, citing it. He often cited it surrounded by American flags—once, in fact, in a flag factory—which was a reference to another of Dukakis's greatest hits: the governor had vetoed a bill requiring students in Massachusetts to recite the Pledge of Allegiance, out of respect for the civil liberties of Jehovah's Witnesses and others who forswore oaths of any sort. It was the sort of nuanced, and deeply American, response that had become quite untenable in the muddy field of TV politics.

In late May, Atwater tried out some of these "issues" on focus groups in Paramus, New Jersey. The sessions would become legendary. The groups were composed exclusively of Democrats who had voted for Reagan and were intending to vote for Dukakis. As soon as they learned about Willie Horton and the Pledge of Allegiance, almost everyone in the room flipped and said they would vote for Bush. Atwater knew he had his campaign, and he knew it wasn't going to be uplifting, and he wondered if Bush would go for it. He brought videotapes of the Paramus sessions to Kennebunkport for the vice president's perusal. Bush told him to fight fiercely.

A few days later, Pinkerton told me that they had discovered what would undoubtedly become one of the key issues of the campaign: the Pledge of Allegiance veto. I laughed. "You're kidding, right?" Later Jim and I would have a more serious conversation about Willie Horton. My gut reaction was that it was unfair, insubstantial, and all about race. His defense was that it was absolutely substantive—an indication of how ridiculously lenient the Democrats were on the crime issue—and therefore fair game (after all, Al Gore had used the furloughs-for-murderers argument against Dukakis during a debate in the Democratic primaries). Pinkerton also argued, accurately, that Bush never mentioned Horton's race. True enough, but disingenuous: an independent group called Americans for Bush, which may or may not have had ties to the Bush campaign, ran a television ad showing a picture of Willie Horton, who

did indeed look like your worst nightmare. The media
picked up on this, and pretty soon almost every civilian in the country who was interested in the presidential campaign knew what color Willie Horton was and
what he had done—and was wondering why Michael
Dukakis had set him free for the weekend to do it.
(And so another of the fetid extracurricular activities of
modern campaign technique was born: the independent campaign committee that would go sleazy against
an opponent, without tarring the candidate—George
W. Bush would have the benefit of several such committees in his 2000 and 2004 presidential campaigns;
and liberal groups like MoveOn.org would spend vast
amounts of money, to little effect, running negative ads
against Bush in 2004.)

For his part, Roger Ailes never showed Willie Horton with a knife. Ailes ran a brilliant advertising campaign that year, but his most important innovation had
nothing to do with what went on the air. He decided
to hire a stable of advertising subcontractors, rather
than a single consultant, to do the Bush ads. The subs
would compete to come up with the best script after
Ailes gave them general marching orders: do something
about the prison furloughs, do something about the
pollution in Boston Harbor. The ads that Ailes eventually selected were devastatingly good. His "Willie Horton" ad didn't even mention Willie Horton. It was shot
by the Republican consultant Sig Rogich in black and
white, and showed convicts in a revolving door exit-
ing a prison. An announcer said, "Michael Dukakis's

revolving-door prison policy gave weekend furloughs to first-degree murderers not eligible for parole . . . Now Michael Dukakis wants to do for America what he has done for Massachusetts. America can't afford that risk."

By contrast, the Dukakis ad campaign was a mess. In fact, every organizational aspect of the Dukakis campaign was a mess. He even had two campaign managers for the general election after he brought back John Sasso—who had been fired for covertly distributing the tape of Joe Biden's oratorical plagiarism during the primaries—to replace the utterly incompetent Susan Estrich. Except that Sasso didn't really replace Estrich: in yet another eruption of liberal sensitivity, Dukakis just couldn't fire the most prominent woman in his campaign. So Sasso and Estrich coexisted—each with his and her own polling and advertising team.

Given the confusion, rapid response was impossible; in fact, given Dukakis's predilections, **any** sort of response was unlikely. The man seemed a political pacifist, fundamentally incapable of defending himself, and when he tried to do so the halfhearted results were pathetic. "I have a question for Mr. Bush," Dukakis tried at one point. "Don't you think it's about time you came out from behind the flag and told us what you intend to do to provide basic health care for 37 million Americans?"

That was snappy. Atwater later confided to a group of **Time** magazine editors how he would have run a campaign against his own candidate. "He would have built TV ads around pictures of George Herbert

Walker Bush as Ambassador to the UN in the early 70s," Brady writes in **Bad Boy**, "with his half-rim glasses, long hair and sideburns, and flashy neckties. Pictures of Bush in tennis whites dancing a silly pirouette to celebrate winning a close match. Pictures of the sprawling oceanfront mansion in Kennebunkport, with a voice-over: 'No wonder he wants to cut capital gains taxes on the wealthy.' "

Actually, the Dukakis campaign staff suggested to the candidate that he consider going after Bush as an elitist who would benefit financially from Republican policies—but Dukakis thought it was unnecessarily personal and distasteful, and refused to do it. After the election, according to Thomas Patterson in his book **The Vanishing Voter**, Dukakis acknowledged "a failure to understand" the forces that had been unleashed against him. "I said in my acceptance speech in Atlanta that the 1988 campaign was . . . about [competence not ideology]. I was wrong. It was about phraseology. It was about 10-second sound bites. And made-for-TV backdrops. And going negative." He was certainly right about the last point. Patterson cites a study by Darrell West of Brown University: about 35 percent of "prominent" campaign ads in 1976 were negative; the number rose to 60 percent in 1980, 74 percent in 1984, and a staggering 83 percent in 1988.

After the 1988 election, President George H. W. Bush asked Lee Atwater if he would like a job in the new administration. Atwater said he wanted to be chairman of the Republican National Committee, and Bush agreed. It was a fitting coda to the Year of the Handlers: Atwater was the first professional consultant to be named chairman of an American political party, an official acknowledgment that the consultants had assumed the traditional role of the political bosses. In 1992, Bush would name his pollster, Bob Teeter, as his campaign chairman—another first.

Atwater, sadly, wasn't around for the 1992 campaign. He was diagnosed with brain cancer in March of 1990 and lived a horrific, painful year—during which he apologized to Dukakis and all the others he'd beaten and slimed—before passing away on March 29, 1991. His absence was very much apparent in 1992, as Bush ran a flabby, toothless, lugubrious effort against Bill Clinton that seemed very much like the Dukakis campaign of 1988. An example: At a fund-raising stop at a gay nightclub in New York, Clinton was asked if he would permit homosexuals to serve openly in the military. He said yes. The statement, which was made late at night after the network news programs were over and most newspapers were put to bed, made no splash at the time. The Bush campaign certainly didn't seem to notice it. Atwater undoubtedly would have—and he undoubtedly would have been slagged by people like me for running a homophobic campaign. But, as Ben Wattenberg later pointed out, gays in the military could have been a perfect window into the much larger problem Clinton had as a prospective commander in chief—just as Willie Horton had illuminated Dukakis's weakness on crime. Clinton's discomfort and unfamiliarity with the military, dating back to his draft avoidance during the Vietnam War, would be a problem throughout his presidency.

But even if Atwater had been around and scurrilous, I'm not sure he could have beaten Bill Clinton in 1992—because many of the tricks that Atwater and Ailes had used to sell George Bush as a candidate in 1988 had come back to haunt George Bush as president. The Bush 1988 campaign remains, to this day, best known in the political community as an example of how a brilliant group of political consultants could succeed with a candidate who was mediocre on his best days. But the real lesson of What Atwater Wrought may be just the opposite: how difficult it is to succeed as president after you've campaigned as someone you're not.

Bush the Elder was a terrific president for people like me—"Eastern establishment, Council on Foreign Relations assholes," in the words of a prominent adviser to Bush the Younger. The old man was prudent, to use his favorite word. His foreign-policy team was eminently responsible, handling the details of landmark events like the reunification of Germany with careful diplomatic rigor. His economic-policy team didn't overreact to what would prove a mild economic downturn. He organized an international coalition to make war against Saddam Hussein, received the approval of the United Nations for that war, and abandoned the battle when his goal—the liberation of Kuwait—was achieved, without attempting to liberate Baghdad. The Gulf War catapulted Bush's public approval ratings to 89 percent, the highest ever recorded by an American president (until his son topped out at 91 percent, after the terrorist attacks of September 11, 2001). But the numbers were a chimera. Bush was now a known quantity—and he wasn't quite the guy people had voted for. He had broken the most famous pledge of his 1988 campaign, which, in retrospect, seems the worst sort of stupid consultant trick. "My opponent won't rule out raising taxes," Bush said in his acceptance speech at the Republican National Convention, which was written by the Reagan speechwriter Peggy Noonan. "But I will and the Congress will push me to raise taxes, and I'll say no, and they'll push, and I'll say no, and they'll push again. And all I can say to them is read my lips: no new taxes."

The convention erupted. In 1990, Bush raised taxes.

An equally serious breach may have been a matter of style rather than substance. Bush had campaigned as an American dude—at least, more American than the Greek guy—a lover of pork rinds and country music, a born-again Episcopalian. But he governed as the aristocrat he was. He seemed unable to understand the public without guidance from his campaign team. Perhaps his most famous statement of the 1992 campaign was his inadvertent reading of a tactical tip from his handlers: "Message: I care." He undoubtedly did care, but he couldn't figure out how to show it—how to respond to the fact that the recession, which he knew to be mild, was scaring the bejeezus out of a great many Americans, especially of the blue-collar Reagan Democrat variety in New Hampshire where the campaign began and the mills were closing. Bush's right-wing challenger in the primaries, Pat Buchanan, was transformed—he became a nativist and a protectionist—after he listened to the hard-luck stories of the workers at a north country paper mill that was about to close. The president, by contrast, seemed incapable of responding spontaneously to a worried and restless public—a contrast that became even starker when the prohibitively human H. Ross Perot flamed into the race.

The Gods of Politics are not oblivious to karma. When Bush began the 1992 campaign with a heavily stage-managed effort to show that he really did care about the economy—a January trip to Japan with desperate American automobile executives, in the hopes that some concessions might be extracted from the primly perfect Japanese auto industry—the president vomited on the prime minister of Japan's leg and fainted in his lap. In **The Reasoning Voter**, Samuel Popkin cites a CBS poll taken after Bush's trip: only 18 percent thought the trip was a success.

And Bush continued to send "low information" signals to the public indicating that he thought the political process was a drag and their concerns were bogus. In one of his final moments on center stage, the second of three debates against Clinton and Perot, Bush was seen glancing at his watch: clearly, he wanted to be elsewhere. And the American people soon gave him his wish.

Not that they loved Bill Clinton. My guess is, they might have preferred Perot—he didn't sound **anything** like a politician; he was a wildly spontaneous antidote to the consultant-driven campaigns of his opponents. He was a one-man turnip festival . . . but very much to a fault. It soon was apparent that the Texas billionaire lacked the ballast to be president. His humanity was flagrant, but brittle and undignified. He was a new phenomenon: the candidate as radio talk-show host, entertaining but ultimately annoying. The inability to modulate is the fatal flaw of political mavericks (a topic to be discussed in greater detail later).

Clinton split the difference between Bush and Perot—more dignified than Perot, more human than Bush. He campaigned as a compendium of his complexities: the smartest guy who ever fell out of a tree in Arkansas, a world-class baloney-slicer who also was a brilliant policy wonk (he could actually explain those policies in everyday English), an indiscriminate consumer of fast food, a womanizer of desperately bad taste, a Rhodes scholar who once owned a pickup truck carpeted with Astroturf in the back. "It wasn't what you think," Clinton said of the Astroturf—a comment that betrayed a perfect understanding of his own penchant for straying from both the truth and his spouse, and which intuited a certain sympathy among people his age, south and north, who had not always done the right and proper thing. Indeed, Clinton's version of

Turnip Day was all about the familiarity of his assorted excesses—the most important of which was his excessive joy in the political process. He ran as who he was: a big, smart, sloppy guy who loved talking to people, loved talking policy, and wanted desperately to be loved in return. And even though he put together a memorably flashy team of consultants to guide him— including James Carville, the Democrats' own lunatic jiggly version of Atwater—and even though, as we'll see, the consultants saved his candidacy at a crucial moment, Clinton's victory in 1992 had almost nothing to do with killer ads or the decision to set up a "rapid response team" that would flash back instantaneously against every Republican canard.

It had everything to do with his often inadvertent authenticity.

4

I Came to Love Our Weekly Polls

★ ★ ★ ★

In December of 1987, Congressman Richard Gephardt had been campaigning in Iowa for two years. He had moved his mother into an apartment in Des Moines. He had worked the state like a plowhorse, listening **hard** to the questions tossed at him by farmers sitting around kitchen tables in deep summer, and responding with disciplined calm. He had frozen through many a wintry morning shift change at the John Deere plant gate in Waterloo and at Quaker Oats in Cedar Rapids. He came across as an honest, unadorned midwestern fellow. He was from a working-class family in the neighboring state of Missouri, and had an even-keeled, strawberry-blond, all-American way about him. His wife was named Jane. They had three blond children (one of whom had survived cancer, although Gephardt wouldn't talk much about that until he ran for president again in 2004, when spilling intimacies had become a preferred shortcut to "authen-

ticity" in an Oprahfied nation). He seemed a formidable candidate and by autumn of 1987 he was running
first in the polls. And then he fell.

He fell precipitously. It wasn't because of a specific
gaffe or incident, if I remember correctly. People just
decided to look around, take a test drive, see if someone else—maybe Senator Paul Simon, the lovely, corn-
pone idealist from Illinois—might be a president. By
mid-December, Gephardt was in last place. He literally
had lost his voice. I remember spending a frigid Sunday going door to door with him in a working-class
neighborhood of Des Moines, blinding sun flashing off
new-fallen snow. The candidate, squinting, sipping hot
water with lemon nonstop, whispered greetings at each
door and handed out leaflets. He seemed utterly pathetic.

And then, he turned it all around again—with a single television spot, which aired on December 26, in the
midst of a huge snowstorm that kept all of Iowa in-
doors watching television. It didn't hurt that his com-
petitors were off the air that day, having figured that
people didn't want to hear from politicians during the
holiday season. And it certainly didn't hurt that the ad
was absolutely boffo. It featured Gephardt standing in
front of a Chrysler assembly line. "They work their
hearts out every day," he began, "but after nine different taxes and tariffs a $10,000 Chrysler K-car costs
$48,000 in South Korea. It's not our fault that we can't
sell cars in a market like that, and I'm tired of hearing
American workers blamed for it." If he were president,

Gephardt concluded, the Koreans would know that "we'll honor our treaties, because that's the kind of country we are. But they'll also be left asking themselves: How many Hyundais are they going to be able to sell in America for $48,000 apiece?" And then, on the screen, Gephardt's feisty slogan: It's Your Fight Too. (The $48,000 was probably inflated—independent trade experts said it was more like $30,000—but nobody was counting.)

Gephardt won the Iowa caucuses, and the Hyundai ad became famous—one of those rare spots to actually turn a campaign around. It also became the defining moment of Bob Shrum's career as a political consultant.

Shrum and David Doak had remained together after their Caddell misadventure. Gephardt was their first presidential campaign. And while there were constant disputes over who got credit for what—including the Hyundai ad—it was probably Doak who came up with the idea of emphasizing the more populist aspects of Gephardt's message. He had managed Mark White's campaign for governor of Texas in 1982, and was amazed by how effective White's fire-and-brimstone, anticorporate, anti–special interest, prairie-populist pitch had been. Gephardt had bought the argument on substance—"fair" trade was one of his issues—but he was reluctant to adopt the classic, tub-thumping populist style. His father had been a cranky populist sort, a milk-truck driver, a member of the Teamsters, always complaining about how the little guy got screwed;

Gephardt had identified more with his mother, the personification of the self-improving, upwardly striving American ideal. She was pink collar, a secretary. She was a strong Baptist and a lover of books. But when Doak and Shrum—and Joe Trippi, who spent two weeks traveling with the candidate—asked Gephardt to reinvent himself as his father, it seemed to strike a deep personal chord. The candidate was transformed. "When he got up to speak, he nailed the lines I'd given him," Trippi wrote in his memoir, **The Revolution Will Not Be Televised**, "including a reference to the Hyundai, an import from Korea. And the room blew up. A huge ovation. Soon Shrum was in Iowa, making what became somewhat famously known as the 'Hyundai' spot."

Trippi and Shrum would spar over who was really responsible for the Hyundai ad. Trippi and Doak and Shrum sparred over almost everything. "Shrum was amazingly creative," Trippi later told me. "But he was not a strategist. He'd rely on Caddell or someone else saying, 'Hey, this is what this campaign is about.' I still think the best spots I ever made were with Shrum. They were total collaborations. We'd sit down in a room, and the sparks would just fly. He'd have an idea, or I would, and we fed off each other. When I left the firm, he was the person I missed the most, which was a total shock to me. In a way, I still miss him."

Shrum was another of life's brilliant misfits—especially before he married Mary Louise Oates, a former society columnist for the **Los Angeles Times**, who transformed Shrum into a fairly spectacular social animal. Pre-Oates, Shrum was a classic political geek, a disheveled loner with an encyclopedic knowledge of political lore and a passionate attachment to idealistic candidates—first the New York mayor John Lindsay, then George McGovern (after a brief stay with Edmund Muskie), but most especially to Ted Kennedy and the extended Kennedy family. Shrum had been born in western Pennsylvania and raised in Southern California, the son of a tool-and-die worker. He went to Georgetown, where he was president of the debate society, and then on to Harvard Law School. There was an air of nervous uncertainty about him, a need to prove himself, which often translated into arrogant dismissal of other people's ideas—and later, into an almost primal need to be close to the candidate, closer than any other aide. He hated situations where he wasn't in complete control. He didn't drive and he hated flying.

"Once Bob and I were coming back from a shoot in Tennessee," Trippi told me, in another of his many accounts of getting fired during the Caddell-Doak-Shrum years. "We're in first class and Wilt Chamberlain is in the aisle seat across from me—and Wilt starts a conversation. He turns out to be a real nice guy and we're talking about this and that. Meanwhile, the plane is bouncing all over the place. And Bob is freaked. He tells me to stop talking to Wilt. I ask him why, and he says, 'This plane is gonna go down.' So I'm like, okay, but Wilt wants to keep talking. Wilt asks me something else and Bob whispers, 'If you say one more word, you're fired.' And Wilt says something innocent like, 'Where you guys from?' And I say, 'D.C.' And Bob, I swear, at full throat in the middle of first class screams: 'YOU'RE FIRED!' It was like a scene out of **Airplane**. I look back and all the people in coach are leaning into the aisle, trying to figure out what's happening."

Trippi eventually decided to leave the firm, he says, for a reason that he found surprising: Shrum and Doak were too successful. They were running campaigns all over the country, and often the campaigns were carbon copies of one another. Trippi realized that what he really loved about politics was the immediacy and co-operative creativity of a campaign; he loved watching someone like Caddell come up with a strategy that no one had ever thought of before; he loved tossing around ideas for implementing that strategy with a really creative guy like Shrum. Trippi figured he was a dopey romantic, that he needed to really believe in a candidate in order to do his best work. "Today, you sit with these guys—the pollster, the media consultant, the manager—and it's all just regurgitated crap from the last one," he told me. "They give every candidate the same advice: 'Don't answer hypothetical questions' and so on. I mean you don't even need a manager. You tell each candidate the same twenty things. Caddell never fell into that. Every campaign was different with him. It wasn't like, 'I did this in the last one and it worked, so let's do it here.' Pat was actually thinking through each race. It wasn't canned . . . I'm not talking bad about Bob and Dave. I'm just saying that the difference now is that people like Bob are running the same campaigns over and over."

That was true, but not quite fair. In races that he really cared about—Ted Kennedy's difficult Senate race in 1994, John Kerry's difficult Senate race in 1996, the birth of John Edwards as a North Carolina politician in 1998—Shrum could deliver great personal attention. He was a terrific editor, a master at sharpening a stump speech; he was excellent at debate prep. But there were so many races, and so little time. All too often, a Shrum candidate would have a populist tinge to him—but of a specific economic sort, which was far less effective than Atwater's social-anger populism.

Populism is one of the more romantic and less admirable American political traditions. It purports to represent the interests of the little guy. More often than not, it has manifested itself as a witlessly reactionary bundle of prejudices: nativist, protectionist, isolationist, and paranoid. The central assumption is that the little guy is so aggrieved that he can only be roused to citizenship by an appeal to his basest suspicions. Exploitation and venality are posited as the central fact of American life: the country is being taken to the cleaners by wicked plutocrats or smoggy-brained intellectuals.

This rather sour ideology had one fleeting moment of high-mindedness in the 1890s. The Populist Party promoted several programs—the progressive income tax, a central banking system with control over the money supply, antitrust regulation—to provide needed controls over an emerging national economy. These were embraced by Theodore Roosevelt's Republicans and Woodrow Wilson's Democrats. And the tendency toward reform—these days, toward reform of government and special-interest power—remains the very best of populism, although very much a minor chord.

There are three major chords. One is bipartisan, one conservative, and one liberal. The bipartisan chord is the most successful: aesthetic populism—the candidate as common man. The log-cabin mythology of the nineteenth century gave way, rather hilariously, to a trailer-park mythology in the twentieth. One didn't necessarily have to be a redneck, of course, one could nibble at being one, as George H. W. Bush nibbled on his pork rinds in 1988. Indeed, an argument can be made that not only does "warm" beat "cold" in latter-day presidential politics but victory goes to the most convincing cracker. In 2000, Al Gore—perhaps the apotheosis of political inauthenticity—made a fool of himself trying to come off as a Tennessee farm boy; George W. Bush, the reformed bourbon drinker and tobacco spitter, was a far more convincing rube. (And it was no contest when Bush ran against John Forbes Kerry in 2004.)

The next most successful strain of populism is Lee Atwater's Republican social conservativism. The little guy turns out to be a Rush Limbaugh listener, a bristling bundle of leave-me-alone resentments about crime and race, incensed by politically correct educrats and feminazis. These populists turn out mostly to be guys, which makes them an unholy attraction to the guy-deprived Democratic Party. In the George W. Bush elections, a feminine version of social populism was introduced, which had to do with sex (gay marriage, untrammeled abortion rights) and religion (school prayer, displaying the Ten Commandments in courthouses). As Pat Caddell—and Scammon and Wattenberg—predicted, married women had slid firmly into the Republican camp by the turn of the twenty-first century.

The least successful form of populism is Shrum's economic class warfare, which has only received majority support during tough times, like the Great Depression (and only when implemented by a sweet, non-angry politician like Franklin Delano Roosevelt). After the Gephardt campaign in 1988—and in far more prosperous times than FDR's—the economic rant became Bob Shrum's hobbyhorse. All too often, a Shrum candidate would be "fighting for working families" and insisting that "health care is a right, not a privilege" and saying that the most important family values were policies that "value families." The Shrum clones often were candidates who tried to preserve the past by "fighting" to protect the manufacturing jobs that were skedaddling to countries with lower labor costs; they opposed free trade agreements like the North American Free Trade Agreement. They weren't as blatant about it as, say, the leftist entertainer-documentarian Michael Moore, but there was a whiff of classic know-

nothingism to Shrum-clone candidates—nativism, iso-
lationism, protectionism, paranoia. They played three-
issue monte, and the issues were all domestic: jobs,
health care, and education. They attacked Republicans
for wanting to "privatize" Social Security and to cripple
Medicare by "herding senior citizens into HMOs."
Shrum clones didn't have all that much to say about
national security, except that they were for "strength"
in the world (though very often not for the **use** of
strength). They were less concerned about environmental issues, like global warming, than about the high
price of gasoline or heating oil (environmental issues
were abstractions to most "working families"). In the
2004 campaign, George W. Bush's opposition research
team produced a twelve-page memo that compiled the
language that every Shrum candidate seemed to use.

Shrum was not alone as an industrial assembly-line
consultant, of course. As the 1980s succumbed to the
1990s, consultancy became an embedded fact of American politics. Twin consulting hierarchies evolved in the
two parties. Each had its distinctive campaign themes,
polling questions, and advertising templates. Most of
the action was congressional. The really crucial political relationships in both parties were between the consultants and the political aides who ran the campaign
committees in the House and Senate. The committees
decided which local candidates would get financial
support from the national party. Hiring the "right"
consultants, along with the ability to raise great gobs of
money, became a threshold issue for a prospective can-

didate. "If a guy came to us and said he had someone like Shrum or Ray Strother doing the media, and Geoff Garin or Mark Mellman to do the polling, we'd look at him more kindly than if he had Uncle Herbie, who ran a local advertising agency, doing his ads," said Bob Kerrey, who ran the Democratic Senatorial Campaign Committee in the 1996 and 1998 elections. "Actually, the guy I had running the DSCC, Paul Johnson, pretty much blackballed Shrum because Paul didn't like how Bob had handled the advertising in my 1992 [presidential] campaign. But the people who ran the committee before and after me were more conventional, and they liked Shrum a lot."

Shrum had tried to turn Kerrey—a free trader—into a Gephardt-like "fighter for working families" in the New Hampshire primary, putting Kerrey in front of a hockey net in one ad, promising to protect America against unfair Japanese trading practices. "I went along because the Japanese trading practices **were** unfair," Kerrey later told me. "But I was sort of irked that I was running second in New Hampshire when we put Bob's ads on the air—and running fourth a week later. It wasn't so much the hockey net as this other spot they'd done on health care, which was the most important issue in the race. They had me in some sterile, frightening hospital room. It was very cold, a real turnoff. I'd never had an advertising buy **lower** my position before. But then, in my campaigns back in Nebraska, I'd always insisted on writing and directing at least one ad myself. That way, I owned it. The language was mine.

But this was the big leagues, and these guys were the pros, and they insisted on doing every ad."

Kerrey was an extremely rare politician, one who was able to keep an ironic distance from the political process. He was a Vietnam veteran, a former Navy SEAL who had lost part of a leg in battle and received the Congressional Medal of Honor (an award he always insisted that he did not deserve). After he lost the 1992 New Hampshire primary, a reporter asked if this was the worst thing that had ever happened to him. Kerrey just laughed. He loved politics, loved the alpha competition of the game—but he was astonished by most of the players, especially those who were unable to step back from the process and see how, well, **strange** it had become. Most of his colleagues were content to follow orders, listen to their handlers, and stay "on message," or better still, "totally on message." He was bemused by the politicians and consultants— none of whom had ever been in combat—who saw politics solely through the metaphor of war. Oh, there were strategic similarities. There were tactical ploys. You wanted to defeat your opponent. But there was an intermediary factor in politics: the people. The actual work of politics was the precise opposite of war. It was talking to people, convincing them, getting them to trust you. And much of that was being lost in the cookie-cutter campaigning that came to dominate politics in the 1990s.

Indeed, among those who dispensed the money at the congressional campaign committees there was an inherent bias against candidates who seemed unconventional. There was even a bias against the more out-there consultants, like Trippi and Minnesota's Bill Hillsman (who did hilarious, unconventional ads for Jesse Ventura and Senator Russ Feingold). Hillsman claimed that the only honorable sort of focus group was to invite a bunch of people together, provide lots of beer and snacks—but never ask them any questions. Just have a TV in the corner, running some political ads. If people stopped their conversations to watch an ad, that was a good one. "Bill is good, but only for certain types of candidates," said Jim Jordan, who ran the DSCC for John Kerry in the late 1990s. "Mavericks, mostly."

Mavericks, however, were mostly not favored by the campaign committees. Occasionally an oddball slipped through. In 2002, Alex Sanders—without doubt the funniest politician I've ever met—was anointed as the Democrats' sacrificial lamb in the race for Strom Thurmond's South Carolina Senate seat. Sanders was an ambrosial Southern storyteller who had served in the state legislature, as a judge, and as the president of the College of Charleston. He promised the local Democratic Party that he would play by the rules and do all the things that the DSCC wanted him to do. And he did try, but it was hard—and when a **New Yorker** writer appeared on the scene, namely me, Sanders could not resist becoming a spy in the house of the consultants.

"Do you want to know what I do all day?" he asked me. "I sit at a desk with a telephone. A woman named

Ashley Newton sits across from me with pieces of paper called focus sheets and a stopwatch. She hands me a focus sheet and a phone number and some vital information about a potential contributor. I call the number. She starts the stopwatch. I have six minutes to make the sale. I'm supposed to make ten calls per hour. So I start out like this, 'Hello, my name is Alex Sanders and I'm running for the United States Senate. Have you ever heard of me in your whole entire life?' Then I chat with him for a moment about life at his horse farm or whatever. I tell him I know about the horse farm because I have a focus sheet with all this information. And then I say, 'I'm not calling to ask for your vote. It'd be a waste of time to ask for a single vote. My purpose is far more humiliating. It's the chemotherapy of a political campaign. It's painful . . . Wouldja give me some money?' If they say yes, I tell them I have two more questions, and these are far more humiliating than the last. 'First, I am so sorry to have to ask but, when you gonna send the money? Can you send it today?' And then I say, 'Now this last question is so embarrassing that I can hardly bring myself to ask it, but . . . How much?' And before they can think about it, I jump in and say, 'How 'bout a thousand bucks?' "

But that wasn't the hardest part of being a postmodern political candidate. Sanders had been a rogue donkey all his life, a flamboyant integrationist, environmentalist, death-penalty opponent, and free-speech proponent. The DSCC sent him a young campaign

manager, Chad Clanton, and some operating instructions. "We had this big meeting," Sanders told me. "All
the consultants. They came from Washington, D.C.,
and from California. One fellow stood at a blackboard
and drew a box. It's called the Message Box. I never
heard of such a thing. Inside the box he wrote, 'Education. Health Care. Personal Experience. Not a fierce
partisan.' Those are the things I'm supposed to talk
about. I'm allowed to have opinions on other things,
but I'm not supposed to bring them up. If that's the
campaign I'm supposed to run, I think I'll die. I will
surely bore myself to death."

It is quite possible that Sanders never had a chance
against Lindsey Graham, a politician with an independent streak of his own, who turned out to be an excellent U.S. senator. ("If I'd known Lindsey was gonna
turn out like that," Sanders later said to me, half joking, "I mighta voted for him myself.") In fact, Sanders
was quite disappointed by his own candidacy, especially by his decision to run the campaign the way the
professionals wanted him to do it. He writhed within
the Message Box; he seemed to campaign in a straitjacket. It was a sad thing to watch, and it was part of a
national disaster for the Democratic Party, an attempt
to run a unified national campaign in 2002, controlled
by the congressional campaign committees.

Jim Jordan denies that the campaign was strictly
unified. Mark Mellman, who had been hired as the
DSCC's pollster, did do extensive research in 2001,

Jordan says, to find out which Republican incumbents might be vulnerable and which themes were strongest for the Democrats. "But what happened in the individual campaigns was up to the individual candidates," Jordan told me.

Somehow, though, the individual campaigns wound up seeming very cookie-cutter. The two most important issues facing the country—the prospect of war in Iraq and the impact of George W. Bush's tax cuts—were, with only a few exceptions, placed **outside** the Message Box. Democrats were instructed, as Alex Sanders was, to talk about jobs (namely, that Bush hadn't created any) and health care (namely, that Bush hadn't passed a prescription-drug benefit for the elderly). They could also run the usual scare campaign about old-age entitlements. It was, in fact, an old-age campaign: a conscious decision was made to fight the Republicans, nationally, over the elderly vote. Old people were reliable voters; if you targeted them, you'd get some bang for your buck. Young people were purposely ignored. "We have tactical elections," the pollster Stan Greenberg told the **Washington Post**. "We don't have big elections, because there is every prospect that you can win by thinking small."

So the Democrats had become the party dedicated to the principle that the most important issues (war, taxes) would not be discussed, and the segment of the population that had once thrilled to the party's idealism (young people) would be ignored. It was a shameful campaign, and rightfully rejected by the public: the

Republicans gained control of the Senate and eleven seats in the House.

Actually, the Democrats were playing catch-up. The Republicans had been the first to try a unified national congressional campaign. In April of 1994, Newt Gingrich—the newly minted leader of the House Republican Caucus—told me that he was going to bring every Republican running for Congress to Washington on September 27 to sign a pledge to enact a "checklist" of reforms "to end politics as usual." This was to stand in contrast with the business-as-usual congressional Democrats, who had been suffering through a series of petty scandals and who were, clearly, played out intellectually. I published Newt's intention to develop this plan, which would come to be known as the "Contract with America," in my **Newsweek** column—and most people thought it was just Newt being Newt, blowing hard. The Republicans had been a minority in the House for forty years; they would, no doubt, remain so in perpetuity.

But Gingrich won a smashing victory in November. The Republicans gained fifty-two seats in the House and also took control of the Senate. Why did Newt succeed with a national campaign in 1994 and the Democrats fail in 2002? Well, Bill Clinton's disastrous first two years as president had something to do with it, just as George W. Bush's leadership after the terrorist attacks of September 11, 2001, had something to do with the Republican success in 2002. Beyond that, however, Newt's national agenda was based on beliefs, not just tactics. It addressed the issues that seemed most important to conservatives and populist reformers at the time—tax cuts, welfare reform, term limits, trimming the congressional bureaucracy—although it did avoid the hotter social issues like school prayer and abortion, and it did include a tablespoon of malarkey (a United Nations–bashing component and some senior-citizen pandering). But most important, it flowed from the bottom up. Early in the year, Gingrich and his second-in-command, Representative Dick Armey of Texas, asked their pollster Frank Luntz to survey the 435 Republicans running for the House and find out what **they** thought was important; about half replied. The Contract with America was **their** top-ten list, Luntz later told me. "There was one exception," he said. "They wanted school prayer on the list and Newt didn't. The reason, Newt said, was 'I will not have Al Hunt [the liberal columnist of the **Wall Street Journal**] define this as a religious document.' "

But even though the Contract with America agenda was one that the candidates themselves—not Newt Gingrich or Frank Luntz—had decided upon, it did have Luntz's fingerprints all over it: every word in the contract had been market-tested and carefully massaged. "We tested the philosophy of each point," Luntz told me, meaning—I think—the popularity of each proposal, "and then we tested the competing words. Every single item had two ways to word the 'contract,' and we used the best language for each of them. Most of the time, one option would get 30 percent and the other would get 65 percent, so it was pretty easy. We used focus groups extensively. We found, for example, that if you told people you were going to give them a $500 tax cut per child, they would say, 'Thanks, but no thanks . . . What you're giving me is meaningless.' But they liked it better when we offered a $1,000 tax credit for a family of four. We learned from focus groups in Colorado that 'Politicians make these promises all the time. We want to know they're serious about it. We want to be able to hold them accountable.' So we added this wording: 'If we break our promise, you throw us out. We mean it.' " (Gingrich's House Republicans passed everything they promised—except a term-limits bill—but the contract died a painless death in the Senate.)

The Contract with America made Frank Luntz a star, which drove his fellow pollsters up a wall: they considered him more a showman than a scientist, a charlatan who—like Pat Caddell—played fast and loose with his data. And there **was** something of the carnival barker to Luntz, especially after he began to stage focus groups on television for MSNBC. He had a taste for the informal and the flamboyant—his first client was the right-wing populist Pat Buchanan, who ran against Bush the Elder in the 1992 Republican primaries; his second client was Ross Perot. But the effect of his work was more often soporific than inflammatory: he scrubbed the partisan edge off the Contract with America, removing the word "Republican" from the title and any mentions of "Democrats" or "Bill Clinton" from the text. He was vehemently opposed to harshness and negativity in politics, a consequence of his use of a relatively new and very controversial survey tool: the dial group—in which civilians were handed a gizmo with a dial, which they could twist right or left, to react instantaneously, positive or negative, to the things they were seeing and hearing.

The first gizmo was a big, clunky machine developed by the Educational Testing Service in the 1940s, to help George Gallup with one of his sideline businesses: Audience Research, Inc., which tested reactions to new movies for the Hollywood studios. The Hopkins Televoter Machine allowed ten people at a time to respond immediately, positive or negative, to the images they saw on the screen—trailers advertising new films, mostly. Eventually, the silicon revolution enabled pollsters to use a smaller, sleeker handheld gizmo that fed its information into a central computer that would, in turn, blend the simultaneous reactions of dozens of people—their consensus would appear as a wavy line at the bottom of a television screen, leaning upward when they liked something and downward when they didn't. Richard Wirthlin was one of the first to use this tool, and of course he gave it one of his fancy names, Pulse-Line: "I could then go back and pinpoint the exact phrases and segments from the President's speech that produced the most and least favorable reactions," Wirthlin wrote.

But there were problems. Humans react to stimuli on a variety of levels, and the dials could only catch the most immediate, superficial responses. If a politician said, "As Abraham Lincoln once said . . ." the dials would take off. Any reference to the American Eagle knocked the dials off the charts. If anything negative was said, the dials would plummet. This was, of course, computerized hokum: people might not like a negative message, but that didn't mean they wouldn't remember it and act on it. The dials could catch momentary reactions but not overall impressions . . . unless they were superficial impressions. In 1988, for example, the Bruce Babbitt campaign hired a dial group to watch the first debate among the Democratic contenders. In real life, Babbitt is not only an extremely decent and thoughtful man, he is also a rather handsome one. On television, however, he came across as slightly jowly and the timbre of his baritone sounded vaguely Nixonian—and every time his face appeared on the screen, before he said a single word, the dials would turn down. Babbitt aides joked that the money would have been better spent on plastic surgery.

Luntz loved the dials. They helped him with his most important work, picking out the right words to convey his client's message. He found, for example, that while people didn't mind paying the "estate tax," they hated paying a "death tax." They liked "tax relief" more than "tax cuts." And the best way to take the edge off of environmental fears was to talk of "climate change" rather than "global warming." His fellow pollsters were convinced that this was flummery and, to be sure, there wasn't much that was scientific about it. But that wasn't really the point. "Luntz has an amazing ear," the cognitive linguist George Lakoff, who would later try to sell his own Luntz-like services to the Democratic Party, told Nicholas Lemann of **The New Yorker**. "As a linguist, I look at him and say, 'He knows how to frame the debate.'"

In 1994, Luntz distributed a pamphlet of suggested usage to Republican candidates around the country. It was a great leap forward in the sterilization of American politics: now every campaign could be virtually the same campaign. And sadly, as Bill Clinton found out to his amazement in November of 1994, the stuff worked.

I've written plenty about Bill Clinton elsewhere, and won't belabor the substance and scandals of his administration here. But a few words about Clinton's relationship with his consultants may be useful, since it was, as was everything about the man, brilliant and occasionally maddening. For one thing, Clinton was a human Turnip Day. He was an immediately identifiable human specimen—even his creative fudgery ("It depends on what your definition of the word 'is' is" and "I didn't inhale") was so clearly a variant on schoolyard bull-tossing that it almost seemed benign. All it took was one visit to McDonald's and the appearance of the perfectly tawdry Gennifer Flowers for most people to understand that this guy was an extreme version of someone they'd met in high school—and when he spoke, it was clear that he was a very smart version. This was clearly a guy who didn't need consultants to tell him how to sell himself.

And yet, he did. He certainly needed consultants to tell him how to organize his campaign—which was an unholy mess until James Carville was put in charge (Carville was a very Republican sort of consultant, the rare Democrat who could also impose order and a strategic plan). Clinton also needed his consultants to rebuild his credibility in the spring of 1992, after he had been caught lying about his avoidance of the military draft within days of the Flowers efflorescence. Then Ross Perot had stormed into the campaign and stolen Clinton's identity—the independent reformer who was a palpable Southern human being. By May of 1992, an odd thing had happened: Clinton had won the Democratic nomination, but he was running third in the polls behind Perot and George H. W. Bush.

Clinton's consultants launched what they called the "Manhattan Project" to undo the damage. There were two major challenges. One was biographical: the draft evasion and the non-smoking of pot while he was a Rhodes scholar at Oxford had left the impression that he was a child of privilege, rather than the scuffling son of a single mother who grew up poor in Arkansas. The public had to be reintroduced to the Man from Hope. Clinton's media consultant Mandy Grunwald pointed the candidate toward the plethora of talk shows and new cable networks, where he could introduce himself to people who weren't necessarily political junkies. He played the sax and talked welfare reform on **The Arsenio Hall Show**, he fielded questions on MTV and with Larry King and Oprah Winfrey. Then, in one of the most effective biographical films ever used to introduce a nominee at a national convention, Grunwald and Clinton friend Linda Bloodworth Thomason provided the mythic image of the candidate as a young delegate to Boys Nation, shaking hands in the Rose Garden with John F. Kennedy.

Clinton's other challenge was political. He had to prove that he wasn't just another liberal Democrat. His policies certainly were not traditionally liberal, but— his consultants knew—most people don't study policy. And so they arranged for Clinton to have an "I paid for this microphone" moment. In late June, Clinton appeared at a meeting of Jesse Jackson's Rainbow Coalition and criticized the rap singer Sister Souljah, who had appeared the evening before, for her violent and racist lyrics. This was a slick solution to what seemed a perennial problem for the Democrats: Jesse Jackson stood for black militancy in the minds of many Americans; his hot, sweaty rhetoric at the 1988 Democratic National Convention was an absolute turnoff for Clinton's target audience, the suburban middle class. After Sister Souljah, members of the "forgotten middle class" could surmise that Clinton stood in a different place from Walter Mondale and Michael Dukakis when it came to the care and feeding of the Reverend Jackson, which sent a coded message that this candidate was going to be tough on crime and welfare—on all the racial issues that had crippled Democrats for twenty years.

The final symbolic act that cemented Bill Clinton's image as "a different kind of Democrat"—a term of art developed in focus groups—was his selection of Al Gore as vice president, which flew in the face of conventional wisdom about ticket balancing. It seemed totally fresh and philosophically consistent. Gore was from the next state over, Tennessee. Like Clinton, he was young and moderate—together, they seemed a crackling departure from the Kennedy-Dukakis-Mondale Dems (and far more fun than Jimmy Carter). Clinton's pollster, Stan Greenberg, was particularly vehement about this path. Two nights before the announcement, I'd had a long airplane chat with Clinton in which I tried a number of methods to elicit some news from the candidate about his impending choice. I asked him who his favorite governor was (he told me how he felt about **every** governor—especially former Florida governor Bob Graham, which led me to make an entirely embarrassing call to my employer Katharine Graham, predicting her cousin would be the pick). I asked him about the people he'd defeated for the nomination, which led to a conversation about what a tough and admirable guy Dick Gephardt was. Clinton never once mentioned Gore. In Little Rock two days later, Greenberg came up to me and started laughing: "Klein, you're a real pain in the ass," he said. "He kept us up all night with that Gephardt business. We almost lost Gore."

Greenberg was right, of course. The burst of enthusiasm that ensued after Clinton selected Gore—and the quickening efforts of the press to expose some of the more erratic aspects of Ross Perot's personality—caused Perot to abruptly drop out of the race when the Democratic convention opened in July. All of which jolted Clinton ahead in the polls, a startling renewal after his spring doldrums. (Perot would attest to the erratic aspects of his personality by dropping back into the race in late September.)

Although James Carville was a walking sound bite, much beloved by journalists, Clinton's most important consultant relationship during the 1992 campaign may have been with Greenberg, who had spent a great deal of time studying the Reagan Democrats, trying to figure out how to lure them back to the party. Greenberg's findings bolstered Clinton's gut sense of what was important; and his focus groups helped Clinton with the Luntzian work of finding the right words. Traditional liberals talked about the needs of "working families." Clinton talked about the "forgotten middle class." (In fact, "working" versus "middle-class" families would become a subtle fault line between the left and the middle of the Democratic Party; in 2004, John Kerry—who had trouble making up his mind about anything—would square the circle by talking about "working and middle-class families.") Greenberg and Clinton also figured out a brilliant euphemism for spending money: they favored "investing" in the future. They took the Republican two-word belief phrases (Strong Military, Low Taxes, Traditional Values) and cut them in half: Opportunity, Responsibility, Community—which first made their appearance on the cover of the Democratic Leadership Council's 1991 manifesto. These were softer and more abstract than Reagan's sentence fragments, but the cold war was over and the nation was ready for a spell of soft.

But not too soft. After he was elected, Clinton seemed to wander leftward, too obviously enthralled by the liberal elite in Hollywood and New York. New Democratic campaign themes like crime and welfare reform were forgotten (and gays in the military was suddenly rediscovered, and augmented by the press and the Republicans). His campaign consultants—who were social and economic populists—hated Clinton's fiscal conservatism (the numbers said that people didn't care about budget deficits) and loved the First Lady's plan to require businesses to provide health insurance for their employees. They encouraged Clinton to push hard on health care, to melodramatically pull his pen from his pocket during a State of the Union address and threaten to veto any bill that didn't provide for universal coverage.

This was a classic stupid consultant trick—and Clinton, privately, kicked himself for not going with his gut sense, which was to stow the pen and figure out some way to woo the Republican leader Bob Dole, compromise, declare victory, and come back later for a gradual expansion of the program. It was a rare strategic lapse, perhaps induced by the president's byzantine relationship with the First Lady, for whom health care was do or die.

Still, Clinton was the slickest presidential strategist the country had seen since Lyndon Johnson, with a sophisticated understanding of how to use his consultants. They could show him the playing field; they could provide numbers and language and sometimes even ideas. They could tell him which issues simply wouldn't fly and, more important, how to sell the ones he cared about. But his innate political sense was better than any poll—and there were times, for reasons of political responsibility or just **feel**, that he would sail against the numbers. After the 1994 election, he bailed out the Mexican government during a currency crisis even though the polls were running overwhelmingly against; in 1995, he refused to give up his support for affirmative action even though his consultants were saying it would hurt with Reagan Democrats and might even cost him the 1996 election. By then, however, Clinton had taken up with a whole new team of consultants.

A few months after the Gingrich triumph, the political scientist Samuel Popkin had lunch with his friend Stan Greenberg, who was no longer working for Bill Clinton. Popkin asked Greenberg what had happened. "People think Clinton does what the consultants tell him to do," Popkin recalled Greenberg saying. "But it's the exact opposite. He picks his consultants according to where he wants to go."

Now he wanted to go—posthaste—back to the po-

litical center. The most obvious person to take him
there was an idiot savant named Dick Morris, who had
helped Clinton regain the governor's mansion in
Arkansas after he was defeated for reelection in 1980.
It should be noted that the First Lady, Hillary Clinton,
was the first to get in touch with the fellow.

Morris was another luftmensch, a courtier whose
smarminess was legendary and ambidextrous—he
worked for Democrats and Republicans alike. In his
grotesque and unintentionally hilarious memoir, **Behind the Oval Office**, written after he had been
caught with a prostitute and dumped from the team in
the midst of the 1996 presidential campaign, Morris
writes that he is probably "mildly autistic" and recalls
that his parents sent him to a "desolate" sleepaway
camp on the "lonely" Maine shore. "Only after years of
therapy did I begin to understand how this early dep-
rivation affected my personality . . . As Eileen"—his
wife—"and my therapist, Dr. Elizabeth Hauser, soft-
ened my rage and brought me inner peace for the first
time in my life, I decided to abandon negative advertising as a metier."

One imagines Uriah Heep on the couch . . . and, for
a time, in the president's ear. There are echoes of Caddellian and Wirthlinian flattery, especially in Morris's
extended rumination on the similarities between Bill
Clinton and Abraham Lincoln: each was a dark-horse
candidate from a small western state, without much
Washington experience; each was elected with about
40 percent of the vote in a three-person race; each was

"deeply suspected by his own party and shunned by the opposition." (Each was pretty tall, too.) Morris goes on, in his memoir, to say that he told Clinton, "You want me to sit right there, on your left shoulder, like a bird, and whisper in your ear, three, four, five, ten times a day." He writes this without recording the president's facial expression at the prospect of a daily decathlon of whispers. "Then, if you choose, you can use my advice to control your staff, your campaign, your dealings with Congress . . . to empower you."

The president, Morris writes, "smiled broadly and said, 'You got it. I'll take what I want.' "

Morris was the ultimate iteration of the consultant as snake-oil salesman. One imagines him spreading his daily selection of policy trinkets and elixirs out on an Indian blanket in the Oval Office. But his medicine worked, in large part because most of his birdlike whispers were based upon the most extensive polling data collected in the history of the presidency, conducted by the firm of Penn, Schoen and Berland Associates. "I came to love our weekly polls," Morris writes. And their daily tracking polls, too: not just during campaign season but also during governmental crises— which, during the Clinton administration, meant most of the time. Morris commissioned "the mother of all polls" to prepare for one of Clinton's State of the Union addresses. "The survey was 259 questions long. It had to be divided into five parts, since no one would willingly stay on the phone for the hours it would have taken to answer every question." Famously, Morris used polling data to send the president on a cowboy vacation in Wyoming rather than having him indulge in his and Hillary's preferred soiree on Martha's Vineyard.

After the health-care debacle of the first term, Clinton was allergic to grand schemes. The most common substantive criticism of Morris was that he tended to produce "bite-sized" programs, and he did luxuriate in the trivial, but that wasn't the entire picture. He was a forceful advocate of welfare reform and of producing a balanced budget, which became two of Clinton's signal achievements (Morris also favored scuttling affirmative action and lowering the capital gains tax rate, which Clinton refused to do). But there was one striking difference between the Morris-Penn-Schoen worldview and the Carville-Greenberg (and Shrum) version: the complete absence of economic populism.

Mark Penn—who became Clinton's most influential consultant after Morris was sent packing—was a shy, mumbling, shambling technocrat. He later told me how he convinced Clinton to strip the class warfare tropes from his language: "Usually, a Democrat will say something like 'the Republicans want to cut Medicare because they want to reduce taxes on the wealthy.' " Penn decided to drop the second half of the sentence. He figured that the stronger part of the argument was preserving Medicare—and that people, no matter what they said to the contrary, had mixed feelings, at the very least, about the prospect of lower taxes (many aspired to being wealthy themselves some day). Furthermore, "the minute you bring in the second half of the sentence, you're bringing in class warfare. And so what I tried was a variation on: 'We believe in Medicare and the Republicans don't.' " It tested better. "It was much better ground to fight on," Penn concluded. "And I won the battle with the president. If you go through his speeches, he cut out 99 percent of that kind of stuff."

Penn and Schoen were more moderate than most Democratic consultants. They had come to prominence working for New York's brilliant neoliberal-and-also-sort-of-conservative-but-really-indescribable mayor Ed Koch—and they were quite innovative, in a rather quirky way. Penn was a drop-dead policy wonk; he disdained the softer, less substantial aspects of politics. "Being human is overrated," he told me. "There are several successful styles of leadership, of which strength, decisiveness, sticking to what you believe in is far more important than anything else." He also hated focus groups, as did Schoen. Didn't run a single one for Clinton . . . and for all the right reasons: "The group dynamic doesn't sufficiently duplicate reality," Penn told me. "People tend to say a lot of socially desirable stuff, like 'We hate negative campaigning.' " (Clinton, who agreed, was more succinct about focus groups: "They're a bunch of bull . . .")

But how to test visual material, like television ads? Penn and Schoen invented a new way—brief one-on-one sessions in shopping-mall offices, in which civilians would be paid to watch competing pairs of ads and respond to a series of questions. In the 1996 campaign,

Penn decided to create a series of negative ads about Clinton to see what might work best against his candidate. "The most effective negative we came up with involved him saying 'I didn't inhale, but I wish I had.' It was sort of the classic, 'Yeah, that's complete bullshit. He has no character.' And then we tested some possible responses." The best pro-Clinton ad concerned the passage of the Brady Bill, a gun control law that required background checks for gun buyers. The script went: "It wasn't about politics. It was about character. He stood up for us when we really needed it . . . The Brady Bill." Penn said, "We'd show people the negative ad and the positive ad—and finally, with Brady, our positive ad won. That's how we do it: we keep testing until we find an ad that wins. Then, in October, when the character attacks began, we put the Brady spot on. We already had it done."

There are two prominent theories about how you win an election: spend most of your energy rousing your devoted followers—your "base"—or spend most of your energy trying to win over the 20 percent or so in the middle of the political spectrum, the "swing" vote. This is, of course, a gross oversimplification. Any successful campaign has to do both. But there are . . . **inclinations**, and in 1996—after Clinton's failed first two years in office, an experiment in trying to govern from the left—both the president and his advisers were inclined toward the center of the political spectrum (especially since the Democratic base had already been roused to a blood boil by the garish Republican attacks on Clinton, the rise of talk-radio entertainers like Rush Limbaugh, and the fat target of Newt Gingrich). If economic populism was the shortest path to the heart of the Democratic Party, social populism was the shortest path to the mythic Reagan Democrats and other assorted swing voters—and quietly, through ads that aired in carefully targeted markets, the Clinton campaign went after the swingers.

Doug Schoen was asked to pay special attention to winning Tennessee, the home state of Vice President Al Gore. "This was obviously going to be the first step in the 2000 presidential campaign," Schoen told me. Penn and Schoen had divided swing voters into two categories: those leaning Democrat (swing I) and those leaning Republican (swing II). Schoen's successful Tennessee campaign was a swing II primer. "We did extensive polling, 3,000-person samples as opposed to the usual 800. I could tell you what played in the suburbs of Memphis as opposed to the suburbs of Nashville," Schoen told me. "One of the things that people don't realize about the 1996 Clinton campaign was that we spent $5 million on Christian radio in the South, and a lot of that went into Tennessee. Clinton was always way ahead of us. He told us to check out the court decisions on school prayer. 'We can go a long way with this,' he said. 'We can use it in the campaign.'" So Schoen concentrated on selling social issues in the Tennessee suburbs—school prayer, limiting abortion, reminding people that Clinton had passed welfare reform and was in the process of adding 100,000 police officers to the streets. And it worked: Clinton-Gore thumped Bob Dole and Jack Kemp in Tennessee, 47 to 41 percent.

Penn and Schoen figured that they'd set the course for Gore's 2000 campaign, but they were mistaken: Gore eventually abandoned them for the Greenberg-Shrum side of the street, a populist campaign on the theme of "The People Versus the Powerful." Penn later acknowledged that the Greenberg-Shrum economic populism aroused more intense reactions than his swing-vote social populism but, he sniffed, "I don't know how much political value there is to having more people say they 'strongly' support you. They're going to vote for you, anyway."

But that's not why Al Gore lost to George W. Bush in 2000. It was all about Turnip Day.

5

The Twenty-Point Kiss

★ ★ ★ ★

I once asked Al Gore if he would have chosen politics as a career if his father hadn't been in the business. Gore thought for a moment and replied, "Probably not." He went on to muse a bit about how he might have been more comfortable in academia. It seemed an **aha!** moment: Gore wasn't thrilled by his chosen profession, which seemed clear enough when you watched him stumble along the campaign trail. (I later learned that Bill Clinton had been nonplussed by Gore's comment.) In retrospect, though, my **aha!** was probably off by at least one level of complexity. I had missed the calculated grinding of the Gorean gears: **Hmmm. If I say that I would've gone into politics anyway, then I'll seem like just another politician. People are sick of politicians. Clinton is a politician. But wait a minute, if I say I only went into politics because my father was a U.S. senator, doesn't that make me seem like daddy's little boy? Not true! And if I say**

academia, that'll seem precious, but then again, Joe likes talking about serious stuff like reinventing government and global warming—and maybe, in a way, it's closer to the truth . . .

Or something like that. One of my smaller regrets in life is that I never thought to ask George W. Bush the same question. My guess is, he probably would have found some way to laugh it off: "Well, I wasn't good enough to pitch for the New York Giants . . ." (which, Bush knew, was something he and I had in common: our favorite childhood baseball team). Or, "Well, I wasn't having much luck in the oil business." But Bush—a natural politician—would never have **answered** the question directly because he would have understood in his central nervous system that it was a trick: there was no good answer. Bush would also have known, without thinking about it, that while his father had been elected president, the old man was never really in the business. He had delegated politics to Lee Atwater and others; he was too decent a man for the hugger-mugger.

Actually, one of Bush the Elder's few political rules did apply here: you don't stretch yourself out on the psychiatrist's couch with a reporter—an especially crucial rule in the 2000 election because, Bush the Younger knew, one of the biggest differences between him and the vice president was Gore's propensity to talk about deep psychological stuff with journalists, including really embarrassing stuff like the impact on his psyche of a book called **The Drama of the Gifted**

Child. Most Americans, Bush understood, would re-
late better to a candidate whose favorite book was **The
Melodrama of the Mediocre Screwup**. After he appeared with his father at the family's Kennebunkport
mansion at the beginning of the campaign, Bush—
who was a big fan of the Austin Powers comedies—
whispered to me, "I was afraid you guys would say,
'There's the President and Mini Me.' "

Early in the campaign, Bush's friend and media consultant Mark McKinnon had given the candidate a
piece called "After Elvis" from **The New Yorker**, in
which the vice president professed an admiration for a
book called **Phenomenology of Perception** by the
French philosopher Maurice Merleau-Ponty and indulged in free-ranging intellectual gobbledygook in
what seemed a desperate effort to impress the writer
Louis Menand. There was a fair amount of New York
and Washington dinner-party chat about the piece after it was published, with opinions divided between
those who swooned over Gore's intellectual flash (New
York, mostly) and those who considered him a
pompous blowhard (Washington). Bush's reaction to
the piece was ecstatic: "Venus and Mars, man! I can't
imagine anybody who's less like me," he told McKinnon. "This makes it easy for me to run against him."

And so, Bush took pains to play it simple. When
asked about his weaknesses in a 1999 **Talk** magazine
interview, Bush aimed a dart at Gore's neck: "Sitting
down and reading a 500-page book on public policy or
philosophy or something." This not only fit Bush's per-

sonality—he had long resented the effete easterners he had bumped into at Andover and Yale (which may have had something to do with his own relationship with his father)—but it also fit perfectly into Gore's apparent disdain for people who weren't smart. Bush figured Gore would "misunderestimate" him and come across, at some crucial moment, as aloof and patronizing. The strategy also placed Bush squarely in a Republican tradition going back to Clem Whitaker and Leone Baxter in California in the 1930s: people didn't want to be burdened with facts and ideas, they wanted to be entertained, and to be led. Bush's application of this principle was by turns charming and demagogic, but it was nonstop effective. Karl Rove modeled the campaign on William McKinley's front-porch candidacy of 1896: Bush would stay in Austin and the world—assorted military, foreign-policy, economic, and political experts—would beat a path to his door. The candidate would concentrate on raising great gobs of money (which he did) and he wouldn't go gallivanting around the country, fielding tough questions and making mistakes.

The 2000 presidential election, then, was all about mind games—and most of them were played at Al Gore's expense. There was something about the vice president that simply demanded couchification. He was successfully analyzed by his opponent. He was unsuccessfully analyzed by his own consultants, who tapped into Gore's frustration with fathers past and presidents present and eventually seduced him into an angry populist campaign theme, "The People Versus the Powerful." And he was analyzed superficially by people like me, who tried to pick through the awkwardness of the public Gore, and the antic jokiness of the private Gore, and drill down to the core Gore—the shy fellow who would rather "sit off by himself with his computer" than glad-hand campaign contributors, as his wife once told me. Worst of all, he was constantly analyzing himself. "There was so much angst," said a Gore associate. "For him, it was: 'Wait a minute. I was a great vice president. We have peace and prosperity. I didn't have sex with Monica Lewinsky. What's happening to me?' "

It isn't easy for a sitting vice president to run for the top job. Only two have succeeded—Martin Van Buren and George H. W. Bush, and the latter, as we've seen, succeeded because of the lameness of his opponent. The problem is largely structural: the vice president's job is to be the First Follower—and the president's job is to lead. Gore had indeed been a terrific vice president, the strongest New Democrat among Clinton's inner circle. He had stiffened Clinton's backbone on issues ranging from the war in Bosnia to welfare reform. His judgment was rock solid, admirable, and visionary. And yes, I really did learn a lot from him in our private conversations about both military and environmental issues. But that was in private; in public, he was the apotheosis of clunky. He had a slightly untethered tendency to go goofy in the spotlight—and, at times, to panic. Early in Clinton's second term, Gore had peremptorily gone to the White House press room to answer questions about his role in a fairly obscure campaign fund-raising scandal, and allowed himself to get caught up in a classic media scrum, in which he endlessly and robotically repeated that there was "no controlling legal authority" that applied to his actions. I'm still not quite sure what he meant—but then, no one in the public really cared about the substance of the controversy. They cared about Gore, who had begun to define himself as the oddest of oxymorons: a panicky robot.

He was also infuriated by the Monica Lewinsky affair. He had **daughters** that age. Clinton had lied to his face about it, and then he had lied to the public—and for six months Al Gore, First Follower, had had no other choice but to be loyal to the guy, going so far as to call him a "great president" in a partisan moment of passion, which the Republicans would use against him in the campaign. Gore's wife, Tipper, was even angrier. At one point, backstage at the charity performance of the Broadway version of **The Lion King**, she had refused to come out from her holding room for a picture with the Clintons. Finally, the First Lady was dispatched to talk to Tipper and bring her out. "People who were there," said a Gore aide, "found the whole thing pretty embarrassing."

The closer the campaign loomed, the more unhinged Gore seemed. The early horse-race polls in the spring of 1999 had him trailing George W. Bush (whom many voters thought was George H. W. Bush).

Gore decided to respond by announcing his candidacy very early, in June of 1999, and he followed the announcement with a spray of detailed policy speeches and position papers—a thoughtful and sometimes even courageous display of policy expertise (he risked disapproval from the party's base with his aggressive positions on national defense and his support for government funding of poverty programs run by religious organizations). But the timing was foolish. It happened too early. No one was listening to his ideas, except for the reporters trailing him, who didn't pay much attention to substance in any case.

Gore was not the most pleasant of bosses. He had a reputation as a ranter, and he didn't inspire much loyalty among the troops. Consequently, he didn't have the hard core of true believers that had propelled Reagan and, to a certain extent, Clinton to the White House. Indeed, there weren't many people on his staff or in the campaign organization who knew him very well—and he fired some of the most prominent of those in the spring and summer of 1999, as his national poll numbers continued to languish. He fired his longtime media adviser Bob Squier in June. There was a superficial reason for this—Squier had produced a bio spot Gore didn't like—but the real cause of the disruption was consultant politics: Gore wanted to add Carter Eskew, a friend from his days as a journalist for the Nashville **Tennessean** and Squier's former partner, to the team. Squier refused to work with Eskew, who had busted up their partnership to join Mandy Grunwald and Mike Donilon in a new, and short-lived, consulting firm after the 1992 election. (Consulting firms are a deck of cards constantly being reshuffled, usually over disputes about money and egomania.) Politicians fire consultants all the time, but this firing had especially bad karma: Squier was diagnosed with an aggressive cancer a few weeks afterward. His widow refused to allow Gore to speak at the funeral.

Mark Penn and Doug Schoen were fired in late summer. They were, after all, Bill Clinton's pollsters—and Gore was feeling an increasing need to separate from Clinton in every possible way. Penn says he was fired because he couldn't find any evidence that Gore was being hurt because of his proximity to Clinton—which the press had begun to call "Clinton fatigue." Others in the Gore campaign said there was also a dispute over the accuracy of Penn's New Hampshire polls, which had Gore ahead of Bill Bradley by ten points. Local polls had Gore ten points behind—according to several Gore staffers, Penn had been extrapolating the New Hampshire results from national polls he had taken. (Penn responded that the New Hampshire polling was done by another firm that had been subcontracted by the Gore campaign.)

Gore continued to thrash about. He was consumed by trivia. He decided to move the campaign headquarters from Washington to Nashville, to seem less an insider. He decided to bring in Tony Coelho, a longtime Democratic professional, to manage the campaign—rather than go with his respected chief of staff, Ron

Klain. He also hired Naomi Wolfe, a friend of his daughter Karenna's, to offer advice on his personal style—at a rate of $15,000 per month, which enraged many people higher up the campaign food chain who were being paid less.

Wolfe is best remembered for suggesting that Gore might appear more comfortable in public if he started wearing "earth tones," which became one of the more risible epitaphs of the campaign. But Wolfe's most basic advice—to let Gore be Gore, and not worry about all the conflicting advice he was getting from the other consultants—was sound. In the autumn, the vice president began holding a series of town meetings in New Hampshire, where he would go on and on (and on) about his various policy passions, and these were among his best work as a candidate. Gore wasn't nearly as good as Clinton at explaining complicated problems—no one is—but the man was smart and creative; his answers didn't seem canned and he was clearly qualified to be president. None of that was getting through to the public, however, for all the clatter of consultants coming, going, and dumping on each other. Wolfe's role was leaked to the press. "Clearly, the other consultants hoped to get rid of her," a Gore aide told me. "She was telling him to talk about the things he cared about. They were trying to get him to go with the issues that polled well. They couldn't control her." And there seemed to be new consultants added by the day. Harrison Hickman came on as a pollster, to replace Penn and Schoen. Stan Greenberg was added later, to augment Hickman. Bob Shrum, with **his** new partners, Tad Devine and Mike Donilon, arrived in the autumn of 1999. Tony Coelho suffered a stress-related physical collapse in the spring of 2000, and was replaced by Donna Brazile.

Few of these people knew Gore well. Press Secretary Chris Lehane and Domestic Policy Director Elaine Kamarck and Foreign Policy Director Leon Fuerth were about the only remaining high-ranking members of Gore's staff involved in the campaign effort—and the consultants did their best to shut the policy advisers out of strategy sessions. "They just didn't know who he was," Kamarck later told me. "At one point, Tony Coelho proposed that Gore cut the defense budget and I had to tell him, 'No, Tony, Gore is actually in favor of **increasing** the defense budget.'"

Kamarck—one of the leading New Democrat thinkers—found an unlikely ally in Donna Brazile, who had managed Jesse Jackson's campaign in 1988. They were roomates in Nashville, Roman Catholics who went to mass together and commiserated endlessly about the stupidity of the guys running the campaign. Brazile fought Shrum over resources: he wanted more money to go into television advertising in Iowa; she knew that ground organization—door-to-door get-out-the-vote efforts—had disproportionate impact in a precinct caucus system where turnout usually is low. Brazile fought the pollsters, too. "It was ridiculous," she later told me. "They had so much data, they couldn't possibly analyze it all. I've got seven cartons of it sitting in my basement. They had focus groups three or four times a week. They had sixteen different categories for white women. Can you imagine that? I didn't know white women came in so many different categories. But the candidate needed it. He was on the phone to the pollsters every five minutes, it seemed."

Given the number of consultants involved and their redundancy, turf battles were inevitable and constant. At one point, Shrum—who was fanatic about controlling debate prep—tried to block Gore's New Hampshire campaign chair, Governor Jean Shaheen, from attending a session. Shaheen had been complaining about the direction of the campaign, and especially about Shrum's ads. "He told me the debate prep was canceled," Shaheen said to me. But she happened to be driving by a local church and saw the Gore campaign caravan parked outside, and decided to drop in. "Jeannie came in and immediately came over to me," Kamarck recalled. "She asked, 'How long has this debate prep been scheduled?' I told her and she said, 'That son of a bitch lied to me.' She was just furious, so I went over to Gore and said, 'You better spend a few minutes with Jeannie.' And I went over to Shrum and said, 'You guys are fucking sexists. You wouldn't do this with a male governor.' " (Shrum refused to be interviewed for this book.)

As 1999 slipped into 2000, there was good news and bad. The good news was that Gore's primary opponent, Bill Bradley, was proving to be a mortal dud, another of the high-minded lugubrious northeasterners that the Democrats seemed to produce in endless supply. The bad news was that the vice president's campaign had terminal cancer; killer cells were metastasizing all over the place, wasting vast amounts of energy on internal struggles. The campaign was consuming itself, strangling him. "You've got to stop firing people," Kamarck told Gore that autumn. "It's becoming an issue."

"Yes," Gore agreed, sighed, and then laughed. "But it feels so good."

In Austin, Texas, Mark McKinnon watched the Gore campaign from a distance and knew exactly what was going on: the Dukakis campaign. It was a distressing spectacle, but also not. McKinnon had spent his life as a philosophical, operational, and (especially) cultural Democrat and now, for the first time, he was working for a Republican . . . although he didn't really think of it that way. He figured he was just helping out a friend, a fellow he believed in: George W. Bush. But that wasn't quite right, either. Very much to his surprise—and to his wife's horror—McKinnon was in the midst of being converted, not so much to the Republican philosophy but more to the Republican way of doing campaigns. It was so much simpler.

Maybe it was because Republicans were more businesslike. (They sure knew how to structure a campaign and make the trains run on time.) Maybe it had to do with the fact that they saw human nature differently, or that they were more homogenous than the Democrats, or that they saw their consultants not as saviors but as employees, or all of the above . . . or maybe it was just the way Bush and Karl Rove went about the practice of politics. But this was, without a doubt, the tidiest campaign he had ever seen. There was none of the backbiting, staff shake-ups, or power struggles, there was none of the constant hand-wringing about whether the shading of a position would offend the party's interest groups. **Issues**, in fact, seemed less prominent than they did in any given Democratic campaign. And McKinnon had come to a slightly guilty realization: maybe that was a good thing. Rove's assumption was that voters had three basic questions about a candidate: Is he a strong leader? Can I trust him? Does he care about people like me?

Politics was all about getting the public to answer "yes" to those three questions (of course, an integral part of the job was aggressively—often stealthily and sometimes disgracefully—painting the opposition as weak, untrustworthy, and effete). Everything flowed from that; every paragraph in the stump speech, every radio spot and direct mail piece was vetted on its relevance to those questions. The last of the three—Does he care about people like me?—was always toughest for a Republican, and Karl Rove had spent the past fifteen years learning how to convince dyed-in-the-wool Texas Democrats, especially suburban women, that Republicans really did care about them. Yes, Bush would run on the same themes that every Republican had run on since Reagan: Military Strength. Lower Taxes. Traditional Values. Beneath those, however, was a Bush-Rove addendum to Traditional Values: "compassionate conservatism." Specific issues were adopted by the campaign only as they illuminated that theme—and this was a big difference from the Democrats.

McKinnon could easily imagine his old colleagues hunkered down and sweaty, arguing over the precise details of Gore's position on global warming—labor needed this, the tree huggers wanted that. Democrats had trouble seeing the forest for the tree huggers; Republicans didn't sweat the details. Oh, the Republican business interests would get their wish-list agenda—especially tort reform, a Bush-Rove favorite. And the religious right would get a nod—funding for faith-based social programs—and a wink on hotter issues like abortion and gay rights. And the National Rifle Association just **knew** that Bush was with them all the way. But the essence of the campaign was the presentation of personality, not policy. Indeed, policy was often merely a tactical reaction to Democratic initiatives. Gore had an elaborate prescription-drug plan for the elderly; Bush was for that, too, and arguably with a better general principle—take care of the poorest old people first—but with none of Gore's heavy, sluggish details. Two or three national reporters might sift through the entrails of the competing drug plans and declare Gore's more comprehensive. But there wasn't a single, breathing swing voter in the fifty United States who would make his or her presidential decision on the basis of which candidate had the better prescription-drug plan for the elderly.

McKinnon was amazed that the Democrats had never quite figured this out. In fact, they had it ass-backwards. A guy like Stan Greenberg would take a poll to learn which issues people cared about—inevitably, jobs, health care, education—and then the Dems would try to figure out the best ways to talk about those policies. They would use these abstractions—government initiatives!—to sell their candidate to a public that no longer trusted the government. The character of the candidate, they believed, would be inferred from the quality of his policies. How quaint. In the television era, fleeting impressions counted far more than cogent policies. Fleeting impressions were all most people had time for. Presidential politics was all about character . . . or rather, the appearance of character. Did he (or she) seem strong? Trustworthy? Care about people like me? The utter simplicity of it was astonishing: it wasn't about the economy, stupid.

It was about the appearance of caring about the economy, stupid.

Presidential politics had been reduced to a handful of moments and gestures. It had been moving this way ever since Reagan paid for his microphone. A presidential campaign could be won or lost in the moment that George H. W. Bush vomited on the Japanese prime minister. (Was he strong?) Or when Michael Dukakis did not get angry at the image of his wife raped and murdered. (Was he trustworthy?) Or when Bill Clinton asked a black woman a question about **her** life in a town-hall format presidential debate. (Did he care about people like me?) The next step was obvious. If campaigns turned on those Turnip Day moments of humanity, Turnip Day could be frozen, packaged, and sold. But you had to be smart about it. You had to be more subtle than pork rinds. You had to be real—the first thing Americans could spot in a politician was whether or not he was a phony.

No less an expert than Bill Clinton watched George W. Bush come out of the box, working the press and the crowds, and touting "compassionate conservatism" in the summer of 1999, and he told his friends: This guy ain't dumb. He's found a simple, reassuring way to connect with the folks. He's saying to them, "Elect me and I'll keep the good times going. I'll do the same stuff as Clinton, only in a more orderly, conservative way . . . and without all that **personal** stuff." Clinton wanted to sit down with Al Gore and warn him. He wanted to tell Gore, "We may be in some trouble here. Let's think about how to deal with it." But he and Gore weren't talking very much anymore.

McKinnon had wandered into the Bush tent quite by accident. He had quit politics a few years earlier, announcing it publicly in a 1996 **Texas Monthly** article: "Maybe it was the candidate for statewide office who got so drunk he came on to a member of our film crew at a public restaurant while his wife and daughter sat horrified across the table . . . Maybe I got tired of candidates asking me what their firmly held convictions should be . . . Maybe I simply lost my political idealism." So McKinnon—who had once written songs with Kris Kristofferson in Nashville, who had written a song, in fact, that Elvis had agreed, just before he died, to record—turned his skills to corporate consulting, owning a local nightclub, raising giant lizards and a family, and making the occasional high-minded documentary. It was in the course of making a documentary about a local charter school that he met George W. Bush. "Given my history, I was institutionally inclined not to like the guy," McKinnon told me. "But he was a really interesting human being. We didn't talk politics at all. He asked me about my daughters. He had daughters, too, and we got into a pretty deep conversation about that. Even when I interviewed him about the charter school, he didn't seem like a politician trying to spin me. He had some interesting things to say about education."

McKinnon was a jogger, and so was Bush, and they began to run together. They became friends, not especially close—but low-key and easy. Bush was a pol, to be sure, but he didn't seem half crazed with ambition like most of them (although he most assuredly was). He did normal well, and so did Laura. And then, early in 1999, Karl Rove called and asked McKinnon if he would run Bush's media in the coming presidential campaign.

Afterward, McKinnon couldn't figure out what was more strange, the fact that Rove—who had been a bitter rival in more than a few Texas campaigns—had called, or that he hadn't told Rove to get lost. McKinnon had said he'd think about it. He was actually sort of tickled by the idea. And the more he thought about it, the more McKinnon realized this was pure Bush. The governor was being set upon by all kinds of Republican media hotshots—Mike Murphy, Phil Dusenberry, and others had all made the pilgrimage down to Austin. But Bush had a healthy skepticism about political consultants, especially those he didn't know very well. Rove was more a family retainer than a hired gun—he had been devoted to young Bush for nearly thirty years. Karen Hughes, his warrior-woman communications director, would stop a bullet with her teeth for the guy. "He knew that if I did it, it wasn't because I was a raging Republican, or that I wanted to be a Republican media guy. I didn't need it financially," McKinnon said. "So, in his mind, I'd be doing it for all the right reasons. I was the one guy who didn't want it. If I did it, it would be about personal loyalty, which is what he cares about most. We both figured that I'd catch a lot of heat from Democrats—my wife, Annie, is still a strong Democrat—but in the end, **he** was the one who took the heat. He got a lot of 'How could you put a Democrat spy in the camp?' and 'How can you trust him?' and so on. And man, he just literally got in their faces and said, 'This is my guy and that's the last word.' "

The governor proved to be more than a fair-weather employer. On the afternoon that John McCain clobbered Bush in the New Hampshire primary, McKinnon was summoned to the governor's hotel suite. "I was putting on my body armor," McKinnon recalled. Stuart Stevens, another of the media consultants, stopped by and said, "I'm packing. We're fired."

The entire Bush inner circle was at the meeting: Rove, Hughes, Laura Bush, old pal and finance chair Don Evans. "Listen, I want to be clear on one thing," Bush told them. "This is my responsibility. You all did a great job, and I apologize to you—I didn't measure up as a candidate. Now, people are going to look at us when we walk out of here. They're going to read our body language, and I just want you to know that I believe in you. I think you're great professionals and we're gonna win this thing. But we have to come out of here strong. We can't show vulnerability. We've got to be optimistic. I don't want anyone blaming anybody else. We came in here as a team and we leave as a team."

That night, McKinnon watched on television in a noisy, crowded room as Bush gave his concession speech. "I couldn't hear what he was saying," McKinnon said, "but it looked like a victory speech. I mean, all his body language and everything said victory."

Which was all well and good, and even admirable— but the tactical decisions that flowed from the New Hampshire loss were scurrilous. What followed, in South Carolina, was one of the most disgraceful campaigns I've ever witnessed. Bush and his minions did a clandestine demolition job on John McCain. Rumors about McCain's mental stability swirled through the state—it was said that he had been brainwashed during the six years he had been imprisoned and tortured by the North Vietnamese; it was said that his wife, Cindy, was a drug addict (she had been addicted to painkillers for a time); it was said that he was the father of a mixed-race child (the McCains had an adopted daughter who came from Bangladesh). There were no fingerprints on any of the dirt, but it was funny how these sorts of rumors always seemed to float about in campaigns run by Bush's chief strategist, Karl Rove. (In the 1994 Texas gubernatorial campaign, for example, there were rumors that the incumbent governor Ann Richards was a lesbian.)

"John, it's just politics," Bush said to McCain when they met backstage before their South Carolina debate.

"George," McCain replied quietly, jaw taut, "**everything** isn't politics."

In fact, Bush was particularly—and heinously—adept at sequestering his behavior in political campaigns from the rest of his life. He had learned from the master, Lee Atwater, and he stood squarely in the Whitaker-Baxter tradition. Politics was spectacle, not substance. It was a blood sport, and there was only one rule: whatever it takes to win.

And so it was entirely disconcerting for me to watch Bush have a perfect Turnip Day moment in the midst of the raw sewage that his campaign was pumping during the South Carolina primary. It came during a town meeting in Hilton Head. A sneering man asked Bush what he would do about "all these bastards" being born to women on welfare. I'd seen many politicians use this question to slag the undeserving poor over the years. But Bush glared at the man—he seemed truly angry— and said, "First, sir, we must remember that it is our duty to love all the children."

There was no political advantage to the statement. The audience was classic country club Republicans, people who fiercely resented the fact that their tax dollars were going to "bastards" on welfare. But there was something about the questioner's arrogance that piqued Bush's hatred of snobs and (usually liberal) self-righteousness. He responded as a human being. For a moment, everything wasn't politics.

Sadly, I never saw Al Gore (or John Kerry, in 2004) have a similar moment—in which he directly challenged the smug assumptions of his supporters— during the course of the campaign. This was a spiritual failure, and it probably cost Gore the presidency. Bush had the ability, on stray occasions when he wasn't reciting his daily message, to pass for a regulation human being.

Gore didn't.

Gore dispatched Bill Bradley easily in the Democratic primaries of 2000, but he was unsatisfied in victory. He trailed Bush in the spring polls. And he didn't know what to do next. Normally this would be the time to introduce an agenda—but Gore had already done that in his excellent speeches the summer before, when no one was listening. A memo from Gore's policy staff to the candidate described the conundrum:

> The Problem: Al Gore outlined a centrist political agenda in the primaries. George Bush did not. George Bush is now putting forth an agenda designed to move to the middle and, in doing so, he looks like he has a strategy and we look like we do not.
>
> The Solution: Go back to a series of meaty policy speeches that are not **dumbed down.** Repeat in their entirety speeches that we gave last year but with one or two new elements. Tell the press there will be a series of speeches laying out the Gore general election policy and message. (If they recognize some of it as from the primaries—so be it.)

Gore decided that what he really wanted to do was give a major speech on global warming. This elicited a chorus of groans from his political consultants, who pointed out that the environment was way down the list of issues people cared about, according to their polls. But Gore ignored them. The environment was the issue he cared more about than any other; he had written a best-selling book about it, **Earth in the Balance.** He wanted to tell the public, as precisely as possible, what he was going to do about it—and he wanted to do a lot: a $150 billion program over ten years, using the Clinton budget surplus to pay for it. "He was saying, 'This is the most important thing I want to do as president. This is what we have to do to limit our dependence on fossil fuels,'" Elaine Kamarck recalled. "We really worked on it all spring. Katie McGinty"—Gore's environmental specialist—"chaired like ten meetings of a task force to come up with the proposal."

He delivered the speech on June 27, in Philadelphia.

And nothing happened. The **New York Times** got the story right, citing Gore's "broad vision" in the lead, but buried it on page 24. The **Washington Post** played it inside as well and, worse, emphasized that this was Gore's attempt to deal with high gasoline prices. The television networks also played the gas-price angle. The speech caused barely a ripple. "What the fuck happened?" the vice president asked his staff the next day, livid. "What went wrong?"

No one was sure . . . but, in the end, Gore came to believe that it was an act of passive resistance on the part of his consultants. They wanted a different campaign from the one he wanted. They wanted an emphasis on the usual Democratic stuff—education, health care, prescription drugs for the elderly. (Bob Shrum, for one, had been pushing for a universal health-care plan, even though Gore favored a more incremental approach.) "The consultants were insistent on running the campaign they wanted to run," Tony Coehlo later told me. "If Gore disagreed with them, or wanted them to do something else, they sand-bagged it."

It was quite astonishing. The consultants would **allow** him the global warming speech, but they would do none of the strategic planning necessary to make Gore's environmentalism a centerpiece of the campaign. There would be none of the photo ops, town meetings, television ads, none of the sustained and repetitive campaign appearances needed to drive the point home. There would be no attempt to grant an exclusive interview to a Grand Panjandrum of the television world in which Al Gore bared his good green soul. Indeed, the larger vision of the speech would not be sold at all by his staff. Lower gas prices would become the press hook. "All of you who drove to work today know that gas prices are simply too high," was the lead quote in the **Washington Post**. Bush quickly responded that the Clinton-Gore administration never had a strategy to keep energy costs low: "[Gore] seems to forget who's been in office for the past seven years."

It must have been infuriating. Gore had just laid out a goddamn visionary energy policy—a real break from bite-sized Clintonism—and no one had noticed. But Gore just didn't have the time or energy to fight his own staff about it. He was in a tunnel, pushed from event to event, day after exhausting day, unable to step back and make strategic decisions about his campaign. (And there wasn't an inner circle of loyalists to sit on the consultants and make sure they provided exactly what the candidate wanted.) The Gore campaign was a supertanker laden with the political equivalent of non-renewable fossil fuels—it would be impossible to turn it in the direction that Gore wanted without another staff massacre.

In fact, the consultants were fighting among themselves. Shrum was pushing populism. He wanted the theme of Gore's convention speech and the fall campaign to be "The People Versus the Powerful." Stan Greenberg disagreed. The phrase was death in focus groups. A better idea was the more expansive—and less combative—notion of "Prosperity for All." Greenberg kept taking "The People Versus the Powerful" out of the convention speech; Shrum kept putting it back in. "After the convention, Gore was supposed to go down the Mississippi on a riverboat," Greenberg recalled. "And there it was, all over the boat—P v. P: The People Versus the Powerful! I had them take all the signs down."

But, ultimately, the vice president, who needed some way to release the anger over **everything** that was roiling within him, sided with Shrum. On some subterranean level, Gore believed that **he** was the people, powerless against fate and Bill Clinton's depredations and the constant Republican ridicule of his (slight) tendency to exaggerate, which the press seemed all too happy to embrace. He had said that he was one of the people who was responsible for the development of the Internet—and it had been twisted into a boast that he had "invented" the Internet, and an opportunity for

Bush to joke about all the other things Gore had invented. (In the first debate that fall, Bush challenged the numbers in Gore's prescription-drug plan and said, "I'm beginning to think not only did he invent the Internet, but he invented the calculator.") They were picking away at his credibility and he lacked the deftness to respond—and worse, his consultants were ignoring this emerging character issue. "Both Greenberg and Shrum were all about issues," Chris Lehane recalled. "They simply didn't understand that presidential campaigns are all about character."

Actually, Gore's convention speech—with only one reference to P v. P—was a huge success. But it wasn't so much the words that made it work. As he arrived at the podium, Gore planted a big wet smooch on his wife, Tipper, who had just introduced him with wit and warmth. It was not a perfunctory kiss; it went on for a while, mouth to mouth. Tongues seemed to be involved. The crowd applauded and then, as the kiss continued, began to cheer. Everyone on Gore's staff was surprised. It was a spontaneous moment, and it was filled with "low-information signals." It said to the world that maybe Al Gore wasn't such a stiff after all. In fact, he seemed a pretty passionate guy. And, unlike Bill Clinton, he was passionate about his wife. "I was standing next to [campaign press secretary] Mark Fabiani when it happened," said Lehane. "And my jaw dropped. I said to Mark, 'That's a twenty-point kiss.'"

Lehane was close. Depending on the poll, Gore bounced twelve to seventeen points after the convention speech. "He walked around for days after that with a smile on his face," Lehane said. "I think it was because he knew—it wasn't the speech, it was the kiss."

Indeed, Gore's two strongest moments in the general election had absolutely nothing to do with issues. They had to do with the strength of his marriage, and his decision to pick the first Jew—the palpably solid, decent, and experienced Senator Joseph Lieberman—ever to run on a national ticket as his vice president. The Lieberman selection came despite Shrum's lobbying for one of his other clients, the inexperienced but photogenic former trial lawyer John Edwards, who had served only two years in the U.S. Senate. "Edwards was a ridiculous idea," said an aide. "Gore was never going to choose someone with so little experience as his vice president."

Indeed, both moves—the kiss and Lieberman—were expressions of passionate, defiant spontaneity. They were Gore at his best, bursting free from his campaign straitjacket. He surged to a nine-point lead in the September polls, which should have been impregnable. But the vice president was still a very angry fellow, frustrated with his handlers and yearning to breathe freely—and the need to break out became the subconscious theme of Gore's disastrous performance in the debates.

In one of his first debates during the 1988 presidential primary campaign, Al Gore's mother gave him a note

card with three words on it: SMILE. RELAX. AT-
TACK. He followed the instructions faithfully. He was
a joyous, exuberant, and at times brilliant warrior when
placed onstage with his fellow candidates, and he
emerged as the clear winner of the 1988 Democratic
primary debate season. Then, as vice president, Gore
had gleefully eviscerated Ross Perot in a debate about
the North American Free Trade Act on Larry King's
CNN program. And he had tidily dismembered Bill
Bradley in the debates during the 2000 primaries. It
was assumed that he wouldn't have much trouble with
an underinformed George W. Bush in the three debates
scheduled for the general-election campaign.

"But there was a huge change in the way debate prep
worked from the primaries to the general," Kamarck
recalled. "In the primaries, it was as it had always been
in the past. A bunch of us would sit around a table with
Gore, coming up with questions and figuring out the
best ways to answer them. He'd have a yellow pad and
a pencil. It was a research project. He'd be saying, 'Find
that out. Get me the best number on that.' And so
forth. It was all pretty loose, a lot of joking around,
putting him at ease. Half the time, he'd give hilarious
answers and we'd all be laughing. But that's not the way
they did it in the general-election campaign."

Bob Shrum had been a champion debater in college,
and he was known for his excellent debate prep. But his
idea of how to do it was far more formal than Gore's.
An exact replica of the debate set was built. The prep
sessions were videotaped, and then the tapes were taken

to a dial group to determine which answers worked—
and also, Shrum later told me, to show Gore how people responded to some of the things he was doing
wrong. Shrum's methods were not unusual. Bill Clinton had been prepped that way in 1992, down to his
body language. ("We encouraged Clinton to move
around, and especially to move toward the audience in
response to questions," Stan Greenberg recalled. "We
figured that Bush would be handcuffed to his chair.")
No doubt, George W. Bush was prepped similarly in
2000—although his consultants would never divulge
the details.

But Gore clearly hated the way Shrum ran debate
prep. Greenberg later wondered if Gore's actual performances in the debates were a purposeful act of
rebellion—he did everything they had warned him
against. They had been concerned about his sighing in
frustration when Bush answered a question. They
showed him how arrogant and petulant it seemed on
videotape. But in the first debate, he sighed early and
often and disastrously. They told him to hold down on
the aggressive body language in the town-meeting
debate—he had a tendency to stalk after Bush (who
was played in the prep sessions by the lawyer Bob Bar-
nett). They replicated the set inch for inch and gave
him a line he could not cross—and then, in the town-
meeting debate, which was the last of the three, he immediately crossed it. Bush turned to face his stalker and
gave him a "what on earth are you doing" look, which
put Gore on the defensive for the rest of the evening.

The first debate was a classic example of the perils of dial groups. "The dials were terrific for us," Lehane recalled. "You could hear the guy who kept track of the machine calling out the numbers—92, 78, 88—fabulous numbers every time Gore spoke. Shrum and some of the other folks were, like, 'The election's over. We're cleaning his clock.' I had my doubts. I just smelled the arrogance thing happening . . . and then I was the guy who had to go out into Spin Alley, and I got killed. The press was going nuts over Gore sighing. When I got back to the hotel, everyone was having a celebration. They were certain we'd won."

The three Bush-Gore debates were singularly dispiriting public events. Three different Gores showed up: the lion, the lamb, and the stalker. There was only one Bush, and he was prohibitively simplistic, demagogic, and quite often wrong on the facts. When he famously accused Gore of "fuzzy math," he was wrong: Gore's numbers were absolutely correct. But Bush paid no price for his inaccuracy and he proceeded to be creatively wrong on a series of issues—like the amount of money his state spent on health care and European participation in peacekeeping operations in the Balkans. (He implied there wasn't any, even though Europeans made up more than 80 percent of the peacekeepers.)

Soon, every time Gore made an effective argument Bush dismissed it as mumbo jumbo from the nation's capital. (Or he claimed that Gore had indulged in an old debater's trick—which in itself was an old debater's trick.) And Gore seemed helpless to respond. When

Bush insisted in the second debate that "nothing" had happened in Washington during the past eight years on an assortment of issues, Gore didn't even suggest that the unpopular Newt Gingrich and the Republican congressional majority might have had something to do with the "bickering" and "finger-pointing" that Bush was criticizing. The omission was deliberate. "It was believed that people wouldn't respond to that," a Gore aide told me. "The research showed they wanted the election to be about the future, not the past."

Ah, the research! Gore seemed all tangled up in polling data. If his sighing and body language in the debates seemed a way to defy his consultants, he was slavishly devoted to their numbers with every word he uttered. A particularly dreadful moment came midway through the second debate, when the discussion turned to the murderous rampage by two students toting a small arsenal of weapons into Columbine High School, in Colorado.

BUSH: Let me say something about Columbine. Listen, we've got gun laws. He says we ought to have gun-free schools. Everybody believes that . . . But there seems to be a lot of preoccupation on—not only in this debate, but just in general—on law. But there's a larger law. Love your neighbor like you would like to be loved yourself.
GORE: I also believe in the Golden Rule.

And I also agree with a lot of the other things the Governor has said.

Gore had given one of the more passionate speeches of his life at the memorial service for the murdered Columbine students. For more than a year, he had attended town meetings across the country where Columbine had been a topic of great concern, often the very first issue raised. Bush had signed a law—speaking of laws—that allowed Texans to carry concealed weapons into church. The vast majority of Americans agreed with Gore on this issue . . . but his consultants wanted him to lowball gun control because there were lots of gun lovers in Pennsylvania and Michigan, crucial states he needed to win if he wanted to be elected president.

Well, he won Michigan and Pennsylvania. But he lost the election, even though the public agreed with him on most issues. He lost the election—actually, it was a dead heat—because he did not seem a credible human being. And he did not seem like a credible human being because he had shoe-horned himself inside the Message Box that had been created for him—because he had been polled and focus-grouped and dial-grouped and market-tested **literally** to the point of distraction.

Two years later, Gore invited a group of friends—his former policy staffers, big fund-raisers, personal friends, about forty in all—to Memphis to discuss his plans for 2004. "If I do this again," he said, "I'm going to speak from my heart. I'm not going to listen to consultants or obsess on the polls. I'm going to tell America what I know from my experience is the right thing to do. Period."

In fact, there had been a candidate who had done precisely that in 2000—John McCain—and he had lost, too. But it was a very **interesting** loss, one that may contain hints of what politics might become . . . if we're lucky.

6

Issues Are the Last Refuge of a Scoundrel

★ ★ ★ ★

During a languorous midsummer stretch in 1975, I traveled across Iowa and Nebraska in a camper with former senator Fred Harris of Oklahoma, who was attempting a seat-of-his-pants populist candidacy for president. It was the first trip of my first presidential campaign. We stayed in campsites; Fred cooked. We drank a fair amount of Jack Daniel's and laughed a lot, especially when Fred's friends Gene and Evelyn Crawford, who were Cherokee, told ethnic jokes about Native Americans. It was Turnip heaven . . . contrasted with the regal sterility of Gerald Ford's press entourage, which I joined in Colorado as the president made his way back across the Midwest, stopping in some of the same places I'd been with Harris. My first campaign trip: the alpha and omega of American politics.

On my last night with Harris, in Scottsbluff, Nebraska, the candidate blew a gasket. He was speaking to a small crowd, no more than twenty people, on an evening when a throng had gathered across the street, waiting in line to buy tickets to see the movie **Jaws**. A woman began to complain about the people on welfare—it's amazing how often this has come up in my thirty-five years of political reporting—and Harris asked her for specifics. "I'm a schoolteacher," she said, tentatively, "and it's the free-lunch program . . ."

"The free-lunch program?"

"Yes, there are kids who are getting free lunches who just shouldn't be."

"And you don't like that? How many kids would you cut out of it? What kind of kids?"

"Well, mostly minority," she said, meaning illegal immigrants from Mexico.

At which point, Harris erupted. "Well, I want you to know, I want you to know this straight out, I want it to be **very** clear, that if I make a mistake as president, I want to make it in favor of those little kids who get the school-lunch program." His face was red, and he was pacing back and forth. "I remember, as a kid, we were very poor. It wasn't that my daddy didn't work hard, either. But we were poor. And I had to stand in line, with a little yellow cardboard, waiting for a free lunch . . ."

He went on, angrier and angrier. The woman's husband, a postal worker, stood up to defend her and Harris went after him: "Maybe we should cut back on the bureaucrats at the post office who do nothing but sit around all day . . ."

Of course, there was no way that anyone so impolitic would ever be elected president. When the Harris campaign fizzled in New Hampshire, he said, "I guess the little people weren't tall enough to reach the voting levers. Maybe next time we should provide stools."

And so began my lifelong love affair with mavericks. As Harris faded in the winter of 1976, California governor Jerry Brown—a hilariously ironic space cadet—bloomed in the spring. Brown's Maryland primary campaign was perhaps the most fun I've ever had on a press bus. The governor, a New Age Jesuit-Buddhist, was the unlikely recipient of the Baltimore ethnic machine's support, courtesy of Governor Marvin Mandel, who happened to hate Jimmy Carter, the prohibitive front-runner. Each night, Brown—whose campaign buttons had no words on them, just the eponymous color—would find himself in crowded community halls, introduced by people with names like Harry "Soft Shoes" McGuirk and Theodore "TV Teddy" Venetoulis, and then he would regale the uncomprehending locals with tales of "A spaceship earth, hurtling through the universe with only limited amounts of air, water, soil . . ."

The governor attracted a particularly eclectic press corps. I was the representative of **Rolling Stone**. My favorite running mates were Joe Lelyveld, who later became the editor of the **New York Times**, and Gary Wills, the erudite former Catholic priest who was writing, I think, for **Time** magazine. The governor regarded us—and his own existential dilemma—with

puckishness and mortal dread. There was a slightly hal-
lucinogenic quality to the whole thing. At one point, I
asked Brown a plodding, journalistic question about
his contradictory positions on several issues. "Issues,"
he proclaimed, "are the last refuge of a scoundrel."
There was a press conference with a dazed-seeming
Muhammad Ali, who was preparing for a fight; he predicted that Jerry Brown would be the first black president. At a rally in east Baltimore, the governor was
endorsed by a local leader named Joe Staszak, who said:
"Elect Jerry Brown president and this country will be
lily-white."

The next day, Wills, Lelyveld, and I sidled up to the
governor—the world's most laconic pack, we were. I
think it was Wills who asked Brown about the incon-
gruity of a reform candidate getting so much machine
support. "In my father's house," the son of Governor
Pat Brown said, "there are many machines."

No way that guy was ever going to be elected president, either. (Although he did beat Carter in Maryland
and five subsequent primaries.)

There has been a voluptuous history of weirdos,
near-weirdos, and plain old mavericks running for
president in the television era. They catch the public
fancy with their impolitic candor, and then flame out.
They live Al Gore's fantasy—unbought, unbossed, un-
coached, and unrestrained . . . but they are also, inevitably, in presidential politics, unvictorious. (Jerry
Brown, by the way, called himself "The Uncandidate.")

But, you might well ask, aren't most of these guys

doing exactly what you want politicians to do? Aren't they having Turnip Day moments up the wazoo? Yes, yes . . . to a fault. An impolitic politician is an oxymoron. Discipline and dignity are every bit as important to the political equation as humanity and, sadly, candor. It is also very curious that in a number of these instances—Jerry Brown, John Anderson in 1980, Ross Perot, and Howard Dean—the candor is unleavened by warmth: American mavericks, especially of the fanatic-reformer variety, tend to be angry loners, cold fish, egomaniacs. I have no idea why that's the case—although the egomania may well be compounded by the lavish early reviews they receive from rogue-lovers like me.

There is another thing that latter-day mavericks have in common. With certain exceptions—Jerry Brown comes to mind—they tend to speak English. They don't use banana-peel words. They don't talk like politicians, and especially not like Washington politicians. A quick story: I was with Senator Bob Dole in New Hampshire during his first run for president in 1980. Over time, Dole became one of my favorite politicians—honorable, reasonable, and with a wicked sense of humor—but he was a smog bank on the stump. Visiting a middle school one day, Dole was asked by a young girl about his plans to combat acid rain. "That bill's in markup," he replied.

A first rule of mavericks: they make a splash because they don't indulge in legispeak. Nor do they bloat gaseously with opaque rhetorical switchbacks of the sort introduced by John Kennedy's lovely speechwriter Ted Sorensen and then pounded into a pulp by the likes of Bob Shrum: "And I say to you, my fellow Americans, you can hack up a political reform, but you can't reform a political hack." As the public has become more aware of banana-peel oratory and market-tested language, plain speaking has taken on a totemic quality in presidential politics. In fact, in the absence of real candor, speaking badly plays better than speaking well: George W. Bush's fractured syntax and malapropisms—even as he read speeches that were focus-grouped extravagantly—gave him a whiff of "authenticity" that neither of his Democratic opponents could muster. Being "misunderestimated" was his most brilliant political ploy. Calling Greeks "Grecians" and flunking a snotty snap quiz on world leaders conducted by a Boston television reporter brought howls of derision from the eastern establishment—an invaluable credibility-builder with the rest of America.

A second rule of mavericks: they become so addled by the power that comes from speaking freely that they tend to lose perspective, become messianic, and slip the rightful bonds of politics. Unlike Reagan and Clinton—who modulated their use of consultants— mavericks tend to think they have unlocked the secrets of the political Rosetta stone, that they have no need for a careful strategy or tactical advice. A successful political campaign has a dramatic structure that often begins with a bang—the candidate makes known his or her distinctive quality—then subsides for a time as the press and opponents pick away at the candidate's weak spots, then builds gradually toward an election-day climax. One of the hoariest political clichés is actually true: it is possible to peak too soon. Mavericks inevitably do. They thrive in the midst of the maelstrom, but lack the perspective needed to make the daily tweaks and weekly adjustments that are necessary in a long campaign.

Ed Rollins, a consultant whose own no-bullshit style has led to more than a few roguish flameouts, allowed himself to be lured into managing the Ross Perot campaign in 1992. He spotted the essential problem from the very beginning. "Perot is the ultimate control freak," he later wrote. "Politics is a world full of things you can't control; what you have to do is manage them. That's why politicians hire experts, and why smart politicians listen to them."

Perot not only didn't listen, he actively mistrusted everything his consultants proposed. Eventually, according to Rollins, Perot came to believe that Rollins had been signed to a "lifetime" CIA contract by former spymaster George H. W. Bush and sent by the Republicans to be a mole in his campaign. Well, there **was** that—but there was also the fact that Rollins came from a different part of the jungle. He spoke a different language, the language of message discipline and direct mail and get-out-the-vote operations, and Perot believed that he didn't need any of those "traditional" mechanisms to win. All he needed was himself. "I don't want to run a traditional campaign," Rollins shouted at

Perot's minions at one point. "I just want to run a fuck-ing **campaign**! You go on television, you tell your mes-sage, you identify your voters, you get them to the polls, you have debates. This is what you do in any campaign."

Yes, but.

Rollins was imperfectly correct: that's how a cam-paign manager sees a campaign, traditional or not. One imagines that Ross Perot saw the process quite differ-ently: you tell people what's wrong, you tell them how to fix it, and they vote for you. A nontraditional cam-paign, ideally, would combine elements of both Rollins and Perot. And some inspiration besides.

For a time, in the winter of 1999–2000, John Mc-Cain seemed to have struck the perfect balance. If Jerry Brown's Maryland campaign was the most fun I've ever had covering politics, McCain's New Hampshire race was the most exhilarating. This was a candidate with-out fear, speaking in the plainest possible language. I never saw him duck a question, and his best responses had a startling clarity. Asked about health-care reform, for example, he said: "The problem is the Democrats are in the pocket of the trial lawyers and we Republi-cans are in the pocket of the insurance companies. And so there is gridlock, and there will continue to be, un-til we get the special-interest influence out of politics."

There is no more compelling spectacle in politics than watching a man on a white horse attempting to traverse a muddy field. McCain drew the largest, and most diverse, crowds I'd ever seen in New Hampshire—

not just Republicans and Independents but also Democrats, including elected Democratic officeholders unable to control their curiosity. "I can't vote for him," State Representative Marjorie Smith told me after watching McCain and falling completely in love with his style. "I'm a liberal, and there's his position on abortion . . . But you listen to him and you think, this is the politician who could do a 'Nixon in China' on wasteful military spending and corporate welfare. You ask him a question and he answers it directly."

Actually, that was only the beginning. He was willing to admit when he didn't know the answer to a question—and if he sensed that his questioner knew more than he did, he would say, "Tell me more about your position. What do you mean?" Instead of hunkering down as the campaign grew hotter, instead of retreating into the robotic "message discipline" that even terrific candidates like Bill Clinton use as a safety net in the latter days of an election, McCain seemed to unfurl himself, testing the limits of political improvisation.

He granted total access to the press, and soon top editors from New York and Washington were trooping up to New Hampshire for rides on the "Straight Talk Express," a road show that was part press conference, part borscht belt comedy routine, and occasional trial by fire. Every time a new big shot boarded the bus, armed with gotcha questions and anxious to challenge the senator's vaunted candor, McCain would disarm him in the simplest possible way: he would admit that he had made a mistake or gotten something wrong, or didn't know the answer. He did this constantly, and it was always successful. One day, Joe Salkowski of the **Arizona Daily Star** asked McCain why he had told National Public Radio, in a moment of un-McCainian braggadocio, that he'd achieved more legislative results than any other member of the U.S. Senate. "That was somewhat disingenuous on my part," the senator confessed immediately. "A lot of times it was just that my name was on bills, some of them pretty nonsensical, that came out of the Commerce Committee."

Which raised an interesting question: Why do most politicians—George W. Bush, for example—seem to believe that any admission of failure or error will cast them immediately into the outer darkness? This is a mystifying reflex, a bit of tradecraft that has almost become a political tradition. It is probably the single greatest contributor to the general impression that politicians are congenital liars. What if, for example, John Kerry had admitted, early in the 2004 campaign, that his vote in favor of the war in Iraq had been misguided, "but we're there now and we have to find a way to win it." The Republicans would have called his judgment into question, no doubt. They would have said he was wishy-washy (they did anyway). But he would have had the advantage of running on the high ground, with a position that was obviously true—as Hillary Clinton later said: No one would have voted for the war if it was known that there were no weapons of mass destruction in Iraq. There wouldn't have been a vote. (Of course, Kerry would still have had an impossible time explaining his craven and idiotic vote against the $87 billion to prosecute the war—but that's a topic for the next chapter.)

McCain's honesty about his own weaknesses was an exceptionally powerful political tool, and it probably stemmed from the fact that running for president was not the defining moment of his life, nor the most difficult thing he had ever done. He had been a prisoner of war in North Vietnam for six years, and had suffered the most excrutiating torture, his arms broken and rebroken several times. His awkward, truncated arms— he couldn't raise them above his shoulder, couldn't comb his own hair—were a constant reminder of his sacrifice. He had refused early release from prison, which had been offered by the North Vietnamese because his father was an admiral (the rule was that the prisoners who had been interned longest must be released first), which led to even more intense torture. Ultimately, under extreme duress, McCain had agreed to sign a war crimes confession—a matter of crushing and enduring shame. (He was the first presidential candidate to admit that he had attempted suicide—twice, after signing the confession.)

Later, McCain was one of five senators investigated in an infamous banking scandal, even though he was probably included among the Keating Five for purely partisan reasons (the other four were Democrats). He was exonerated after two years, but he later told me that the experience was more difficult, in some ways, than being a prisoner of war. "My honor was being called into question," he said. "There were days when I was so depressed I couldn't leave the house."

McCain's honor was a rare, vestigial military thing and quite unrelenting. It was one of the oddest qualities I'd ever seen in a candidate—entirely sincere and yet politically brilliant, with the effect of neutering any argument that could be made against him. In one fairly dramatic example, McCain told me, unbidden, that the breakup of his first marriage was all his fault: "I've lived a very, very flawed life. I don't think people would think so well of me if they knew more about that part of it."

McCain let that drop during one of our few formal interviews—most of the time we were just spritzing—in an airplane headed to New Hampshire. I wasn't sure how to react. There was no way I was going to ask him, "What do you mean, specifically?" In fact, I was so embarrassed that we had wandered onto such personal turf that I stopped taking notes, and then—incredibly—tried to comfort him. "There aren't many of us who haven't done things we're ashamed of over the past twenty-five years," I said.

McCain shook his head and replied, "Yeah, but . . ."

"Why are you so hard on yourself?" I asked, realizing that McCain's candor had accomplished a complete reversal of the traditional reportorial situation. Usually, the implicit question was directed the other way, from politician to reporter: "Why are you being so hard on me?"

McCain beat George W. Bush—who seemed a cardboard candidate, ghostly pale in the face of his opponent's florid humanity—by nineteen points in New Hampshire. He was a national hero, a political phenomenon. Money began to flow into his campaign via the Internet. And then his candidacy began to disintegrate.

To be sure, Bush's disgraceful South Carolina campaign had a great deal to do with McCain's decline. There was also the stark political reality that McCain just wasn't very popular among members of his own party; all his successes came in states where Democrats and Independents could cross over and vote for him.

But McCain had a hand in his own demise as well. It began with a single word. On the night of his New Hampshire victory, he called his campaign a "crusade." A very loaded word in American politics. The intimations of stiff righteousness were soon apparent in his candidacy. The self-deprecating humor disappeared, and so did some of the humility. Granted, it is fairly hard to be funny when a bunch of jerks claiming to be war heroes are saying you were brainwashed by the North Vietnamese, and you are being "accused" of fathering a mixed-race child—but grace under that sort of pressure is the defining test of a presidential campaign. Ultimately, McCain's dudgeon led to a revealing moment after Bush defeated him in South Carolina. In a speech that he delivered in the Reverend Pat Robertson's hometown of Virginia Beach, Virginia, McCain assaulted Robertson and other selected shamans of political Christianity as "Agents of Intolerance."

Hooray, you say? Wasn't this just the inevitable man-
ifestation of McCain's relentless candor? Didn't someone need to take the sleazy tele-charlatans down a peg?
Yes, but.

The Virginia Beach speech was more a product of
McCain's pride and temper than his candor. He didn't
bother to build a case against the bad guys. Their main
offense was that they had misrepresented him. "I am a
pro-life, pro-family fiscal conservative and advocate
of a strong defense. And yet Pat Robertson and Jerry
Falwell and a few Washington leaders of the pro-life
movement call me an unacceptable presidential candidate. They distort my pro-life positions and smear the
reputations of my supporters. Why?"

He repeated that same point over and over again.
He had been attacked unfairly. It was purely personal.
There was a slapdash injudiciousness to the speech that
betrayed a certain self-absorption. McCain had gotten
all caught up in McCain . . . and his handlers, who
should have deepened or dampened or deep-sixed the
speech, had gotten all caught up in McCain, too.

"We didn't do our jobs," said John Weaver, a consultant who was as candid as McCain was about his
own flaws. "We made some real mistakes in South Carolina. We started thinking like John. When the Bush
campaign began to spread those rumors, we responded
the way we thought John would. We had our morning
conference call and decided we were going to rip Bush
a new you-know-what, we were going to run an ad
comparing him to Bill Clinton—and we just went

ahead and did it because we figured that was what John would want. We didn't test it. The only focus group was six angry white male consultants. And it turned out to be a very bad idea—it really compromised the high-road campaign John was running. After the ad appeared, he asked me, 'Why did we put that thing on, anyway?' "

McCain was complicit in another mistake his consultants made, which also dishonored the campaign: he agreed to make a statement supporting South Carolina's right to fly the Confederate battle flag atop the state capitol. "We were trying to be cautious," Weaver told me. "It took days of arguing to get him to do it, and when he finally agreed, he read the statement we gave him as if it was his North Vietnamese confession. It hurt us with everyone on both sides of the flag dispute. As soon as the campaign folded, McCain told me, 'We've got to apologize for that,' and he went back to South Carolina and apologized."

But McCain's most basic problem was similar to, though not so extreme as, Perot's: he thought that he was enough, that the campaign didn't need the ballast that came with careful strategic planning. "We prepared big thick briefing books on each state and each issue, but he wouldn't read them," Weaver said. "They got thinner and thinner as the campaign went on. We couldn't use polling to hone the message, because he wouldn't cooperate."

It is probable that even if McCain had done everything right, he still would have lost to George W. Bush.

The Republican Party is not comfortable with insurgencies. It has a tendency toward primogeniture—the most senior candidate inherits the throne. Bush had vicarious seniority; he had raised lots of money and he had his father's name. And McCain was simply too popular among Democrats to be trusted.

But the freshness of the McCain campaign lingered long after he withdrew from the race. He had broken through the consultant-industrial straitjacket—and there was a strong suspicion, in the political community, that a candidate like McCain, who appealed across party lines, could beat George W. Bush in a general election, that the folks were hungry for someone who didn't talk like a focus group.

And now, a few words about the role of the press in presidential politics and, well, about me. I "retired" after the 2000 campaign. My intention was to write books and occasional pieces for **The New Yorker**. This was probably never realistic, given my addiction, but sitting on the sidelines became impossibly painful after the terrorist attacks of September 11, 2001. And so I found myself back at the old stand in the summer of 2002, watching an early Democratic cattle show, staged by the Democratic Leadership Council (DLC)—and amazed that Senator John Kerry of Massachusetts seemed the most compelling of the bunch.

I was amazed because I'd known Kerry for a long

time and had never been impressed by his political skills. I covered his first congressional race in 1972; he was dreadful. I covered his 1996 Senate race against William Weld; he had improved some, but he still wasn't a house on fire. We'd had lunch fairly regularly over the years, especially in the 1990s—and I came to appreciate him as I did the other five Vietnam combat veterans serving in the U.S. Senate: Bob Kerrey, John McCain, Max Cleland, Chuck Hagel, and Chuck Robb. They were my favorite politicians in Washington. They had a swagger, and an integrity, and a sense of perspective that most of their colleagues—many of whom had evaded military service in the 1960s (as I had)—could not match. They were a quiet caucus, which met frequently and informally, especially regarding issues of war and peace—and to defend each other when their service in Vietnam was called into question, attacks which came with nauseating frequency, since the war in Vietnam corroded almost everything it touched. Over time, I came to realize that when one of the others was attacked, it was John Kerry who organized the posse to provide for their mutual defense.

John McCain was most passionate on the subject of Kerry. They had been named co-chairs of a commission to investigate the possibility that American prisoners of war were still being held in Vietnam. "I gained a lot of respect and affection for John during those POW-MIA hearings," McCain told me. "He was a lot more mature." Kerry was especially helpful when some of the more extreme POW-movement types testified before the committee. "I'd see the way some of these guys were exploiting the families of those missing in action, and I'd begin to get angry," McCain said, "and John would sense it and put his hand on my arm to calm me down before I'd lose"—McCain paused and smiled—"my effectiveness."

Kerry had organized the Senate combat vets—Democrats and Republicans alike—in McCain's defense during the South Carolina primary. He organized op-ed pieces and television interviews in support of Bob Kerrey when he was accused of having taken part in a massacre during the war. He organized support for Max Cleland, after Cleland was defeated for reelection in a particularly nasty campaign in 2002. These acts, and the love of his colleagues—"It's the closest thing to love that I can feel for another man," Bob Kerrey told me—were more impressive than anything Kerry ever said or did as a politician.

But he was saying the right things in the summer of 2002. At the DLC cattle show, he was the only candidate to talk extensively about foreign and national security policy. In fact, he derided "a new conventional wisdom of consultants, pollsters, and strategists who argue . . . that Democrats should be the party of domestic issues only."

Music to my ears. I decided to write a profile of Kerry for **The New Yorker**. This had become something of a tradition. I had written an early profile of

Michael Dukakis, a cover story in **New York** magazine in August of 1987; it wasn't a very flattering piece but, I was told later, it opened a vein of Wall Street money that gave Dukakis greater credibility as the primary season approached. I did the same thing in early 1992—the candidate was Bill Clinton—which led the militantly myopic Howell Raines of the **New York Times** to write that I was in the tank for Clinton because I had called him a "master politician."

Was I "in the tank" for Clinton? Perhaps. It was a conundrum most journalists, and all columnists, face. I certainly agreed with most of Clinton's policy positions, which seemed a creative departure from the old liberal Democratic rut; his early DLC domestic and economic policy advisers—Elaine Kamarck, Bill Galston, Bruce Reed, Rob Shapiro, Roger Altman—were among my best friends in politics. But that didn't mean I was uncritical, especially when Clinton strayed away from policies he had supported. In fact, a month before Raines attacked me, I had written a column slamming Clinton for pandering to the public employees unions (who opposed many of the bureaucratic reforms he had backed).

Still, the "in the tank" question was—and remains—an uncomfortable aspect of my job. I was being paid for my opinions and yet when I made a decision to write a profile of, say, John Kerry, it seemed that I was playing favorites, picking winners. After the profile appeared, Howard Kurtz of the **Washington Post** noted that Kerry had won "the Joe Klein primary." Which was true, and not. I had known Kerry a long time; I felt close to him in the same way I felt close to McCain, Kerrey, Hagel, and the other combat vets whom I so admired. But it did not mean that he was going to get a free pass from me as the campaign progressed—in fact, as with Clinton, I may have held Kerry to a higher standard than the other candidates since my expectations for him were higher.

I did give Kerry the benefit of the doubt in the beginning, though, when we talked about the impact that John McCain's candidacy might have on his own campaign. "I've reached the point where I'm just going to do what I'm going to do, and to hell with whatever the conventional wisdom is," he said, and it almost seemed credible, given his closeness to McCain, especially when he added, "I mean, if I screw up, what are they going to do—send me to Vietnam?" (In fact, that's exactly what they—the Bush-related Swift Boat Veterans for Truth—ultimately and scurrilously did.)

Kerry proceeded to run one of the most conventional, consultant-driven, market-tested campaigns imaginable—and it was soon clear that if there was a Democrat intent on emulating John McCain's free-wheeling style, it was the governor of Vermont, Howard Dean.

Dean's finest moment came early in the campaign. The Democratic National Committee had gathered for its annual winter meeting in Washington, D.C. A cattle show was on offer—all the candidates for president would be speaking, and all but one of the plausible contenders delivered their standard stump speeches.*

Dean did not. His entire pre-speech prep went something like this, according to his campaign manager, Joe Trippi.

> **TRIPPI:** You know what they really want? They're waiting for someone to walk up to that podium and say, "What the fuck is going on here? What the fuck happened to our party?"
>
> **DEAN:** Joe, I can't go out there and ask, "What the fuck is going on here?" How about if I say, "What I want to know is?"

Dean sat down, wrote a series of bulleted points on index cards. There was no prepared text, no practice sessions—but that didn't mean the candidate was unprepared. Dean clearly had planned his entrance. When he walked onstage, he went directly to the podium, didn't wave, didn't say hello to the assembled dignitaries, didn't acknowledge DNC chair Terry McAuliffe or the other candidates. He just started speaking, in a conversational tone. These were the first words out of his mouth:

---

*I'm not counting vanity candidates like Al Sharpton, Carol Moseley Braun, and Congressman Dennis Kucinich.

What I want to know is why the Democratic Party leadership is supporting the President's unilateral attack on Iraq?

What I want to know is why are Democratic Party leaders supporting tax cuts? . . .

What I want to know is why we're fighting in Congress for a Patient's Bill of Rights when the Democratic Party ought to be standing up for health care for every single man, woman and child in this country?

What I want to know is why our folks are voting for the President's No Child Left Behind bill that leaves every child behind, every teacher behind, every school board behind and every property tax-payer behind?

The committee members were up, cheering, whooping, bellowing. Dean allowed them to subside and then he dropped the hammer: "I'm Howard Dean . . . and I'm here to represent the democratic wing of the Democratic Party."

What followed for much of the next year was another exhilarating rogue-ride and flameout. I wasn't as sympathetic toward this one as I'd been toward Mc-Cain, however, because it was apparent to me from the very start that Dr. Dean had the most prohibitively cold and arrogant bedside manner I'd seen in a candidate since . . . well, since Ross Perot, and he was a bit of a policy opportunist besides. He blithely abandoned moderate positions he had staked out as governor of

Vermont and pandered to the "democratic" wing of the Democratic Party—a formulation that Dean had borrowed from the late Senator Paul Wellstone of Minnesota. Unlike most mavericks, he took no inconvenient positions. With the exception of his position on the war—which placed him nicely to the left of his opponents in the Democratic primaries—Dean's roguery had everything to do with style and not much to do with substance. He backed away from raising the retirement age for Social Security, and from his support for Medicare reform. His incendiary and fundamentally irresponsible position on George W. Bush's "No Child Left Behind" education bill was a sop to the teachers unions, who were opposed to educational accountability of any sort. A few weeks after his DNC triumph, I interviewed Dean one-on-one before a live audience at the Kennedy Library in Boston. He didn't seem to know very much, a deficit he filled with demagogic bluster. At one point, I asked him if health insurance should work like auto insurance— that is, everyone should be required to have it. The government would subsidize those who couldn't afford it, but the estimated fifteen million who can afford it but choose not to buy in—healthy young adults, for the most part—would be required to purchase some form of insurance and expand the risk pool. "Don't they have a moral responsibility to buy in?" I asked.

"I don't talk about moral responsibility," he snapped. "That's what the current president does."

"But shouldn't health insurance work like auto insurance?"

"Auto insurance doesn't work," he said. At which point, I crossed Dean off my list of potential presidents.

None of that was important to the rest of the world, though. The only thing that mattered was that the governor had taken a clear, cogent—and ultimately correct—position against the war in Iraq, which was enough to rouse the antiwar left wing of the Democratic Party, especially the younger voters who had been ignored for so long. It didn't hurt that Dean was using plain old unadorned English to express himself, or that he just **reeked** of spontaneity—in fact, spontaneity turned out to be the only way to reach a new generation of political activists who communicated via the Internet. For them, the ancient, sludgy pace and cautious, fudgy language of, say, John Kerry seemed everything that was wrong with politics . . . and they made themselves known to the Dean campaign in droves by e-mail in the spring of 2003. More than a few just showed up in the Burlington, Vermont, offices, willing to eat cold pizza and work all night (and sleep on the floor when they weren't working).

Trippi, who had always seemed a descendant of either Sacco or Vanzetti, had finally found his métier. He was leading an anarchist cult rebellion. He recruited an inspired group of computer geeks—including a woman whose name, Zephyr Teachout, seemed to sum up **everything**—and made it plain that he was willing to try just about anything new. After noticing that there was a fair amount of Dean activity at a new Web site called Meetup.org, Trippi linked the Dean Web site to Meetup and quickly signed a $2,500 contract with the founders to promote his candidate. Meetup was an elegant idea, a brilliant use of the Internet: it organized monthly meetings across the country, as demand required, for local affinity groups of lonely enthusiasts—balalaika players, knitters, vegans, Wiccans . . . whatever. It seemed a classic political organizing tool, and it exploded for Dean in the spring of 2003. By March, thousands of people were turning out across the country for the monthly Dean meetups. It was the sort of outpouring that politicians dream about. Indeed, Dean was the first Democratic **primary** candidate in a long time to cross an essential political threshold: he could create his own crowds. He didn't have to rely on the local Rotary club or senior-citizen center to provide an audience. People, by the thousands, were dying to see him; those sorts of crowds usually don't appear until the general-election campaigns in the fall, if then.

The candidate seemed astonished by all the attention—and bemused by the new technology that was turning his campaign into the hippest thing in politics. When I caught up with Dean in California in late spring, he told me: "I have no idea how any of this works . . . but the Meetup folks are the core of our organization out here in California. In New York, they're working to get us on the primary ballot, which is not

an easy thing. This campaign is totally decentralized.
There are probably fifteen or twenty different kinds of
bumper stickers because people in different states tend
to print their own."

The heart of the campaign was its Web site, which
proved a living, breathing thing, a virtual headquarters—
unlike the passive pages produced by most politicians.
It was the locus of fund-raising, organizing, news, gossip (there were several blogs running), and, when the
campaign turned sour, griping. The fund-raising was
astonishing. By the second quarter of 2004, Dean was
raising more than John Edwards and John Kerry, who
had led the pack in the first quarter. By the end of the
year, Dean had raised more than any other Democratic
presidential candidate in history. And, at first, very
little of the money was going to the now standard consultant preoccupations. In fact, it wasn't until the autumn, when Dick Gephardt began running a series of
negative ads in Iowa, criticizing Dean for his formerly
responsible positions on Social Security and Medicare,
that Trippi started polling. "We've used polling differ-
ently from any campaign I've ever been associated
with," Trippi told me at the time. "When Gephardt
starting banging on us, we wanted to see if it hurt. And
I think we've done one focus group. We ran a three-
minute tape of Dean at his most passionate to see if
people thought he seemed angry. They didn't, by the
way. They thought he seemed strong. Anyway, we've
got better ways to find out what people think. When
we step in it, our supporters let us know immediately,

by e-mail. We get flooded." (In fact, one of Trippi's new measures of success was crashing the Web site—which would occur when so many people responded simultaneously to a posting on the Blog for America that the Web site shut down. This happened more than once, and every crash was seen as a triumph.)

But there was a problem, which had become apparent as early as the spring. The Dean campaign was about process—about the blog, the meetups, the Internet fund-raising—more than it was about substance. "It's time to shift gears," Dean had told me in June, "to become a more presidential candidate with an inclusive vision, not just a bomb thrower."

The gears were stuck, though. As Dean began a cross-country "Sleepless Summer" tour, the crowds were huge—but the message seemed to be: "Hey, isn't this a huge crowd? Aren't we great? Aren't we raising lots of money?" It was the Perot/McCain problem one step removed: the campaign was about . . . the campaign. Which was understandable in a way: it was a marvelous campaign. The monthly meetups were truly impressive—they had expanded from Dean organizing to community service in some places, and supporting local candidates in others. The enthusiasm, the lack of cynicism, the sense of community, the pure joy of the movement was almost euphoric. But building his campaign on a movement rather than a message had a perverse side effect as well: Dean was trying to cultivate inevitability in 2004 the same way that Bush had in 2000—by convincing the press that his poll numbers were impregnable and his fund-raising overwhelming, and that there was a gathering snowball of endorsements. And the press, for the most part, went along: polling, fund-raising, and endorsements were the only quantifiable, safely reportable aspects of the campaign before the voting started. On the evening in December that Al Gore endorsed Dean, an otherwise sane television anchor asked me, "Joe, is it over?"

Yes it was, but not in the way most of my colleagues thought: Trippi later said that the Gore endorsement was the beginning of the end. Indeed, his old mentor Pat Caddell was firing off flaming e-mails saying: you don't want endorsements from the Democratic establishment, you don't want your ads to look like everyone else's ads, you don't want to look like every other politician. (In fact, Dean had started a course of negative ads responding to Gephardt's attacks, which were uniformly awful—same old, same old type of ads. Dean didn't run a single creative television spot during the campaign; this, Trippi later admitted, was caused by his contractual and personal allegiance to his partners in his consulting firm.)

To my mind, though, the end had begun a month earlier. Dean gave a speech at Cooper Union in New York City, a hallowed place in American politics, the place where a little-known midwesterner named Abraham Lincoln had established himself as a national candidate for president in 1860 by delivering an intellectually rigorous dismantling of the constitutional arguments for slavery. "A house divided against itself cannot stand," Lincoln said—and, ever since, politicians had stood at the same podium and given immortality their best shot. This was the moment for Dean to reach out to the rest of the Democratic Party, offer a comprehensive vision of a Dean presidency, get **bigger**. Instead, he talked about fund-raising. He announced that he wanted to abandon the public campaign finance system, as George W. Bush had done, and test his campaign's amazing ability to raise money from the grass roots against the president's ability to raise money from the Sun Belt's moneyed elite. In a nice touch, he offered his supporters the chance to vote on this decision—but there was no question they would follow his lead (which they promptly did).

Dean thus became the first Democrat to opt out of the public campaign finance system, which had been introduced as a post-Watergate political reform in 1974. It seemed the ultimate irony—the righteous crusader abandoning a reform intended to take the money out of politics. Dean had a point, of course: the campaign finance strictures made it hard for a Democrat to compete against the Republican money machine (although he was jumping the rules mostly because his enormous stash would give him a major advantage against his Democratic rivals in the primaries). But Dean's decision to use the Cooper Union podium to discuss a matter of pelf rather than the commonweal sent a strong subliminal signal that he had nothing of substance to say, that he lacked the size and grace to be president—that his campaign would have difficulty breaking out from its cult status. Indeed, Trippi admitted to me that the phenomenal growth in the campaign had stalled; he had predicted one million Deaniacs by January 1, 2004, and the campaign was stuck at little more than half that.

The collapse that ensued was historic. It was all but complete by the time Dean concluded caucus night with his infamous scream—which was intended to rally his supporters but was heard round the world as an animal yelp of anguish. The press would find all sorts of process-driven reasons for Dean's fall. His campaign was out-organized on the ground in Iowa by Kerry's legendary get-out-the-vote magician Michael Whouley. It was also said that Dean wasted resources— he whipped through $40 million in about a day and a half, it seemed—setting up headquarters, organizing, and advertising in irrelevant states. And then there were the gaffes. He said the capture of Saddam Hussein on December 13, 2003, had not made America any safer (which was absolutely true; the real problem was that Dean didn't seem particularly **happy** that Saddam had been captured—in fact, he seemed disappointed that the president's war effort had succeeded in any way). Dean also, and rather suspiciously, refused to release his gubernatorial papers to the press. And then, on the eve of the Iowa caucuses, an old interview surfaced in which he slagged the relevance of the arcane Iowa process.

But there was a more subtle and substantial process going on among the Democratic Party voters in

Iowa. The political professionals—the candidates, the reporters—had been wandering through the cornfields for more than a year, but, with the exception of a handful of activists, the civilians hadn't really fixed on the race yet. Oh, they had vague impressions of the candidates—John Edwards seemed young, Dick Gephardt seemed tired, John Kerry seemed stiff, Dean seemed fresh—but they hadn't begun to concentrate on their choice, to really think it through. The actual campaign in Iowa lasted less than three weeks, from New Year's Day to January 19, 2004, when the local precinct caucuses were held. The candidates were inescapable during that time; they hurtled across the state, all day and through the night; their ads cluttered TV screens.

January in Iowa is, quadrennially, one of those rare moments when politics becomes an obsessive topic of kitchen-table conversation; the intensity of the process becomes surreal and almost dreamlike, a closeness magnified by the terrible weather, slippery roads, and a universal lack of sleep. Most sentient humans in the state bump into some candidate or other in a mall or coffee shop during that month. They receive truckloads of mail from the candidates. They have no choice but to pay close attention to this bizarre public ritual—and, in 2004, they decided that Howard Dean just wasn't up to snuff.

Their decision was ineffable. It had little to do with issues. In fact, they agreed with Dean on the issues—especially the war. His crowds remained large and enthusiastic. His poll numbers were drifting down, but slowly, slowly, and no one seemed to be surging up to challenge him. In fact, the most important issue in Iowa existed somewhere beyond the concrete measures of politics. The polls said that Democratic voters were interested in the usual stuff—the economy, education, health care—and most of the questions in town meetings were about those things. The John Edwards campaign, for example, was deluded into thinking that domestic issues were all that mattered. (When I asked a key Edwards adviser why the candidate never talked about foreign policy, I was told: "Because the people don't care about that.")

But, of course, they did. The nation was at war. The Democrats were going to need a candidate who had the stature and gravity to discuss matters of national security on the same stage as the Republican president. And even if the voters were asking about Social Security and college scholarships—things that were close to their daily lives—they were reading body language, looking for stability and authority. They enjoyed Howard Dean's anger. They were angry, too. But he was too . . . fast, too precipitous and undignified to be a plausible president in a serious time. Furthermore, they understood that John Edwards was too inexperienced to be convincing, and that Dick Gephardt had been around too long.

Which left John Kerry. Who certainly looked like a president. And had the military experience to question Bush's foreign policy. And if there was still a question about his humanity, it seemed to be answered two days before the caucuses when an old buddy from Vietnam, whose life Kerry had saved in the Mekong Delta, suddenly appeared in Des Moines.

The timing of Jim Rassmann's appearance was suspicious, and spectacular. Rassmann, a California Republican, said he had tried to reach Kerry in the past, and that as the Iowa vote approached he tried again, and this time got through; the campaign staff rushed him to Des Moines. But the moment when he and Kerry met—for the first time in thirty-seven years—was unplanned and quite moving. It took place in a community center in an African American neighborhood. I was standing onstage as Kerry and Rassmann met, surrounded by a blinding aurora of television lights and cameras. Rassmann began to cry; Kerry took the man's face in his hands and spoke to him quietly, intently. They hugged. Kerry's eyes were glistening, but he controlled his emotions—and, for just a moment, he seemed to recapture the easy authority that his shipmates in Vietnam had always talked about.

For just a moment, he slipped the bonds of politics—the careful calculations that seemed to lock him in a perpetual state of aloof paralysis—and became the natural leader he once had been.

The rest of his campaign was pretty much an embarrassment.

7

We're Going to Meet the People Where They Are

★ ★ ★ ★

John Kerry did have one other impressive moment in Iowa—but it came vicariously, with the best television ad of his campaign. It featured a crewmate of Kerry's from Vietnam named Del Sandusky. There was footage of a young John Kerry as a swift-boat captain in the Mekong Delta, carrying a rifle, hanging out with his men—and Sandusky, a salt-of-the-earth blue-collar guy saying, "The decisions that he made saved our lives. He had unfailing instincts and unchallengeable leadership."

And then, Senator Kerry himself: "There's this sense after Vietnam that every other day is extra. That you have to do what's right and let the chips fall where they may. Because it's right to guarantee all Americans health care. You know it's right to roll back the Bush tax cuts for the wealthy and invest in our kids. That's why I'm running for president."

Then back to Sandusky: "This is a good American."

This is a good American.

In a season of crass and hyperbolic television ads—most of them negative—the Sandusky spot was transcendent. It established John Kerry's character; it linked his past and present; Sandusky was an unimpeachable witness. In twenty seconds, Kerry seemed to answer the three Karl Rove questions: he was strong, he was trustworthy, and he cared about blue-collar guys like Del Sandusky. A Republican version of the ad probably wouldn't have included all the promises—health care for all, roll back the tax cuts, invest in kids—but they were secondary to the most important, and elegantly understated, point of the ad: This is a good American.

It was a line that confronted the prevailing caricature of Kerry: that he was "French"—aloof, effete, narcissistic, the sort of guy you'd never want to have over for dinner. Indeed, had John Kerry proved to be "a good American," he might well have defeated George W. Bush—but he wasn't even close. He proved weak, indecisive, and, yes, aloof. At six feet, four inches tall, with a head of hair that came out of central casting and a sonorous baritone that slouched toward drone, he literally seemed to have his head in the clouds; there was a distressing, unfocused, soporific quality to the man. The prevailing mystery of the Kerry campaign, especially for those who had known him longest—the Vietnam veterans he had led in war (and in peace marches)—was: Whatever happened to the courageous young leader who had risked his life to protect his crew

in Vietnam and risked his political career to oppose the
war when he came home? For me, there was an additional question: What happened to the quietly con-
fident senator who had taken charge when John
McCain, Bob Kerrey, and Max Cleland needed to be
defended? And for George W. Bush's campaign team,
there was another question, too. "I watched those early
ads in Iowa and I thought, uh-oh, these guys get
what this is all about," said Matthew Dowd, the strategist who coordinated Bush's polling. "It wasn't just
Del Sandusky. They had a woman with health-care
problems"—Elizabeth Hendrix—"who said, 'John
Kerry understands what's going on in my life.' But we
didn't see those ads, or that very clear focus, after the
primaries. What happened?"

The Del Sandusky ad was not an accident. It was the
result of hard work, long hours of research, and conversations with the candidate by Jim Margolis, a political
consultant whose role in the Kerry candidacy was a
case study in the value that professionals can add to
a campaign, if they do their homework. Margolis—a
partner in the firm of Greer, Margolis, Mitchell, Burns
and Associates—was hired by Kerry in 2001, after a
rigorous search process. Kerry had always depended on
his old pals from Boston for help in his campaigns—
pollster Tom Kiley, consultants John Marttila and Dan
Payne (as well as his best friend, former brother-in-law,
and fellow veteran David Thorne, who had been a
partner of Marttila, Kiley and Payne for a time). But
the Boston crew faltered in Kerry's difficult 1996 Sen-

ate reelection campaign against popular governor William Weld. Bob Shrum was brought in, and proved invaluable in sharpening Kerry's message, which immediately became more partisan, linking Weld to Newt Gingrich and the radical Republicans in Washington. Shrum also prepped Kerry through an exhilarating, substantive, and fairly feisty series of debates against the governor.

But Kerry was wary about giving Shrum control of a presidential campaign. Shrum's reputation was in tatters after the 2000 Gore disaster. His track record in presidential races was infamous: he had participated in seven, and never won one. This was somewhat unfair. Shrum could hardly be blamed for the defeats of Edmund Muskie, George McGovern, Ted Kennedy, or even Richard Gephardt, whose campaign he helped resuscitate. But he certainly hadn't done much, as a senior strategist, for Bob Kerrey in 1992 or Al Gore in 2000—and John Kerry seemed well aware of Shrum's strengths and weaknesses. "I'd never use him as a strategist," Kerry told friends. "But I would like to have him around for speeches and debate prep."

And so, in the winter of 2001–2002, Jim Jordan—who had been Kerry's choice to run the Democratic Senatorial Campaign Committee and his second choice for campaign manager (Boston pro John Sasso was first, but he was in the midst of a divorce and refused the offer)—organized a series of dinners with leading Democratic political consultants for the senator. "Kerry liked Bill Knapp"—the late Bob Squier's partner—

"but he really clicked with Margolis," said an aide. "He thought Margolis was a good listener. He really liked that."

Margolis elicited Kerry's life story in a series of long conversations. At one point, he asked the senator why he was so interested in foreign affairs, and Kerry told him about growing up the son of a U.S. diplomat, living in Berlin, riding his bike through the Brandenburg Gate as a child, and how he came to understand, in a deep and personal way, the threat of communism. "You should use that in speeches, make your interest in national security into something that's human and part of your personal story," Margolis told him, and Kerry did. Indeed, Kerry's closest staffers—his press aide David Wade and chief of staff David McKean—were impressed by how easily Margolis fit in, and how clearly he understood what the senator's interests, strengths, and weaknesses were. And they were also impressed by how hard Margolis was working, how he traveled around the country, interviewing Kerry's brother and two sisters, and his war buddies (the Sandusky interview was done more than a year before the ad aired). The work was particularly admirable because it was being done "on the come." Margolis wouldn't really be paid until the spots appeared on television, when he would receive a fixed percentage of the money spent on advertising.*

---

*There are conflicting accounts of the size of this percentage, ranging from 9 to 15 percent.

In fact, Kerry seemed off to a good start. He was raising money and beginning to put together credible local organizations in the early-primary states. His national security pitch was unique among the Democrats; he actually flanked Bush on the right, criticizing the president for not using the U.S. Army to capture Osama bin Laden when the terrorist was surrounded at Tora Bora, in the mountains of Afghanistan (the United States had paid local warlords to capture bin Laden, who apparently paid the warlords to let him escape). At the end of 2002, James Carville told me, "I think Kerry's had a hell of a year. Why? Because he's actually saying something . . . The other thing is, 9/11 made the commander-in-chief part of the presidency important again, and that's helped him, too, because of his military background."

But there were troubling aspects to his candidacy as well. Kerry was, after all, a Massachusetts liberal—Ted Kennedy's junior partner—in an increasingly conservative country where "Ted Kennedy" had become an epithet. His wife, Teresa, the ridiculously wealthy widow of Senator John Heinz, was a wifty narcissist who had a reputation for saying the wrong thing in public and for getting her way in private. Together, the Kerrys led a prohibitively fancy life. There were fabulous homes in Boston, Washington, Nantucket, Sun Valley, Idaho, and Pittsburgh. There were private airplanes (Kerry was a pilot) and stunt flying, fine wines, and the sort of sports favored by the super-rich: skiing, snowboarding, motorcycle riding, and—infamously—windsurfing.

"We lost John ten years ago," said one of Kerry's Vietnam buddies after the campaign was over, "when he married Teresa."

Most important, there was Iraq. In October of 2002, Kerry voted to give the president authorization to use force against Saddam Hussein. It was not an easy vote. Kerry had opposed the first Gulf War, even though Saddam had invaded Kuwait, and even though Bush the Elder had assembled an impressive international coalition and won the approval of the United Nations for the counterattack. The truth was, Vietnam had turned Kerry into a mortal dove; opposition was his gut reaction to the prospective use of military power. But as he grew older, and the possibility of running for president loomed, the senator seemed to realize that his reflexive resistance to the use of force would have to be overcome—and so would his seemingly foolish vote against the first Gulf War. When Saddam Hussein thwarted the UN weapons inspectors in 1998, Kerry was among those who led the charge to give Bill Clinton the authority to take military action. It seemed obvious that he would give George W. Bush the same authority in 2002—even though Bush the Younger had neither the provocation, the coalition, nor the support of the United Nations for an invasion. Most Democrats believed the timing of the vote was a transparently political ploy, orchestrated by Karl Rove. It would occur in the last weeks of the 2002 congressional campaign. A "no" vote would reinforce both the Democrats' perceived weakness on national security matters and the president's post-9/11 reputation for strength in fighting the campaign against Islamist terrorism. "The resolution was clearly going to pass. The Bushies clearly wanted John to vote no," said Jonathan Winer, one of Kerry's foreign policy advisers, who argued for the "pragmatic" position. "Why should he give them what they wanted?"

Because you don't play politics with wars. Kerry's speech announcing his vote was filled with caveats and escape hatches, which—I suspect—was an accurate reflection of his inner turmoil. He demanded UN support for any invasion, and only if Saddam refused to cooperate with weapons inspections. But he gave George W. Bush the power to take military action in Iraq. He gave it reluctantly, almost guiltily, and his conflicted feelings about the war—which only grew more conflicted as the disaster unfolded—would be the single most debilitating factor in his attempt to win the presidency.

In May of 2002, I wrote a piece about Bob Shrum for the online magazine **Slate**, in which I surmised that the race for the Democratic nomination in 2004 wouldn't really begin until Shrum chose his candidate:

> He will be in a unique position in 2004, with connections to no fewer than four prominent Democratic hopefuls. He was Al Gore's consultant in 2000. He has a long-standing relationship with

Richard Gephardt . . . He helped with both John Kerry's difficult Senate race in 1996 . . . and John Edwards's difficult Senate campaign against Lauch Faircloth in 1998 . . . No political consultant has ever had so many options.

And so, the first contest of 2004 will be the Shrum primary. The winner, however, will be in a real pickle: If history is any guide, Shrum's choice will lose either a) the nomination or b) the general election.

Obviously, Bob and I were not close friends. But we did have friends in common—especially Anne Wexler, my unlikely partner in the **Rolling Stone** Washington bureau in the mid-1970s before she went on to become Jimmy Carter's commerce secretary, and her husband, Joe Duffy, who had been the director of the U.S. Information Agency under Bill Clinton. In the autumn of 2003, under the auspices of Wexler and Duffy, Shrum and I had dinner (as always, Shrum's hilarious, generous, and entirely compelling wife, the writer Mary Louise Oates, played a major role in the festivities). We got along famously.

No doubt, there were ulterior motives on both sides. It seemed clear to me that John Kerry was going to be the winner of the Shrum primary, and I hoped for a fresh source of campaign information; I'd guess that Shrum was probably hoping to neutralize a longtime critic. In the end, we were both disappointed. Shrum was a lousy source; his loyalty to his candidate and his discretion were impeccable. And I was as critical of Shrum's strategic decisions in 2004 as I'd been in the past.

There was, however, a very good argument—in principle—for adding Shrum to Kerry's campaign team. Shrum's strength as a consultant was honing a candidate's public presentation, which was among Kerry's greatest weaknesses: how to build a stump speech, how to answer difficult questions on specific issues, how to respond to the events of the day. He immediately impressed the Kerry staff with his ability to weed through, edit, and sharpen a foreign-policy speech that the candidate had planned to deliver at Georgetown University—although Shrum's rhetorical inclinations, his weakness for Kennedyesque orotundities, would ultimately reinforce Kerry's anachronistic formality on the stump.

Even before Shrum arrived, there was an odd, patched-together quality to the Kerry campaign staff, none of whom had close or long-term relationships with the senator. The campaign manager, Jim Jordan, was very much a hired hand. He was a volatile North Carolinian, who did not suffer fools gladly—and, in Jordan's mind, the fools surrounding Kerry included most of the old Boston gang, most of Kerry's major fund-raisers, the senator's brother and closest adviser, Cam, and, fatally, the senator's wife. Jordan deserved credit for the orderly creation of a campaign team—he brought in Margolis, hired Mark Mellman as the lead pollster and Chris Lehane, a hardball tactician who specialized in the lethal leak—but Jordan's authority, and perhaps his confidence, was subtly undermined by the results of the congressional elections in November of 2002. As director of the Democratic Senatorial Campaign Committee, he had presided over the party's historic defeat. Among the Washington chatterati, there was a strong belief not only that Jordan had been badly outfoxed by Karl Rove and the Republicans but that he—and Mellman, who served as pollster—had encouraged candidates not to fight the Republicans on Iraq or the Bush tax cuts, arguably the two biggest issues in the race. Jordan maintained that the local candidates had the option to do whatever they wanted, but his distribution of campaign funds and Mellman's polling had shaped the race.

Shrum arrived in the Kerry camp within weeks after Jordan's humiliation. He came with his two partners, Mike Donilon and Tad Devine, whose roles were unclear and quite possibly redundant (Devine was another veteran member of Jordan's hit parade—fellows not to be suffered gladly). Far more worrisome to the existing campaign staff, though, was Shrum's reputation as a disruptive force, an inside operator who would do anything to gain absolute control over the candidate. And the Kerry campaign seemed ripe for disruption. There were too many cooks, and there was no clear sense of the broth. The prevailing vagueness, the lack of planning, the absence of clear lines of authority, the peremptory addition of the big-name consultant—all these were familiar symptoms of the Democrats' quadrennial campaign management miasma. Very early on, the whispering began: "This is just like the Gore campaign" or, among the Boston crowd, "This is looking just like Dukakis."

It seems remarkable that John Kerry could have navigated his entire life toward a presidential run, and been so lazy—and uninformed—about what works and what doesn't when building a campaign staff. He seemed eerily intent on replicating every last Democratic mistake of the television era. He was told this constantly—by Democratic pros like James Carville, Bob Kerrey, Bill Clinton, and some of his old Vietnam pals. Kerry would listen carefully, often agree, and then do nothing. There was a regal negligence to the man; he was all dignity and no details. He had "plenty of policies, but no ideas," as one campaign-staff member put it. Indeed, he had a history of political uncertainty. He would test bold positions—favoring reform of affirmative action (he suggested that preferences should be granted according to class, not race) or curbing the power of the teachers unions—and then he would backtrack. No one doubted his intelligence, and his close friends were vehement about the quality of his character, especially when times were tough. But there was a pervasive weakness, a cautiousness to Kerry as well. It was a conundrum: the man was a hero under fire and a coward when he wasn't.

In this case, Kerry's bold initial plan for his

candidacy—to challenge Bush on his perceived strengths, national security and foreign policy—was in modified backtrack mode by the time Shrum arrived. Bush was a hero after September 11; he stood a strong chance of being seen as an even bigger hero after getting rid of Saddam Hussein. The poll numbers, and his handlers, pushed Kerry toward the more familiar Democratic terrain of domestic and economic issues. More than two million jobs had been lost in the post-Clinton recession, and recovery was slow in coming, especially after the terrorist attacks of September 11. Shrum pushed economic populism at every opportunity. Jordan couldn't understand why Kerry kept harping on the failure to capture Osama bin Laden at Tora Bora. Tad Devine suggested that Kerry's position on Iraq should be that it was unpatriotic to criticize a president's foreign policy during wartime. "It was amazing," said an old Kerry hand. "Tad didn't seem to realize that Kerry had made his name criticizing Nixon during Vietnam."

Of course, the consultant who stood to lose the most by Shrum's arrival was the one who had worked the hardest to learn who the candidate was. Kerry asked Margolis over to his Georgetown home on a Sunday morning in early 2003, and announced that he wanted Shrum to come aboard. Margolis would remain in charge of producing the television spots—although Shrum's firm would take half the fees from the advertising buy. Margolis wasn't thrilled, but he figured that presidential campaigns were cooperative ventures. He had worked other races with Shrum, Devine and Donilon, and considered them friends.

Before Shrum arrived, the consultants—aided by the young speechwriter and New Democrat thinker Andrei Cherny—had begun to work on a theme that seemed to fit Kerry perfectly: the New Patriotism. Kerry would argue that a new era had begun with the terrorist attacks of September 11, 2001, that the nation really was at war against Islamist terrorism, and that war demanded sacrifices. He would criticize the president for not taking the threat seriously enough, for not mobilizing the public to fight the war. He would propose an aggressive energy-independence program as a matter of national security, environmental sanity, and economic development. ("Young American men and women should not be asked to die for Middle Eastern oil," was one of the strongest lines in his stump speech.) He would propose a rollback of Bush tax cuts for the wealthy. He would propose a serious program of national service for young people. He would demonstrate the strength of his character not by talking about his service in Vietnam but by telling inconvenient truths. He would go to Detroit and challenge the automakers to raise fuel-efficiency standards. He would return to his alma mater, Yale University, and challenge the Ivy League colleges to reinstate the Reserve Officers Training Corps (ROTC) programs they had dropped during Vietnam. Cherny wanted Kerry to go even further, to call for mandatory national service for young people.

"That's ludicrous," Shrum said, when the plan was presented to the candidate in early April of 2003. In fact, Shrum pretty much hated the New Patriotism theme. The public didn't care about fuel-efficiency standards or national service. Democratic primary voters—and they **were** the target audience—cared about jobs, health care, education. There was no point in stepping out, taking risks now; the political situation was too uncertain; the war in Iraq was about to begin. The polling showed that Kerry was the lowest common denominator, everyone's second choice—which was another way of saying that he was the most acceptable candidate to the most Democrats. Why mess with that? Why risk alienating the peace movement by touting ROTC? Why risk alienating young people by calling for universal national service? Why challenge the American love affair with SUVs? And "Patriotism" was sort of a loaded word to the left wing of the Democratic Party, wasn't it? It implied those who didn't agree were unpatriotic.

Kerry listened carefully when the New Patriotism was presented, but he sided with Shrum. Andrei Cherny, crushed, later asked—pleaded with—the candidate: "You know you're going to have to step out and take a risk at some point, right?"

Kerry said yes, he knew that. But national service, Cherny's obsession, wasn't the right issue to pick a fight on. "What do you think the right issue will be?" Cherny pressed.

"Early education and child care," Kerry responded.

The staff was mystified and depressed. This was the strong leader, the warrior-candidate? It was quite possible, his Senate staff thought, that Kerry was exhausted and preoccupied, still recovering from prostate cancer surgery. Jordan, however, sensed the X factor was Shrum—and, as Kerry's weird caution persisted into the summer, the rest of the staff came to agree.

Shrum, it turned out, was an ancient sort: a medieval courtier, a flatterer. He was also a superb intuitive psychoanalyst. He had an unerring ability to locate a candidate's insecurities and find a way to massage them. Lehane called it the "Shrum Security Blanket." With Gore in 2000, Shrum had sensed the candidate's anger—at Clinton, at the press, at his existential fate—and so he served up an angry theme: "The People Versus the Powerful." With Kerry, Shrum sensed the candidate's uncertainty about his political instincts and he played to Kerry's cautious side. He also sensed the senator's proper New England discomfort with Jordan's in-your-face style. The campaign manager's relationship with Kerry's family, friends, and fund-raisers was getting worse. At one point, Jordan actually called Cam Kerry an asshole to his face. Jordan was growing ever more frustrated with the constant Kerry dithering, the fact that the candidate had to call half the known world on his cell phone before a decision could be made. The campaign manager resented any and all ideas from people he regarded as amateurs—these included some major-league fund-raisers—sometimes defiantly so, to the point of ridiculousness. He scorned David Thorne's suggestion that they gin up the Internet operation. "There isn't a single vote to be had on the Internet," he said. And worst of all, he was brusque with Teresa.

Shrum wasn't. He commiserated with the candidate's wife, fawned over her, whispered sweet somethings—Jordan doesn't understand John, Jordan is tactless with the fund-raisers, Jordan is wrong—in her ear. This infuriated the other consultants. "It is just an absolute no-no to backdoor through the candidate's wife," said one of the Kerry team. "It drove the rest of us crazy."

A more charitable, and probably more accurate, reason for Shrum's growing influence was that, unlike Jordan, Shrum was a constant source of optimism and support for the candidate. If Jordan's essential message to Kerry was "You're screwing up," Shrum's message was "You're doing fine, you seemed more comfortable on the stump today, you handled that question about nuclear proliferation brilliantly, you might think about tightening the health-care section a bit . . . Why don't you try this?"

And Kerry was, essentially, optimistic about his chances. He assumed that Howard Dean's candidacy, the only real cloud on his horizon, would evaporate when Bush won the war. But Bush didn't quite win the war, didn't find weapons of mass destruction, and, for most of the year, didn't find Saddam, either.

As the weeks passed and the situation in Iraq deteri-
orated, Kerry anguished over his vote on the war.
Had he been wrong? At one strategy meeting, a staffer
asked: What if there were no weapons of mass destruction? "Then we were all misled," the senator replied.
But should he say that? Do you admit error on something so profound as a decision to go to war? In late
August, I spent a day with Kerry in New Hampshire
and he mused, "They're going to find WMD, don't you
think?" (In fact, the fruitless search for WMD diverted
U.S. intelligence resources away from the insurgency,
which only made the situation on the ground worse.)

I told Kerry about Elaine Kamarck's great line, "The
reason why Howard Dean got Iraq right was that he
was the only one of the major candidates who **didn't**
get a classified intelligence briefing from the CIA."

Kerry laughed and then he frowned. "There's more
than a little truth to that," he said.

Dean certainly wasn't going away. In fact, he was
pulling away—racing past Kerry in the Iowa and
New Hampshire polls, raising tons of money, drawing
huge crowds, stealing the idealistic young people Kerry
had assumed were his natural supporters. Jordan and
Lehane wanted to go after Dean, draw some distinc-
tions, cut him up a little. Shrum was opposed. "You
want to hand John Edwards the nomination?" he
asked. Let someone else go after Dean—someone inevitably would, Shrum figured—and Kerry could
maintain his status as everyone's second choice, ready
to pick up the pieces when Dean faltered.

The Shrum-induced passivity demoralized the campaign staff, which drifted toward paralysis. The Dean question festered through the summer of 2003. The New Patriotism remained on the table as well. The question of who was actually running the campaign—Jordan or Shrum or a player to be named later—festered most of all. As early as July, Kerry began a cell-phone roundelay, starting with Ted Kennedy, about whether he should fire Jordan. Meanwhile, the various campaign factions were loading up to do battle over Kerry's official announcement of his candidacy, scheduled for September 2 in South Carolina, in front of the battleship **Yorktown**, a not-too-subtle reminder of Kerry's military past and of Bush's premature "Mission Accomplished" victory speech delivered from the deck of the carrier **Abraham Lincoln** in May.

Andrei Cherny was once again trying to sell a "New Patriotism" announcement speech, and he was supported by most of the staff; Shrum, who seemed to take special pleasure in deriding the young speechwriter ("John Kerry will never say that!" was one of his favorite lines), figured that famous moments like the announcement of a candidacy were his personal preserve—although it was somewhat ironic that Shrum's most famous moment had been Ted Kennedy's **concession** speech to the 1980 Democratic convention. And so, two competing announcement speeches found their way to John Kerry's Boston town house on Labor Day weekend, 2003.

Cherny's wasn't as elegant as Shrum's, but it was much more compelling. It began with a stupid line, "Spring training is over." But it soon turned snappy and conversational:

> The sad fact is that—so far—both political parties have failed to measure up to the big jobs of dealing with September 11th and the Bush [economic] bust . . . Instead of fixing problems, they've spent their time—our time—arguing. All of us in government share the blame for this. There's plenty of it to go around.
>
> I know very well what you're supposed to say when you give speeches like this. You're supposed to promise sunshine and the moon. But I'm starting this campaign by telling you that's not what I'm going to do. I'm going to be a different kind of candidate—and, if you elect me, a different kind of President.
>
> I'm going to give you some hard truths. I'm not going to pander to you or tell you what you want to hear. Maybe that kind of campaign used to work. Maybe it still does. Either way, the stakes are too high in this election for old politics.

And Cherny proceeded to take a fairly decent shot at laying out the New Patriotism—energy independence, a larger military, (non-mandatory) national service, rescinding the Bush tax cuts, closing loopholes for corporations using offshore tax shelters to avoid paying their fair share—but Cherny also, and this seemed especially courageous and admirable, acknowledged some of the less popular aspects of Kerry's liberalism:

> I am against the death penalty. I think it is unjust and unfair. 111 innocent people have been released from death row. As President, I'll enforce the law but I'll also have a national moratorium on federal executions until we use DNA evidence to make sure those on death row are guilty. This is not an issue to fudge and it's time Democrats stopped being afraid.
>
> And I know Democrats are not supposed to mention common-sense gun laws like the Brady Bill . . . I know some people say mentioning gun safety cost us the last election, but I'd rather lose votes in West Virginia than lives in West Virginia . . . I believe in the Second Amendment, but the Democratic Party isn't the party of the NRA—and we never should be.

The speech concluded with a McCainian note of humility:

> I'll be the first to say it: I don't have all the answers. I'm nowhere near perfect. But I know our country and our government can do better . . . I'll be a President who tries every day to be worthy of the courage I've witnessed in my life.

By contrast, Shrum's speech was a disappointment, a laundry list of standard Democratic positions and rhetoric. Kerry called Shrum at his Cape Cod home on September 1, the night before the announcement, and told him that both his speech and Cherny's had merits, and that he wanted an amalgam of the two. "Well, there's some edits we can make, but the speech I gave you is great," Shrum replied. "I wouldn't change it." Furthermore, Shrum argued that Cherny's speech was not dignified, was not **him**. Unsure that he had made his case, Shrum called a taxi and sped from his Cape Cod home to Kerry's Boston mansion, arriving late in the evening. A frantic round of rewriting ensued. Shrum, Cam Kerry, David Wade, and the senator sat in Kerry's kitchen, with Cherny, Jordan, and Lehane on speakerphone—a perfect geographic metaphor.

The final draft preserved some of Cherny's language, but it eliminated many of the inconvenient truths, eliminated the conversational tone, and sanded down all the feisty language, adding such Shrumian flannel as: "But every time our country has faced great challenges, we have come through—and come out stronger—because courageous Americans have done what's right for America." The energy-independence section remained strong—although it began with a dreadful line about the threats to America not just coming from "gun barrels; they also come from oil barrels"—but gun control was barely mentioned and the death penalty not at all. Which was ironic: Cherny was a New Democrat but his speech was more liberal than

Shrum's (with the exception of Shrum's beefed-up jobs, health-care, and blah-blah-blah section); indeed, the real difference between the speeches was not ideological. The difference was between boldness and caution.

Shrum was right: the final, patched-together speech was more dignified and more Kerrified—and it fell flat as a spent balloon. After Kerry made the speech on a sweltering day in South Carolina, he traveled to Iowa to show the flag there. Late in the afternoon, he was doing a photo op at a soft-serve ice-cream stand, buying cones for the press, when Margolis heard a buzzing: all the reporters' cell phones and pagers were going off simultaneously. Suddenly, Kerry—holding ice-cream cones in both hands—was besieged by questions: Was he about to fire Jim Jordan? He gave a mushy answer— "I don't have any plans to make changes"—which only led to a more frantic round of questions. Margolis watched in horror as Kerry stood there, ice cream dripping down his hands, allowing his announcement speech to be hijacked by a staff-shake-up rumor. Another perfect metaphor. Meltdown.

Chris Lehane was fired/quit soon after the announcement debacle. Jordan, who kept pushing Kerry to be more decisive, was clearly on his way out as well. The campaign was running out of money. ("I can't raise another penny for that guy," a prominent New York fund-raiser told me. "He's just an awful candidate.") Kerry had to decide whether to mortgage his Boston home—his prime financial asset—and use the money to keep his campaign afloat. He also had to decide on a strategy: the staff was suggesting that he abandon New Hampshire and put all of his resources in Iowa, where Mellman's polls were showing a firmer base of support. And he had to decide what to do about Jordan.

And then, with his back against the wall in late October, the warrior-candidate emerged from hibernation and decisions came in a rush: Jordan was fired, replaced by Ted Kennedy's super-orderly chief of staff Mary Beth Cahill. Kerry mortgaged his home and put the money into Iowa. These were gutsy moves. The Boston home represented his sole potential contribution to his daughters' inheritance; his brother, Cam, counseled him to think twice about spending more money in what seemed an increasingly unlikely campaign. The decision to go for broke in Iowa was also risky; the state was an unknown quantity, polling for the caucuses was notoriously unreliable—and what would it say if he abandoned New Hampshire, a neighboring state where he was well known?

But another decision was also made in October: Kerry decided to vote against $87 billion in additional funding for the war and reconstruction in Iraq. He said it was a protest vote; he didn't like the way Bush was handling the war. He wanted the administration to make a greater effort to get the United Nations, neighboring countries, and Europe to help—an altogether unlikely scenario, since the United Nations, the neighbors, and many of the Europeans had opposed the war in the first place. What's more, Kerry's opposition to the $87 billion wasn't absolute: in an odd dither, he said he would vote for the money if it was paid for by rescinding the Bush tax cuts for the wealthy.

Kerry's arguments were transparent and foolish. His vote was all about Howard Dean. Kerry and Shrum hoped that a "no" vote on the $87 billion might help in the peaceable kingdom of Iowa, where antiwar sentiment seemed to grow with the corn. The trouble was, if Kerry actually made it past the primaries and won the nomination, the Republicans would attack him for being inconsistent. Kerry had now cast three contradictory votes on Iraq—against the first Gulf War, for the second Gulf War, and against the money to fight the war for which he had voted. Taken together, they were a devastating flip-flop . . . flip. Kerry loyalists had blamed Jordan for convincing the senator to vote for the war, and now they blamed Shrum for convincing him to vote against the $87 billion—but the fault was Kerry's own, and his inconsistency had exposed a fatal character flaw. "John has a good mind for policy, but he has no faith in his political instincts," Kerry's friend Senator Joe Biden said in a classic instance of damning with faint praise. And now Kerry was trapped; any attempt to explain his Iraq votes would sound dodgy, political, futile. He would no longer be able to run a credible national-security campaign against Bush. If he argued—as he later tried to do—that the administration was irresponsible because it hadn't provided the troops with sufficient body armor, the Bushies could respond that Kerry had voted against the money for the body armor. He had destroyed the original rationale, the moral and intellectual basis for his candidacy.

It is a withering commentary on the feeble condition of the Democratic Party that John Kerry went on to win the nomination almost by acclamation.

In fact, things began to get better almost immediately after the tumult of autumn decisions. Gephardt proceeded to launch a kamikaze raid against Dean, using the ancient and dishonorable Democratic canard that Dean wanted to destroy Medicare (in the Democratic lexicon, reform of old-age entitlements equals destruction of old-age entitlements). Dean fired back, with a series of inept negative ads. Shrum's wisdom was becoming apparent, even to his detractors in the Kerry campaign: Dean and Gephardt were destroying each other. Kerry was considered dead in the water by the national press—I wrote that his "sell-by date had passed"—but Mellman noted a mild but persistent buoyancy in the Iowa numbers.

There was a looseness to the campaign now. Decisions were being made. One tiny but significant decision was to buy a lot of tickets, round up as many supporters as possible, and make a real show of force at the Iowa Democratic Party's Jefferson-Jackson Dinner, a major annual fund-raiser, in Des Moines on November 15, 2003. Kerry turned out to have nearly as many partisans in the Veterans Memorial Auditorium that night as Howard Dean, and far more than the other contenders. He also had a new speech.

Cherny had finally won a battle within the campaign. He had been pushing for months to build a speech around the two great Bush gaffes of the Iraq war. The president had declared victory, in effect, standing in front of the infamous "Mission Accomplished" banner before the insurgency even began, and then he had cavalierly responded "Bring 'em on" when asked about the continuing guerrilla attacks against American troops. (Combat veterans found the latter comment particularly offensive: no one who'd ever been in battle would actually encourage an enemy to attack.) Shrum had opposed Cherny's approach in the past, but there seemed nothing to lose now. Kerry was itching to get aggressive against someone—and the Jefferson-Jackson speech was nothing if not aggressive. It began with a brisk proclamation:

> Iowa Democrats, it's time to get real. George Bush thought he could play dress up on an aircraft carrier in front of a sign saying "Mission Accomplished" and we wouldn't notice our troops are dying every day . . . You want to talk about Mission Accomplished? When it comes to coddling big oil, serving up tax giveaways for the wealthiest Americans and opening up doors for lobbyists and polluters, that's the only Mission Accomplished by George W. Bush. When it comes to health care, to

education, to jobs, to the security of our nation, it's not only Mission Not Accomplished, it's Mission Not Even Attempted, it's Mission Abandoned.

. . . I know something about aircraft carriers for real. And if George W. Bush wants to make this election about national security, I have three words for him that he will understand. Bring. It. On.

It was Kerry's first effective rhetorical moment since Tora Bora, even if it wasn't a spontaneous one. It combined things he cared about (national security) with things the consultants cared about (economic populism). And in the weeks that followed, Kerry augmented the populism with a very clever attack on "Benedict Arnold" corporations who were moving their headquarters to Bermuda and the Cayman Islands in order to avoid U.S. taxes. But even here, there was conflict with the consultants—especially Shrum. Kerry was a fervent free-trader. He felt comfortable making the case against phony tax havens, but not against companies who took jobs overseas, which he believed was a natural, if unfortunate, consequence of globalization. "Bob kept adding that Benedict Arnold companies took jobs overseas," said a longtime aide. "Kerry usually took it out, but it kept sneaking back in, especially in formal speeches. And then the **Wall Street Journal** hammered us for shifting from free trade to protectionism, and the whole Benedict Arnold bit— even the really effective part about companies not paying their fair share of taxes—got scrapped."

But Shrum was riding high. He was a prophet. He had predicted the Dean disintegration. And he was out there, on the trail with the candidate, providing constant encouragement, working hard. Even the members of Kerry's staff who were most skeptical about Shrum had come to admire his doggedness. "John was going to these nonstop town meetings across Iowa, and Shrum was just a trouper. He's what? Sixty-one years old, a hundred pounds overweight? And he's out there on the bus all night and up for the first event every morning. And he's pumping John up, 'You were great! Let's just change this line . . .' Even when John was exhausted and cranky and acting like an asshole, Shrum handled him perfectly. We were all tremendously grateful for that."

Indeed, for a moment it seemed that anything was possible. Money began to flood the Kerry campaign. After the nomination was secured, a record $38 million was received in March alone—nearly as much as Dean had raised in all of 2003; more than Al Gore raised in the 2000 campaign—and most of it came via the Internet. The Democratic Party was ready for war, propelled mostly by unmitigated disgust for the president of the United States. But there was also a momentary bubbling of enthusiasm for Kerry. The senator was, after all, on national television every Tuesday, amidst balloons and confetti, winning primary after primary. The president, by contrast, was caught in a bum economy and a bum war. Kerry took a slim lead in the horse-race polls, and the internals—Bush's favorable rating was dropping below 50 percent, an allegedly crucial measure—were looking even better. The consultants were telling Kerry that the election was his to lose.

On the night of his Iowa victory, John Kerry pulled Jim Margolis aside and said, "I just want you to know, I take the measure of a person by how they are in the tough times, not the good times. And you were there with me every step of the way. And I'll never forget it."

And then he forgot it, or didn't bother to remember it, as Shrum and his partners—with the help of Mary Beth Cahill—pushed Margolis out of the campaign. Margolis could sense it coming. Shrum was now the indispensable man: he had been right about the strategy in the primaries and Margolis—who had been part of the Attack Dean caucus—had been wrong. He wasn't very close to Cahill, who was now considered a miracle worker, having rescued the campaign from chaos. According to a Kerry Senate staff member, Cahill was actively working against Margolis, telling the candidate, "I don't think Margolis is so good. Mike Donilon had an awful lot to do with those Iowa ads."

Margolis could sense that a move against him was coming, and so he wasn't surprised when Cahill told him that she wanted to rewrite the money part of the contract. Cahill had a point: even the low-end estimate of Margolis's share of the television buy—9 percent—was an obscene amount of money (she would reduce the consultants' percentage two more times during the course of the campaign, ultimately getting it down to 4.5 percent, which still represented more money than the Republican consultants were getting). There was another problem. Shrum, Devine and Donilon had been working without a contract, just the handshake deal with Margolis to split the profits with them fifty-fifty. Now they decided to push back. "There are three of us and one of you," Donilon told Margolis in March. "We believe the deal should reflect that."

"You guys have to be kidding," Margolis replied. "For two years, I've been putting money into this, buying equipment, hiring staff. And it's not just me. My partners have been working on production and ad buys 24-7. The deal was your firm and my firm coming together, working together, equal partners, and nothing else is going to be acceptable."

Margolis then went to Cahill, who shrugged and tossed it right back at him. "This is for the consultants to work out," she said. Margolis told her that the consultants were at an impasse. If the decision went Shrum's way, Margolis said, he would leave the campaign. "You should talk to John about this," suggested Cahill, who was appalled by the greediness of all the consultants. "I'm not going to touch it."

A few days later, Margolis and Kerry had a lengthy phone conversation about the situation, in which Margolis said that he was probably going to have to leave the campaign. "Look, that just isn't going to happen,"

Kerry reassured him. "I'll make sure that this is all right."

It was the last Margolis heard from Kerry. There was never a clear decision from the campaign, but Margolis understood the non-decision that had been made. He left in late March of 2004. Shrum, Devine and Donilon were now completely in charge of strategy, message, and advertising—which was precisely what John Kerry had told friends would never happen. The Del Sandusky ad, so effective in Iowa, was aired only a few more times during the course of the campaign. It was never seen by most of the country. In fact, after a run of rather mediocre biographical spots in the spring, the emphasis of the Kerry campaign ads shifted markedly from character to the same old issues— health care, education, jobs. They were quite dreadful. "They were," CNN's Jeff Greenfield would later say, "the sort of ads that Bulworth was watching when he decided to commit suicide," a reference to Warren Beatty's political comedy about a senator who decided to end his life after viewing his reelection ads.

Andrei Cherny, a rather lonely figure by now, was trying to sell a new speech for the general-election campaign. His version would build on Kerry's "Mission Accomplished" and "Bring It On" forays, which seemed to energize both the candidate and his audiences. There would be a series of "Bring It On"s—about health care,

the economy, energy independence. It would build
upon Kerry's latter-day aggressiveness in the primary
campaign, and augment the assault on Bush with substantial policy alternatives. Cherny hoped that Kerry
would introduce the new speech at the March 25,
2004, Democratic Unity Dinner in Washington, where
all the candidates that Kerry had defeated, and presidents Jimmy Carter and Bill Clinton, would speak.

Shrum was opposed. He had fallen in love with caution in the primaries—and so had Kerry—and both
men would grow even more cautious now. Indeed,
Shrum decided to shelve Kerry's best lines. Both "Mission Accomplished" and "Bring It On" were deemed
too partisan, inappropriate for the general electorate.
What was left were ancient Shrumian platitudes, like
"Health care is a right not a privilege." The Unity Dinner speech was a dreadful bust (all the more so because
Kerry took the stage immediately after Bill Clinton had
set the house afire). It was stuffed with classic Kerry
mattress ticking like: "For more than thirty-five years,
I've been privileged to be part of the public dialogue in
our country."

Why on earth, one might legitimately ask, did Kerry
suddenly decide—or allow his consultants to decide—
to quarantine the thimbleful of passion at his disposal?
Shrum was concerned that a frontal assault on the president might alienate independent, middle-of-the-road
voters. He was convinced that the election would be a
referendum on Bush. The polls were indicating that
slightly more than half the people had an unfavorable

opinion of the president, and the situation in Iraq was growing worse. So there was no need to get too bold or crazy. "We are going to meet the voters where they are," Shrum told me, which sounded innocent enough—but what it really meant was this: We're going to follow the numbers, follow our focus groups, emphasize the things voters think are important—jobs, health care, education.

The Kerry campaign's devotion to focus groups was slavish, historic, and ridiculous in the extreme. Diane Feldman, a low-key and well-respected pollster—and a friend of Mary Beth Cahill's—did fifty-four of them. And Feldman discovered this amazing thing: people didn't like negative campaigning.

Or so they said.

"I never heard of a focus group that said they **liked** negative advertising," James Carville said. "But they sure do remember it." Feldman and Mellman were aware of that, of course, and they were not opposed to finding clever ways to criticize the president. But there were two complicating factors: one was that the nation was at war—and criticizing the president during a war that seemed to be going badly in the spring of 2004 seemed unpatriotic to many independent voters—and the other was that most people, unlike most Democrats, **liked** George W. Bush as a human being, even if they had doubts about his policies. "The notion that you could dump a lot of negatives on George W. Bush and change a lot of people's minds was fundamentally wrong," Shrum said after the election at a conference about the campaign at Harvard's Kennedy School of Government.

Which was one way to look at it. Mellman and Feldman believed that Shrum was both over- and under-reading the data. Mellman was particularly frustrated. He didn't have much access to Kerry, in part because the candidate simply didn't seem very interested in the numbers—which was refreshing, in a way, but also disastrous: the closest Kerry came to the data was via Shrum's interpretation of it. Mellman, for example, had a view different from Shrum's about the classic economic populism issues. "If you asked people what they were most interested in, they would say jobs, health care, and education," Mellman said at the Harvard conference. "But that's not what they thought the **president** should be interested in. They thought the president should be interested in national security."

In fact, Shrum had it completely wrong. Presidential elections are not about "meeting the voters where they are." They are about leadership. Passivity had worked in the primaries—and Shrum probably thought not only that his cleverness put to rest his reputation as a lousy strategist but also that he had figured out the mood of the people in 2004. He would insist on a positive campaign. He would insist, as his onstage operative Tad Devine, who had a tendency to speak only in market-tested language, would repeat incessantly on television and radio, that "the American people are sick of negative politics. They want an optimistic candidate with a positive plan for the future."

And so the stage was set for a general-election campaign historic in length—instead of the usual Labor Day start, it went full bore from April until election day—with a public that seemed extremely interested in politics for a change, an incumbent president whose ineptitude in waging a foreign war was unprecedented in American history . . . and a Democratic challenger who refused to criticize the president or offer a coherent alternative (beyond the stalest of liberal nostrums). It is no small testimony to George W. Bush's substantive failures that John Kerry almost won. It is no small testimony to Bush's political skill that Kerry didn't.

The Bush campaign was, once again, a model of simplicity. The lines of management were clear. Karl Rove provided the game plan—and this time he was obsessed with getting out every last evangelical and exurban vote possible (Rove believed the 2000 election proved so close because the Democrats had run an unexpectedly superior get-out-the-vote operation, and that four million evangelicals hadn't turned out, perhaps because they were offended by the late-breaking news of Bush's ancient arrest for drunk driving). Ken Mehlman was the campaign manager, but he delegated important parts of his authority. Once again, Mark McKinnon would have a consortium of consultants competing for advertising contracts. Once again, Matthew Dowd would distribute work among a consortium of pollsters. Almost every major Republican consultant had some small piece of the action. "If a consultant came to me and said, 'Hey, I've got this great idea for an ad,'" Mehlman told me later, "I'd say, 'Go see McKinnon. I don't control that money.' It worked incredibly smoothly."

And once again, the Bush strategy was elegant. It was the latest iteration of the campaign that Pat Caddell had designed for Alan Cranston against Ed Zschau in 1986. The election, the Bushies believed, was not a referendum on the president. It was a choice between Bush and this other guy, who most people didn't know very well. "We figured that people knew everything they needed to know about the president," Dowd told me. "Our campaign had to be all about Kerry. The big surprise was that their campaign turned out to be all about Kerry, too."

It was not difficult to discern what the two main lines of attack would be: Kerry the elitist and Kerry the flip-flopper. And Mr. Flip-Flop immediately handed the president a most remarkable gift. It involved the most important flip of them all: Kerry's votes for the war and against the $87 billion.

"We knew that he had a tendency to chase the rabbit," Mehlman told me. "If we hit him on something, he'd probably respond." And respond, and respond. The Bush campaign's highest priority was to get Kerry explaining, and entangling himself, and diminishing his credibility on Iraq, which would be the most important issue in the campaign. Kerry was headed to West Virginia on March 17 for a speech to local veterans. The Bushies decided to seed the clouds, preparing a nasty ad about the $87 billion in which a sonorous announcer calls the roll, "Mr. Kerry?" And Kerry votes "no" on the money over and over again. The ad was on the air in West Virginia on March 16.

In Charleston, West Virginia's capital, the next day, Kerry was hounded by a heckler—perhaps another bit of strategy from the Bush campaign—who kept asking about the $87 billion. Kerry launched into a filibuster of explication and then, to ingratiate himself, he said: "I actually did vote for the $87 billion before I voted against it," referring to the amendment he and Joe Biden had offered to pay for the war with a tax on the wealthy.

The Bushies couldn't believe their good fortune. Within twenty-four hours, they had a new ad on the air, which included Kerry's gaffe. "It was the most important 11 seconds of the campaign," Karl Rove later said.

The next month, as the Kerry flip-flop ads filled the air, was crucial in laying the predicate of the campaign, but not many people noticed—at least, not at first. All attention was on Iraq, which seemed to be disintegrating. The United States had had three extremely successful months after the capture of Saddam Hussein, rolling up dozens of the dictator's associates—Saddam's attaché case had been a cornucopia of useful information. But in April rebellions broke out among the Shia in the south, and among the Sunni in the city of Fallujah. The U.S. military attempted to take Fallujah, then retreated—a disastrous show of weakness. And then, at the end of the month, came the Abu Ghraib prison scandal: photos of U.S. soldiers abusing Iraqi prisoners, a historic calamity for America's image in the Muslim world and, it seemed, a turning point on the ground in Iraq. (U.S. intelligence officials later told me that by late spring of 2004 they had come to the conclusion that the war could not be won militarily, and that they were making a major effort to reach out and negotiate with some of the less extreme insurgents.)

None of which did very much for George W. Bush's standing in the polls. The race remained close. The Kerry consultants, myopically focused on the role of television advertising in the campaign, assumed that the Bush flip-flop ads weren't working. "We began to win because we started to spend more money from the end of April till July," Devine said at the Harvard conference, blissfully unaware that the news from Iraq might have had something to do with Kerry's mild good fortune. Indeed, as the campaign progressed, Kerry's Boston friends began to notice that Shrum, Devine and Donilon had an ad-centric view of the campaign. They were happiest when they could buy television time, which of course was their biggest moneymaker. Unfortunately, none of the humdrum Shrum ads had the slightest impact on the campaign.

The candidate himself was infuriated by the Bush ads. "We've got to respond to this," Kerry said, at a staff meeting in April, and pointed out that Bush was a more egregious flip-flopper than he was.

"Are we really going to get into a debate about who's the biggest flip-flopper?" Shrum replied, according to several people who attended the meeting. "Is that what this campaign is going to be about? These attacks aren't sticking. We're ahead in the polls."

At the Harvard Conference, Mary Beth Cahill said that Kerry's "story"—his biography—was the campaign's response to the flip-flop ads, and Shrum was running "bio" ads that spring. But there was one crucial part of Kerry's biography that was avoided: his role as a leading antiwar protester after he returned from Vietnam. Several of the senator's longtime aides wanted to "own" this controversial moment, to define it, explain it, and take pride in it before the Bush campaign attacked Kerry as unpatriotic, a stratagem the Kerry staffers considered inevitable. They wanted to commemorate the anniversary of Kerry's stirring testimony against the war before the Senate Committee on Foreign Relations in April of 1971. But the Shrum crowd voted no. The testimony was controversial. Kerry had spoken of American atrocities, torture, and murder in Vietnam. Indeed, a few months before his 1971 testimony, Kerry had attended a remarkable meeting in Detroit sponsored by Vietnam Veterans Against the War, an emotional catharsis called the "Winter Soldier" investigation, in which recently returned veterans confessed to atrocities that they had committed.

And now, thirty-three years later, there was Abu Ghraib. What to do? Hold a focus group, of course.

Hold a bunch of them. At a focus group in Arkansas, Diane Feldman asked the participants to draw a picture that conveyed their feelings about Abu Ghraib. The results were very intense: a skull and crossbones, a hand squeezing the world out of shape, America encircled by fingers pointing at it. But in the end, everyone in the group supported the president. The message was, "We've got to finish the job we started."

Indeed, the public seemed quite conflicted about Abu Ghraib—appalled by the scenes of torture, supportive of the troops, infuriated by the Islamic extremists, and open to the argument that traditional boundaries needed to be breached in dealing with the terrorist enemy. The Kerry advisers weren't at all conflicted, however. They told the senator to stay away from Abu Ghraib, even though it would have been his most natural impulse as a human being and as a veteran—and as the former leader of Vietnam Veterans Against the War—to protest the outrage. Any criticism of the Bush administration would make it into a **political** story, his advisers insisted; standard political tradecraft dictates that when your opponent stabs himself in the groin, you just let him bleed. But this was no ordinary stabbing. It was the United States of America acting in a manner that violated the accepted bounds of morality and civilization—a point that Kerry's friend John McCain, a victim of North Vietnamese torture, would vehemently assert in the Senate.

No one seemed to recognize the possibility that if John Kerry spoke from his heart on an issue that he

found momentous and appalling, he might become
something less of a cardboard character, less a typical
politician, in the minds of voters. This might not
"move the numbers" in the polls, at least not at first,
but there was the possibility of grudging public admiration, which might, in turn, lead to votes—especially
if the senator began to speak his mind, not the polling
data, on other issues. If Kerry had been able to establish himself in the spring of 2004 as a politician who,
unlike the president, wasn't afraid to defend himself in
front of unfriendly audiences, who was actually trying
to force a dialogue on the most important issues facing the country, he might have had the credibility to
withstand the attacks on his character—and his war
record—that were soon to come.

But John Kerry remained silent on Abu Ghraib,
aside from boilerplate expressions of concern. And it
was a conscious, **market-tested** silence, which made it
so much worse. He remained silent in June when the
Washington Post revealed that a memo from Bush's
Department of Justice—a memo that was reviewed by
the White House staff—had offered the Department of
Defense a rationale for loosening the standards for prisoner interrogations. In other words, there was direct
evidence—a paper trail—that the Bush White House
had approved the use of torture against detainees in the
war on terror.

And still Kerry remained silent. He did not mention
Abu Ghraib or the torture memo in his acceptance
speech at the Democratic National Convention in

Boston, or in three debates with the president in October. It was a stunning abandonment of the moral principles that had defined his adult life. He was without
definition now. He was an optimistic candidate with a
positive plan for the future.

I liked John Kerry's acceptance speech at the 2004
Democratic National Convention. I liked the brisk
way he delivered it. I thought he made an effective case
against the president, for a change, although that was
mostly by contrast—the rest of the Democratic convention had been terminally bland, the speakers vehemently censored by Shrum's minions, forbidden to
attack Bush in all but the vaguest terms. I liked the tes-
timonials from Kerry's Vietnam War buddies and assorted generals that preceded the speech. I even liked
the fact that the candidate saluted when he approached
the podium and said, "Reporting for duty." I am a
sucker for mission, duty, and service to country. And
Kerry seemed so much more energetic than usual.

"You watched it in the hall, right?" Jeff Greenfield
asked. I nodded. "Big mistake," he said.

Right. It is standard tradecraft for political reporters
to always watch a big speech or a debate on television,
the way most citizens do. But I had been trapped in the
hall for the worst of all possible reasons—I was expected to do an instant analysis of the speech for CNN,
and the network had plunked me in a skybox overlook-
ing the festivities. And so I was swept away by the del-

egates' enthusiasm and missed some of the subtleties. Like the fact that Kerry still didn't have a coherent narrative message. Like the fact that he used the words "strong" or "strength" seventeen times . . . without ever showing his alleged strength by telling the nation an inconvenient truth. (No doubt, every line that registered the slightest hint of disapproval had been scrubbed when the speech had been videotaped and dial-grouped.)

Actually, the most memorable moment of the speech may have occurred backstage and without Kerry's knowledge. It involved his wife and his vice presidential choice.

The Bush campaign had always believed that Teresa Heinz Kerry was a major asset . . . for the Bush campaign. "We decided to put Laura Bush out front as often as possible," said a campaign strategist. "In part because she really was a huge asset. But also because we figured Teresa would demand equal time." It wasn't so much that Mrs. Bush was all-American and Mrs. Kerry was a foreigner; it was that Mrs. Bush was charming and self-effacing, and Mrs. Kerry was a woman with upward of $500 million who acted like it.

During her solipsistic convention speech, Teresa Kerry had vamped in a stagey whisper mostly about herself and her past, not her husband. And now, as her husband was concluding his acceptance speech, she repaired to an area behind the podium for the ceremonial

balloon drop. This is one of the most carefully choreographed moments in American politics. It has worked
the same way for decades: the vice presidential candidate enters first, joining the presidential nominee center stage—they raise their hands together in triumph.
Then the spouses arrive, then the children, followed by
the other candidates who had contested the presidency
and lost, followed by other prominent party members
until the stage is completely filled.

Teresa Heinz Kerry would have none of that,
though. "I will go out first," she told the young campaign aide who was in charge backstage. An argument
between spouse and aide ensued as the vice presidential
nominee, John Edwards, stood by. Spouse insisted, vehemently, on going first. Aide called Mary Beth Cahill
at the headquarters truck, who told him that the order
of battle was set in stone: Edwards went first.

"I am the spouse," Teresa persisted. "I go first."

There was no way to dispute the woman and so,
when Kerry finished the speech and the appointed time
came, the aide blocked Teresa with both his arms,
turned his head, and yelled to Edwards, "Run!"

This was the beginning of a hilariously awful month
for the Kerry campaign. The next bit of business was
the postconvention trip, a recent Democratic tradition
that had begun with Clinton and Gore's spectacular
bus tour through middle America after the 1992 convention. In 2000, Gore—ever anxious to distance himself from the Clintonian past—had abjured the bus
and taken a riverboat down the Mississippi.

That left trains . . . as well as buses and airplanes—
the campaign seemed as indecisive about means of conveyance as it was about everything else. On August 4,
as Kerry prepared to leave on a whistle-stop tour of the
Midwest, an "independent" group called Swift Boat
Veterans for Truth announced that it would air a television ad in which fellow swift-boat captains who
"served with John Kerry" would claim that "Kerry is lying about his record," and that "Kerry is no war hero,"
and that Kerry "dishonored his country."

In a year when Democratic interest groups would
eventually spend $188 million on television ads that
had practically no impact on the campaign, this one
spot—which aired only a few times—dominated all
political discourse for the month of August. The
Swifties, as they were soon called, were given prominent play first on Fox News, and then in the rest of the
media. Almost all their claims about Kerry's war record
were ultimately proven false, but it took more than a
week for the mainstream media to do the meticulous
reporting necessary to make that case. By that time, it
hardly mattered: Kerry's war record, the rock upon
which Shrum had built his candidate, was now in dispute. A second round of very effective Swiftie ads,
which got more airplay, featured widows and Vietnam
war heroes complaining about Kerry's antiwar activism,
especially his—accurate—claims of American atrocities. It almost seemed divine retribution for Kerry's
silent spring. (Eventually Swift Boat Veterans for Truth
would spend $62 million on advertising.)

Mellman immediately noticed the effect of the ads in his tracking polls. Kerry's favorable ratings were down, Bush was taking the lead in the horse-race numbers, and the response to one question—"From what you've seen lately, are you feeling more positive or negative about the Kerry campaign?"—was way negative, especially among independent voters. There was a conference call. A meeting. Another meeting. Most of the consultants were reluctant to take the bait. Shrum thought the Republicans were trying to get them to chase another rabbit. Cahill thought an aggressive response would only balloon the story. And then there were the inevitable money complaints: they were working within federal spending guidelines now, much to Shrum's dismay, with only $74.6 million to spend between the convention and election day. Bush had a five-week spending advantage; the federal strictures wouldn't kick in for the president until he was officially nominated by the Republican Party in early September.* Shrum and Devine didn't want to spend money on advertising until Labor Day. "We had no assets," they later said, as if the candidate himself—and his battalion of Vietnam veteran supporters—weren't an asset; as if a **human** response by the candidate, an appropriate blast of indignation over the smearing of his good name, weren't even an option. (But then, why on earth

---

*The incumbent party traditionally has its convention after the out-of-power party, and Karl Rove had stretched the distance between the Republican and Democratic conventions as far as it would go.

didn't Kerry just go out and do it himself? His censorship of his own humanity was both pathetic and infuriating.) The consultants were quite bereft of ideas that didn't involve putting advertising on the air, and reaping 4.5 percent of the take—and they were inept even at that: in the end, the Kerry campaign had a preposterous $15 million left in the bank.

Meanwhile, the candidate was going slightly berserk. His Vietnam service had been called into question before, in 1984 and 1996, and he had slapped back effectively both times, with emotional rallies featuring a gamey, angry army of fellow veterans. But Kerry was locked on a train now, traveling through parts of the country where the cellular phone service was iffy at best—and his Vietnam pals had been dispatched to the far periphery of the campaign by the ever managerial Cahill. Just about everything else was awful, too. His wife was unhappy; she was constantly complaining of headaches; they had a fight, witnessed by park rangers and some reporters, at the Grand Canyon. He was making mistakes. At the Grand Canyon, he said that even if he had known there were no weapons of mass destruction in Iraq, he would have cast the same vote on the war (a position he would change a month later). So now he was entangled in two wars, still trying to figure out his position on Iraq—and he was calling everyone he could find, whenever he could, trying to mount a defense of his most prized political possession, his record as a Vietnam war hero.

It was not until August 19, two weeks after the Swift

Boat Veterans had surfaced, that the **Washington Post** printed a story proving that Larry Thurlow, one of the most outspoken of the Swifties, had given testimony in the past that supported Kerry's account of one key incident. On that same day, finally liberated from his never-ending cross-country trip, Kerry launched a direct attack on the Swift Boat Veterans and on the Bush administration for covertly supporting the group— a charge that was never quite proved—in an angry speech before a friendly audience in Boston. Over the next week, most of the mainstream media produced stories that confirmed Kerry's account of his war record and raised serious questions about the veracity and motivation of the Swifties. But it was too late. John Kerry's war record had become a matter of opinion: it depended on whom you trusted. People tended not to trust a guy who voted for the $87 billion before he voted against it. Kerry, who claimed incessantly that he was "fighting" for middle-class and working families, had proved incapable of fighting for his own good name.

At which point, chaos. A consultant riot ensued. James Carville—and Bill Clinton—tried to convince Kerry to make major changes in his campaign. In one phone conversation, Clinton told Kerry, "If I hear you say one more word about Vietnam, I'll vote for George goddamn Bush." Carville was even more aggressive, calling for the firing of Shrum, Cahill, press secretary Stephanie Cutter, and the rest of the crew. He succeeded only in getting a raft of new-old consultants

hired: famed Clintonites like Mike McCurry, Joe Lock-
hart, and Stan Greenberg added another layer to the already overstuffed campaign bureaucracy. John Sasso
was brought back as a senior adviser—exactly as he had
in 1988, he received a desperate Labor Day phone call
from the candidate, pleading with him to come back to
the campaign. Meanwhile, some of Kerry's old Vietnam buddies, led by David Thorne, were backdooring
Shrum from a different direction. They made a series
of ads defending Kerry's character and war record
against the Swifties' claims—using the widow of one of
Kerry's closest buddies and Pete Peterson, a former
POW and the first U.S. ambassador to Vietnam. The
ads were powerful and emotional, but only a few
ever made it to air. They were very much unlike the
Shrum ads, which seemed coarse and desperate political bribery aimed at "working and middle class families." They promised college scholarships and a $1,000
reduction in health insurance costs. They were literally
incredible.

The Republicans hammered more nails into Kerry's
coffin at their convention, which was far more negative, vitriolic, and entertaining than the Democrats'
had been. On the third night of the convention, Georgia senator Zell Miller—a putative Democrat—and
Vice President Dick Cheney gave speeches that im-
pugned John Kerry's patriotism, ridiculed his conti-
nental charms and pastimes, and pretty much accused
him of being soft on terrorism. Afterward, CNN's
Wolf Blitzer offered the Kerry campaign a response and

the Kerry campaign produced Tad Devine as the re-
spondent. It would have been an appropriate moment
for a heartfelt blast: "Wolf, this was one of the most
disgusting evenings of politics I've ever witnessed. How
dare the vice president—who skipped out of Vietnam
on a student deferment—question John Kerry's strength
and patriotism? And who can believe Zell Miller? I
mean, twelve years ago he keynoted the **Democratic**
convention and said that Republicans dealt in—and
I'm quoting here, Wolf—'cynicism and skepticism.
They have mastered the art of division and diversion.'
Well, by Zell's own definition, he gave a perfect Republican speech tonight. A cynical diversion. These guys
have made mistake after mistake in Iraq—and they're
trying to divert attention from their own failures by
making outrageous charges about John Kerry. It's just
appalling. They should be ashamed of themselves. The
president's men are playing the scuzziest sort of politics!"

Or something like that. Anything that was real.
What happened instead was this:

Wolf, I think what we heard tonight was the difference between the politics of hope and the politics
of fear.

I mean, I think of John Edwards' acceptance
speech in Boston which was all about hope, the
hope for the future of this country, for jobs, for
health care, for the possibilities of America, and
tonight, with both Senator Miller and then with

the Vice President, the politics of fear, smear, and attack . . .

So we've seen a great difference between these two parties. The Republican Party for three nights talking nothing at all about the agenda for America, for jobs, for health care, and I think these differences are like night and day.

Eventually, Devine got off a few good lines. He noted that Zell Miller had once introduced Kerry in Georgia as "an authentic American hero." He noted that Cheney had voted against many of the same weapons systems that he had slammed Kerry for voting against. But . . .

The politics of hope and the politics of fear.

The politics of fear, smear, and attack.

The agenda for America, for jobs, for health care.

Yecch. Who could believe anyone who talked like that?

Kerry's last chance was in the debates against Bush. Shrum did an excellent job of preparing his candidate. The president seemed ungracious and impatient in the first debate; Kerry was calm, well-informed, plausible— and the expectations for him were so low that he was bound to exceed them. Kerry held his own in the other debates as well, but his "victory" was a formal, intellectual one. There were no moments when he betrayed a spontaneous strand of humanity, when he made a di-

rect emotional contact with the audience—except, perhaps, for his gratuitous mention of the fact that Dick
Cheney had a lesbian daughter, which was a classic
negative Turnip Day moment, a spontaneous comment which revealed the candidate's insensitivity. He
proved himself intelligent, but he remained aloof, a
distant figure, a politician in all the worst senses of
the word.

And throughout, George W. Bush maintained his discipline. He gave the same speech over and over, and
quite effectively, with a country lilt and great conviction. He spoke in simple sentences. Saddam was a
threat. The world was a safer place now that he was in
jail. We must attack the terrorists before they attack us.
Freedom has the "transformational power" to make the
world a better place. We're not conquerors; we're agents
of freedom.

But there was one sentence that surpassed all the
others, that summed up the essence of the Bush campaign: "You may not always agree with me, but you'll
always know where I stand."

The Republicans—with pathetic Democratic com-
plicity—had managed to strip an entire presidential
election down to a choice between two sentences.

Bush: "You may not always agree with me, but you'll
always know where I stand."

Kerry: "I actually voted for the $87 billion before I
voted against it."

At a moment of real consequence in American history, the 2004 presidential election wasn't about issues, or values, or positive plans for America's future. It was about character, as all presidential campaigns are. Character was expressed in the most limited, non-positive way imaginable: I know you don't agree with me, but at least I'm telling some vague version of the truth as I sort of, kind of see it—oh, and by the way, you can't trust a thing the other guy says. This was the clinching argument at a time of war in the world's oldest, and grandest, democracy.

After the election there was a momentary confusion when the exit polls showed that about one-quarter of the electorate said that "moral values" had been the most important consideration in casting their vote. On closer inspection, in a subsequent Pew poll, it turned out that most people who cited "moral values" weren't primarily concerned about the candidates' positions on abortion or gay marriage. They were concerned about simpler and more profound values. They considered "straight talk" a moral value, and they simply did not believe John Kerry talked straight. And they were right.

8

And So, My Fellow Americans, in Conclusion . . .

★ ★ ★ ★

The presidency of George W. Bush represented the final, squalid perfection of the Permanent Campaign that Pat Caddell first suggested to Jimmy Carter in 1976. It was an odd mix of ideology and cynicism, a visionary nihilism, if such a thing is possible. It assumed—correctly—that the public wouldn't be paying all that much attention to the details. It assumed that grand proclamations of principle, the casual tossing about of marching words like "freedom" and "moral" and "evil," would suffice, that the public would never look beyond the high-minded pronouncements to see the cronyism, inattention to basic governance, crude politics, and self-delusional manipulation of reality that lay beneath.

The Bush style seemed a fresh breeze at first, especially after the defensive minimalism of the latter Clinton years. Bush was bold. He seemed unafraid of the vicissitudes of public opinion. His rhetoric was at once

plainspoken and uplifting, and he earned the full support of a frightened country after the terrorist attacks
of September 11, 2001. The foolish burlesques of the
Clinton years, the media obsession with peccadilleos,
seemed ancient history and so did the vast, gaseous
partisan battles over trivialities. It appeared possible
that the president might seize the moment and call for
the changes necessary to make the nation whole and secure in the twenty-first century. He seemed all vision,
smitten with moral purpose. But, sadly, it was only
words, not deeds—all spin, all talking points.

Power in the Bush administration seemed carefully
balanced between serious conservatives like Vice President Dick Cheney and killer politicians like Karl Rove.
Ultimately, though, the pols ruled—because the conservatives were merely ideologues, and even their most
important policy initiatives were little more than
bumper stickers. The White House was overpopulated
with executives and bereft of managers. It was the precise opposite of the small-bore, detail-oriented Clinton
administration: Bush was about big ideas, badly exe-
cuted. Indeed, the pedestrian disciplines of governance
had become alien to the essence of the Republican
Party. Government **was** the enemy, wasn't it? The very
notion of planning, especially long-term planning, for
the common good seemed vaguely . . . socialist, didn't
it? The bedrock text was provided by the redoubtable
British prime minister Margaret Thatcher, who once
told an interviewer, "There is no such thing as society.
There are only families and individuals."

And markets. The inherent prejudice against **society** left only markets and power and politics as appropriate subjects for executive leadership. The only real priority was reelection. The way you got reelected was to keep your coalition happy. And since the principle of responsible governance was not valued—indeed, it seemed a bit musty—you pretty much had a free hand. You could pass massive tax cuts, massive farm subsidies, a massive prescription drug plan for the elderly (and you could flat out lie about the cost of the latter). You didn't have to veto anything, not even the most extreme effusions of congressional vanity. After all, as Cheney pointed out, Reagan had proved that "deficits didn't matter." (Which was, of course, nonsense: Reagan had raised taxes three times after his initial tax cuts.) Important government agencies—like the Federal Emergency Management Agency (FEMA), the Food and Drug Administration, the Environmental Protection Agency— were given over to political cronies or, worse, to special-interest allies of the president intent on eviscerating the regulatory power of the agencies they had been sent to manage. There was an arrogant slovenliness to it all that neutered the essential truth of the conservative vision: that efficient markets were the best way to create wealth. The Bush administration reveled in inefficient markets, skewed to the interests of its campaign contributors.

Everything was politics, even war.

The fecklessness of George W. Bush's Iraq adventure may go down as the defining moment of a generation, my generation—the baby boomers—which had been so coddled, so protected from the awful realities of human existence, that the horrors of war and the martial metaphors of politics had become indistinguishable. A library will be written about the reasons for the president's fateful decision to preempt the nonexistent threat of Saddam Hussein's chemical, biological, and nuclear weapons. It was a complicated decision, with principled arguments on both sides. The belief that there were WMD in Iraq was practically universal. Even the French believed the weapons were there. Given Saddam's past use of chemicals against the Kurds and Iranians, a strong argument could be made that he would use them again. But there was nothing principled about the administration's failure to recognize that lethal chaos was likely to follow the invasion. There was a delusional unwillingness to plan for a guerrilla insurgency. The incompetence of Secretary of Defense Donald Rumsfeld, and of his designated field commander, General Tommy Franks—both of whom simply refused to recognize the difficulty of the struggle—will stand as one of the most irresponsible moments in the history of the American military and its civilian leadership. And it will be seen, I suspect, as part of the larger pattern of governmental negligence that defined the Bush administration.

But worse, far worse, was the tendency of the White House—particularly Karl Rove and the political "message" apparatus—to see the war first as a political opportunity and then, as the news turned bad, as merely another issue to be massaged. At the highest levels of the White House, more effort went into spinning the war than fighting it. The purpose of the White House Iraq Group (WHIG)—which was led by Rove and by Cheney's chief of staff I. Lewis "Scooter" Libby—was not to review and analyze the military or political situation in Iraq but to fight media fires, smear the president's enemies, provide talking points and photo ops that aggrandized the president's tough-guy image. The war was a great opportunity, Rove thought. In January of 2002, he told the Republican National Committee that congressional candidates "can go to the country on this issue" because voters "trust the Republican Party to do a better job of protecting and strengthening America's military might and thereby protecting America."

The decision to ask the Senate for a war resolution in the fall of 2002, just before the congressional elections—and before the matter had been voted upon in the United Nations—was a marketing ploy.* Every Democrat who voted against the war could be bludgeoned as a draft dodger in the war on terror; successfully intimidated, most Democrats chose to avoid the fight. The simultaneous decision to bring the Iraq issue to the United Nations was also a marketing ploy. Chief of staff Andrew Card famously let slip in August 2002 that this tactic would not be announced until September: "You don't announce new products until after La-

---

*This, in stark contrast to Bush the Elder's decision to win UN approval for the first Gulf War before taking the matter to Congress.

bor Day." This particular product was a chimera, however, a response to polls that indicated overwhelming public support for taking the Iraq standoff to the United Nations. Both Cheney and Rumsfeld were opposed to the move, and Rumsfeld pretty much ignored it—he proceeded full speed ahead with his plan to deploy his forces for the late-winter invasion that he favored.

The rush to war was followed by a rush to peace, dictated by public relations needs and wishful thinking. Somehow General Franks was allowed to abandon the war zone, permanently moving his headquarters from Qatar to Tampa, Florida, on May 1—the same day that Bush announced the end of "major combat operations" on board the USS **Abraham Lincoln**. The Bush event was planned meticulously. The aircraft carrier was pre-positioned just off the coast of California. The president co-piloted a plane onto the deck and emerged wearing a jaunty flight suit. As a golden dusk settled over the Pacific Ocean, he reemerged wearing a business suit to make his speech, the camera angles carefully planned to include the "Mission Accomplished" banner in the background.

Franks's departure from the theater of battle also assumed that "major combat operations" were over, an assumption apparently shared by Secretary of Defense Rumsfeld, who tossed off concerns about looting and chaos in Baghdad in a press conference a few weeks earlier. "Freedom's untidy," said Rumsfeld, who had grossly underestimated the number of troops necessary for the operation, "and free people are free to make mistakes and commit crimes and do bad things."

Even as it became increasingly apparent in May that the United States was facing an organized Iraqi insurgency, Franks allowed Lieutenant General David Mc-Kiernan, commander of the coalition land forces, to remove his headquarters staff, including hundreds of intelligence officers, from Baghdad a month later. "It may have been the worst decision of the war," one of Franks's superiors told me. "Tommy just figured the war was over." He left his successor, the new commander of U.S. forces in Iraq, Lieutenant General Ricardo Sanchez, with only twenty-seven intelligence officers to figure out the nature of the enemy. "We left Rick with chocolate mess," a general admitted to me.

The month that Sanchez took over, June 2003, was a fateful one. It was the month that the vexing realities of the Iraq adventure were first discerned, and vehemently ignored, by the Bush administration. It was in June of 2003 that the president and his top aides were told in a CIA briefing that they were facing a full-blown insurgency in Iraq. And yet Rumsfeld continued to insist that there was no insurgency until one of his top generals, John Abizaid, publicly disputed the secretary's evasions a month later, in July, saying that the U.S. military was facing a "classic guerrilla-type" situation in Iraq.

In sum, June 2003 was the month that the White House began to act as if the war in Iraq was a public relations problem first and a military problem second.

The biggest public relations problem had to do with the absence of weapons of mass destruction. They had to be there somewhere.* Bush sent 1,200 intelligence officers and WMD specialists to Iraq to find them, led by former arms inspector David Kay—and Kay took his mission literally. He refused to help General Sanchez, who was still drastically understaffed in the fight against the insurgency; Kay actually ordered his covert intelligence officers to break off contact with Iraqi informants who didn't have WMD information, **even if they did have information about the insurgency**. (In one instance, an Iraqi source who was providing valuable information about terrorist activities in Mosul—safe houses, arms caches, money distribution— was simply cut off.) Months passed. The insurgency organized itself—with little opposition from U.S. forces—and Kay continued to monopolize U.S. intelligence resources in a search for nonexistent WMD, a search whose main purpose had become the avoidance of embarrassment to a sitting president facing reelection.

Also in June, WHIG became obsessed with a former U.S. ambassador named Joseph Wilson who had disputed the claim, made by Bush in his 2003 State of the Union address, that Iraq had attempted to buy uranium in Niger. Wilson was right: the claim was false.

---

*Bush later performed a tasteless comedy routine for the radio and television correspondents' dinner in which he searched under tables in the Oval Office for WMD.

There had been no uranium deal. WHIG concluded
that something had to be done: the president was now
getting hammered for making the Niger assertion in
his speech. And so a major White House effort began
to "take down" Wilson as a credible source. The ambassador was a fat target: a Kerry supporter, and a distress-
ingly flamboyant fellow. But WHIG took a rather
oblique and bizarre path in smearing Wilson. Rove and
Libby, and perhaps others, implied in off-the-record
conversations with reporters that Wilson's trip to Niger
had been a matter of nepotism, that he had been sent
by the CIA at the behest of his wife, Valerie Plame Wilson, a WMD analyst who had once been a covert operative working under nonofficial cover (a secret agent,
in other words). It is a crime to divulge the name of a
covert operative. And so the scandal that caused the indictment and resignation of Scooter Libby was yet another debacle conceived by the Permanent Campaign
apparatus.

By the time the Libby indictment in the CIA scandal was returned, in late October of 2005, the president's fitful efforts to defend his war were pretty much
ignored by the American public, which had gradually
turned against the effort. Bush never seemed to say
anything **new** or interesting about Iraq. He recited the
same limited, indisputable platitudes that had worked
for him in the 2004 campaign. The terrorists were evildoers. They were hoping to weaken American resolve.
Freedom was God's gift to humankind. The United
States had to "stay the course" in Iraq. Not only did the

platitudes remain the same but so did the policy—few major adjustments in strategy were made to confront the successful insurgency. "There is a peacetime mentality, even here in the Pentagon," a senior military intelligence officer told me in the summer of 2005. And a retired four-star general who had supervised the early stages of the war told me that Iraq was a lesser priority for the Defense Intelligence Agency than Iran, North Korea, and China. The leaders of the uniformed military were thoroughly disgusted with Rumsfeld by then—and fearful that the all-volunteer army they had carefully built was being crippled by an ill-conceived war. "We have never taken this operation seriously enough," the retired general told me. "We have never provided enough troops. We have never provided enough equipment, or the right kind of equipment. We have never worked the intelligence part of the war in a serious, sustained fashion. We have failed the Iraqi people, and we have failed our troops."

Indeed, the Bush administration's cynicism and delusions about Iraq had been neatly summarized—by a photo op, of course, which occurred in the White House shortly after the 2004 election: Tommy Franks, CIA director George Tenet, and Coalition Provisional Authority director L. Paul Bremer were awarded the Presidential Medal of Freedom. It was a perfect Orwellian moment. Along with Cheney and Rumsfeld, these had been the prime architects of the Iraq disaster.

Predictably, though, it wasn't Iraq that finally revealed, in a way the public could easily grasp, the substantive bankruptcy of the Bush administration. It was an act of nature, Hurricane Katrina, which ravaged New Orleans and the Gulf Coast toward the end of Bush's annual August vacation in 2005. The federal government—which allegedly had bolstered its ability to deal with disasters after the 9/11 terrorist attacks—proved quite incapable of rescuing the homeless and hungry residents of the flooded city. The Department of Homeland Security, which housed FEMA, was exposed as a muscle-bound and disorganized chaos of agencies hastily slapped together—as an election ploy, another decision by the Permanent Campaign apparatus—during the 2002 congressional race. No real thought had ever been given to how to coordinate or manage the various bureaucracies which had been transferred to the new department from other cabinet agencies—that was the sort of governmental scut work disdained by the Bushies. And FEMA was run by the perfect Bush crony, Michael Brown, whose last known job was as a director of an organization promoting Arabian horses.

Predictably, too, the White House seemed to believe that the Katrina debacle could be ameliorated with an inspired photo op—something like Bush standing in the rubble of the World Trade Center after 9/11, speaking over a bullhorn to rally the rescue workers, his arm draped over the shoulder of a perfectly picturesque firefighter. But there were no such images to be had in New Orleans. The press and the administration seemed to believe, at first, that Bush's failure to rally the nation was a consequence of poor atmospherics. His belated arrival at the scene of the disaster was blamed, as were some casual verbal mistakes he made along the way (like celebrating New Orleans as the preferred party town of his misspent youth). There was a general belief that the president had to show more concern. And so he returned to New Orleans time and again during the month of September 2005. But his stature seemed to diminish, and he seemed more desperate, with each trip. He gave a prime-time television speech about relief efforts, which actually did raise the possibility of a creative response to the rebuilding of New Orleans, but the substance of the speech was overpowered by the obtrusive choreography—the president, in shirtsleeves, standing in Jackson Square, a ghostly, blue-lit cathedral in the distance over his right shoulder.

The Jackson Square speech—indeed, Bush's entire response to Katrina, including the infamous encomium to FEMA director Michael Brown, "You're doing a heck of a job, Brownie"—seemed the end of an era. The expectation of spin had deafened the public to the possibility of substance. Americans were inured to market-tested political speech and carefully stage-managed events. Stories began to appear about the frustration in the White House: the things that had always worked for the Bush administration were no longer working. But the things that had always worked were campaign-style tactics, attacks, and ephemera. Bush's Permanent

Campaign was over, with only history—a realm beyond the reach of consultants—left to judge his legacy.

As I write this, in the autumn of 2005, the Bush administration—perhaps the most efficient political machine in a quarter century—is in tatters and still has three years left to run. If the president is to resuscitate himself, the path will not be paved with spin. He will have to regain respect the old-fashioned way: through careful management and thoughtful responses to public problems. But those are the very things that the administration and the president seem least capable of doing.

And not just the administration. The Democratic Party shuffles between witless partisanship and nervous silence—with its silence coming on the most important issues, like the war in Iraq. The party's leaders are second-rate, at best; their policy thinkers have grown stale and defensive; there isn't a prominent Democrat with the moral authority of Republican senators like John McCain and Chuck Hagel, or former New York mayor Rudy Giuliani, for that matter. The baby boom generation has proved a fairly significant trough in the history of American political leadership; our greatest—our only—contribution to the Republic has been the rise of political consultancy.

I've given my adult life to the study of policy and politicians. I've enjoyed both immensely, and I've tried not to judge them too harshly. I do not expect every day to be Turnip Day. Nor am I one of those who predicts impending disasters—not for this country, not for this system, not for a people so gloriously diverse, informal, and iconoclastic. Stability is the democratic quality that journalists value least, and the United States—despite occasional burps and hiccups—has mastered the art of dynamic stability in a wobbly world. And so it seems curmudgeonly to carp, given all the wonders we behold. Those who argue the waning of America have an unblemished track record: they've always been wrong. Yes, it is now possible to make a case, with good reason if not complete credibility, that America's famed social mobility is hardening into economic stratification, that our culture has been undermined by commercialism, that we've grown too soft (or too rigid, or too xenophobic) to maintain our status in the world—but I've always preferred to celebrate the ingenuity of successive immigrant waves, the boundless chaotic entrepreneurial creativity of our businesses and our arts, the persistent tropism toward a multiracial society, the essential decency of America's global presence, especially when compared with other superpowers throughout history. I've traveled enough, seen what life is like in too many other countries, seen the long lines at the U.S. embassy visa offices around the world, to be anything other than wildly proud to be an American and profoundly optimistic about our future.

And yet only a fool could fail to notice a certain wilting in our public life. American politics is gangrenous with cynicism. It suffers an ideological rigor mortis imposed by the power of special interests and the caution of consultants. The two essential democratic traits—humanity and compromise—are in eclipse.

I came to politics as a liberal and became a moderate, a common enough journey. But to be moderate is to be homeless in twenty-first-century American politics. Indeed, it isn't easy to be a classic liberal or conservative these days, either. The Democratic Party, once the home of democracy's more gracious impulses, has become a reactionary bastion—its signature issues of health, education, and welfare held hostage by teaching and social-work bureaucracies that are utterly resistant to change; its spiritual vigor sapped by vehement secularism and an overdependence on the judicial system, symbolized by the fanatic defense of abortion rights; its soggy internationalism spineless in the face of a dangerous world. The Republican Party, once the home of a prudent conservatism, has gone foolishly radical—fiscally irresponsible at home, intemperate and bullying abroad, purveyors of an intrusive religiosity that is shockingly intolerant of science or reason. Both parties swan toward their extremes, since the extremists are the most adept at raising money and crowds, using direct mail, negative advertising, and the other dark arts of political consultancy. And individual politicians, ever mindful of the dangers on all sides, terrified that the next thing they say will become the fodder for a thermonuclear negative ad, grow ever more cautious. We are drifting, I fear, toward a flaccid, hollowed-out democracy where honest debate is impossible—a democracy without citizenship.

But there is also the possibility that, out of dissatisfaction with the current dreadfulness . . . or sheer boredom—the eternal itchiness of the American electorate—we will begin to drift in a more creative direction. It's certainly well past time for a change. Nothing drastic, mind you. Political consultants are here to stay. Indeed, they've always been around: from Merlin to Iago to Rove, there has been a need for the wizard adviser who inevitably warns, "My crystal ball says, don't go there," or "If you say that, your majesty, the Goths won't be happy."

And we have seen that there is a place for prudent consultancy in American politics—from the Clinton consultants' inspired efforts to rebuild their candidate's public image, on the basis of his real strengths, in the spring of 1992 to Karl Rove's brilliant efficiency at structuring and defining a campaign. Reagan could never have been Reagan without a stage manager like Michael Deaver; Al Gore or John Kerry might have seemed more plausible as human beings if they'd had advisers who'd understood them better (and, in Jim Margolis, Kerry nearly did) . . . well, on second thought, best not go **that** far.

There is an art to politics, and neither Kerry nor Gore had it. The art is largely unteachable; it exists well beyond the capabilities of consultants. It is rooted in personal strength, and confidence—the confidence that, left to your own devices, you probably won't make a fool of yourself. The confidence that Harry Truman displayed when, on the most important evening of his most important campaign, he decided to just wing it . . . to say what was on his mind in the way he wanted to say it. Even if you do screw up and say something embarrassing (but not **too** embarrassing), you can often leverage the mistake to your benefit by appealing to the public's sense of common humanity. Bill Clinton recouped his disastrous, overlong keynote speech at the 1988 Democratic National Convention by lampooning himself on the **Tonight Show**—which is exactly what John Kerry should have done, in spades, after he said he'd voted for the $87 billion before he voted against it. "When I make a mistake," Fiorello La Guardia used to say, "it's a beaut." Why is this so hard for politicians nowadays?

The tyranny of numbers is a good part of it, I suspect. Polling has replaced crystal balls with the patina of science. Numbers seem a lot more authoritative than they actually are—they are skewed by the way the questions are asked, the options offered, the questions **not** asked. And the sum of political knowledge possessed by pollsters is almost entirely dependent upon what has gone before . . . not what might be. Even Pat Caddell's predictive questions are deeply flawed indicators of which policy positions and locutions the public might accept from a candidate. You really need the human touch—the personal qualities of the candidate himself—to evaluate what the traffic will bear. A great politician, acting creatively, can overturn existing public opinion. A good politician, acting out of principle, can win respect for his or her position, even if the public disagrees with it.

In 1982, I traveled through New York State with Mario Cuomo, who was more than thirty points behind Ed Koch in the Democratic primary for governor. The biggest issue in the race was the death penalty, and Cuomo was on the wrong side of it. And yet, at every stop, Cuomo insisted on explaining his position; if the audience didn't ask him about the death penalty, he'd bring it up himself. "You might well ask me how I'd react if a member of my family were the victim of a brutal crime," he would posit, in an eerie prediction of the question that would boggle Dukakis in 1988. "Well, my daughter was recently assaulted on the street in our neighborhood by a man who burned her breast with a cigarette. My son Andrew got into the car with a baseball bat and looked all over the neighborhood for the guy—and I've got to say, if I'd ever caught up with him . . . well, I can't guarantee what I would have done. But I'd be acting on my worst impulses, my momentary anger. One of the purposes of the state is to protect us from our worst impulses—and the desire for vengeance is one of the very worst. So, lock 'em up. Throw away the key. But don't succumb to our worst impulses, our vengeance."

Afterward, I would ask people in the audience about Cuomo's response—and most still favored the death penalty, but they had been given a peek into his mind and his heart and they appreciated that. "I respect his position," they would say. And gradually—helped along by a flippant and hubristic opponent—Cuomo parlayed that respect into votes, and was elected governor. The manner in which he had explained himself was far more important than the position he had taken.

Polling has replaced thinking and feeling, and not just for politicians. Political journalism, especially on television, has become little more than the slavish devotion to polls. The processes of politics—the crosstabs, the buys, the ground war, the weird fetish of numeric expectations ("If Edwards can stay within ten points of Kerry, he will blah-blah-blah)—is the stuff of news now, as opposed to the qualities of the candidates. Or rather, the **positive** qualities of the candidates. We report their gaffes and tactics endlessly; but any reporter who dares to say "Bill Clinton has a really good national service proposal" or "George W. Bush is courageous to talk so much about the poor to country club Republican audiences" is in danger of being accused of being "in the tank" for that candidate. Believe me, I know this from experience.

The banalities of political punditry have become so commonplace that in 2004 we saw the birth of a new electoral species—the citizen-pundit. Instead of voters, we now have handicappers. I noticed this early on during the Democratic primaries, after watching Howard Dean give a rollicking performance in a New Hampshire backyard. "I really like him," a middle-aged gentleman told me, "but I'm not sure how he'll do down

South, and so I'm still shopping." This is a form of pragmatism, I suppose, but it is another factor that creates distance, that makes the political process less compelling. The fact that pundits—people like me—are so often crashingly wrong makes it all the more pathetic. Pundits, like pollsters, get most of their information by looking in the rearview mirror. We cannot predict what will work, or what won't, no matter how certain we sound. Figuring out the future is the job of leaders, and we are merely observers: we are never more foolish than when we make predictions. Real leadership throughout history has involved the defiance of conventional wisdom, the breaking of rules. This has become much more difficult in the age of the consultants, and in-your-face 24-7 mass media, but it is not impossible— as Ronald Reagan and, to a lesser extent, Bill Clinton proved.

Normally, this would be the point where the author makes some specific recommendations about how to heal American politics and create a vibrant public square in the information age. Inevitably this would include various suggestions about ways to increase voter participation, creative notions about the possible uses of the Internet, a full-throated cry for reform of the campaign-finance system, and a plea for more high-minded public debate. Sorry. Not this time, not this book. I find most of the worthy suggestions packed into the last chapters of political books to be insufferably boring. I believe that the **politicians themselves** have to figure out new ways to engage and inspire us . . . or maybe just some simple old ways, like saying what they think as plainly as possible.

But there are a couple of things I'd like to mention—one tiny, and the other impossibly broad and abstract.

The tiny thing is this: given the immense power and authority of the hired guns—the pollsters, strategists, and ad makers—no politician should ever go to battle without a "better angel" at his or her side. The better angel can be a longtime aide, a spouse, a personal friend, but it must be someone who can be trusted implicitly, someone who can say: "John, do you really want to avoid Abu Ghraib as an issue?" or "Mr. Vice President, do you really think you should make so sweeping a statement about no new taxes—you don't really believe that, do you?" A better angel should also be a buffer, someone who rides herd on the hired guns, someone who says, "Look, Vice President Gore's top priority really is global warming, and if you don't agree, if you can't figure out creative ways to follow up on this speech and to keep on hammering away at it, you'd best find yourself another campaign." Ideally, a better angel would be someone who can keep the candidate relaxed and sunny, someone who can gently puncture pretense, tell a joke, play some cards. Indeed, I would suggest that any politician who does not come equipped with a better angel is someone incapable of forging the most basic human connections—someone who doesn't know how to make or keep friends—and therefore someone too isolated to succeed as a leader.

The broader point came to me in, of all places, a focus group that the pollster Peter Hart generously allowed me to attend in late September of 2004, in Kansas City. The members of the group were, nominally, undecided between John Kerry and George W. Bush—and a handful actually were still trying to make up their minds, although most seemed to be leaning toward one or the other of the candidates. Hart plied them with Kansas City barbecue, a distressing variety of cookies, brownies, and candy, and all manner of nonalcoholic beverages. He was a calm, pleasant, skillful interlocutor. I sat behind a two-way mirror with several other journalists.

For most of the two-hour session, the participants said nothing very interesting. They were entirely predictable citizen-pundits. They thought Bush seemed a regular guy and Kerry was aloof. They said they wanted more specifics from the candidates and more high-minded coverage from the media, but the information they possessed seemed to come mostly from negative ads. The conversation was, at bottom, synthetic—the kind of false intimacy common to reality TV shows—and yet I sensed some frustration among the participants. They were searching for a quality in the presidential candidates that they couldn't describe. Finally, Hart asked: "It's the morning after the election. You have exclusive access to the next president of the United States. What advice would you whisper in his ear?"

Silence. Not a single hand was raised. "Anyone?" Hart pleaded. And finally a middle-aged white man, a Bush-leaner named John Kenny, said, "My opinion doesn't have to count."

Again, silence. No one seemed to understand what he was saying. But then I realized that Kenny was delivering a revolutionary message, undermining the very purpose of the focus group. He was saying: Don't listen to me! The next president, he said, has to "stand up on his own and do what he thinks is right."

John Kenny was pleading for leadership. It was the missing piece, the source of the frustration I had sensed, unable to be described by Hart's handpicked civilians because true leadership means taking the country to a new place, and describing the journey in words that are fresh, specific, and real. It means telling us things we don't know and things we don't want to hear—the very opposite qualities from the market-tested political speech that arises out of polling and focus groups.

I once attended a meeting of the Christian Coalition, featuring a Republican presidential cattle show. The master of ceremonies was the oft-controversial former secretary of education and drug czar William Bennett, who prepared the audience for the event with the best political advice I've ever heard: "Some of the people who follow me onto the stage are going to say things that you will find very pleasing. They will speak about 'our' virtues and the vices of the other party. They will speak about 'us' and 'them.' But in America there is no 'us' and 'them.' There is only 'us.' And if a candidate tells you only things that you want to hear, if he asks nothing of you—then give him nothing in return, certainly not your vote, because he is not telling you the truth."

Not one of the candidates said anything vaguely interesting, or challenging, that day. Which is the way it is almost every day on the campaign trail—unless a candidate loses "message discipline" and makes a mistake. It would be wonderful if that could change, if politicians understood that their credibility depended on the Bill Bennett standard—that they must tell the public at least one unpleasant truth or, at the very least, something substantive they hadn't heard from a politician before. It would be wonderful if the public, too passive for too long, held politicians to that standard. Of course, the only way for this to happen is if the public chooses not to vote for those who indulge in the prevailing political banality.

In the beginning—in 1968—there was Roger Ailes predicting that in the future all politicians "will have to be performers." But there has been a problem with that. Politicians are, for the most part, lousy performers. They are far more clunky, and much less credible, than most of the real performers we see on TV. Their advisers—the ad makers, the strategists—are pretty aw-

ful at what they do, too; they lack the iconoclastic creativity that produces great advertising and great performances. In the absence of inspiration, they have
fixed upon the crudest and easiest forms of communication: they've gone negative, they've counseled the robotic repetition of market-tested phrases. They've put
democracy in a Styrofoam cage. And the politicians—
who tend to see caution as an aphrodisiac—have gone
along.

I am hopeful that we are coming to the end of the
era that Ailes began. The ceremonies of consultancy
have become threadbare and transparent; they may still
work, but only in the absence of a real alternative.

And what might that alternative be?

A politician who refuses to be a "performer," at least
in the current sense. Who doesn't orate. Who never
holds a press conference in front of an aircraft carrier or
in a flag factory. Who doesn't assume the public is stupid or uncaring. Who believes in at least one idea, or
program, that has less than 40 percent support in the
polls. Who can tell a joke—at his or her own expense,
if possible. Who gets angry, within reason; gets weepy,
within reason . . . but only if those emotions are rare
and real. Who is capable of a spontaneous, untrammeled belly laugh. Who indulges a guilty pleasure or
two, especially ones that may not "test" well. Who isn't
averse to kicking his or her opponent in the shins, but
does it gently and cleverly. Who radiates good sense,
common decency, and calm. Who is not afraid to deliver bad news. Who is not afraid to admit a mistake.

Who abides by the sign that graced Franklin Delano Roosevelt's Oval Office: "Let Unconquerable Gladness Dwell."

Such a politician might not win, but he or she will be respected. Actually, let me amend that. Any politician who can communicate strength, originality, and a vibrant humanity—and who has the confidence to celebrate the occasional Turnip Day—probably **will** win . . . and so will we.

Acknowledgments

★ ★ ★ ★

I haven't included source notes or a bibliography for **Politics Lost** for several reasons. For one thing, how can you list all the books and conversations that go into a political education? I barely mention Theodore Roosevelt, Winston Churchill, or Robert Moses in this book, but biographies of those men by Edmund Morris, William Manchester, and Robert Caro were quite important in helping form my opinions about what works and what doesn't in politics. There were countless others, too. But I have tried to be scrupulous in the text about citations from the works of other writers. The source for much of the information in this book consisted of interviews I conducted over the past thirty-five years with politicians, consultants, and aides who wanted to have their identities protected for obvious reasons. The hundred or so people interviewed specifically for this book, and the thousands I've spoken with over the years, have my enduring appreciation for their cooperation and insights. In some cases, I've depended on my memories of conversations and events that happened long ago; in many other cases, I've lifted scenes and observations from my own work that appeared in **Rolling Stone**, **New York** magazine, **Newsweek**, **The New Yorker**, and **Time**. The credit for this book, therefore, should go not only to my superb book editor, Peter Gethers, but also to a string of terrific editors, going all the way back to Paul Solman of the **Real Paper**. Paul also deserves credit for the wonderful line "You can hack up a political reform, but you can't reform a political hack," which he created and falsely attributed to Jane Jacobs for reasons too perverse, hilarious, and complicated to be recounted here.

I'd like to thank Jim Kelly, the managing editor of **Time** magazine, for giving me the time and space to write this book. I'll never be able to thank Jim enough for granting me the privilege of a weekly column about politics in one of the great institutions of American journalism. I should thank Jim's bosses at Time Inc., too—Norman Pearlstine and John Huey—for their faith in me and support for my work. (And while we're on the subject of bosses, I can't neglect Peter Gethers's bosses at Doubleday, Bill Thomas and Steve Rubin, who do such a fine job of publishing my books.)

As for editors, there is an inspired sector of the species that warrants more attention than it usually gets. For some reason, in my case, this sector consists entirely of women—the women who, from the very beginning of my career, have edited me line by line, called me on my intellectual shortcuts, questioned my more overwrought passages, and, as Mario Cuomo might say, saved me from my worst impulses. Priscilla Painton is my current savior, and great friend, at **Time**. Dorothy Wickenden played this role at both **The New Yorker** and **Newsweek**, as did Marianne Partridge at **Rolling Stone** and Jan Freeman at the **Real Paper**.

Then there are the people with whom I talk politics, my friends and mentors. First and foremost is Elaine Kamarck, the sister I never had; her husband, Tino; and the rest of the Kamarck clan. Elaine has a rowdy intelligence, a raucous laugh, and a healthy disdain for pretense of any sort; she is all exuberance, all endorphins, just the best pal imaginable. For four weeks each summer, William Galston joins Elaine and me on Cape Cod for a fabulously discursive, often gin-soaked, bull session; Bill is a constant reminder that brilliance need not be self-involved, that it can be humble and thoughtful and kind. Mandy Grunwald is not only the most honorable political consultant I've ever met but also the most honorable human being, which makes her a real pain in the ass at times and an invaluable friend. Adam Walinsky is a mentor in the classic sense, with a passion for excellence in all things that has never diminished; he has **lived** Robert Kennedy's unique combination of toughness and idealism, and he has tried to teach it to me. Richard Holbrooke and Leslie H. Gelb have schooled me, for decades now, on world affairs and national defense, their lessons leavened by ruminations on the Farrelly brothers' ouvre, the New

York Knicks, and great dollops of foreign-policy priest-hood gossip.

Politicians from Kevin White and Tip O'Neill in Boston, to Ed Koch and Mario Cuomo in New York, to the late Paul Wellstone and Bob Kerrey in the Senate, to Newt Gingrich, Governor Bruce Babbitt and his wife, Hattie, and, of course, Bill Clinton have shared the tricks of their trade with me. And there are my colleagues—Jeff Greenfield deserves special mention, for all the time on the road we've spent together, the tribal dinners we've arranged, the never-ending spritz; Walter Shapiro and I have put in a fair number of miles and dinners together, too. Also Mike Allen, Jay Carney, Matt Cooper, Michael Duffy, and Karen Tumulty at **Time**; Dan Baltz, Gloria Borger, David Broder, Aaron Brown, Tina Brown and Harry Evans, Ron Brownstein, Richard Cohen, Nina Easton, Al Hunt and Judy Woodruff, Gwen Ifill, David Kuo, Laura Palmer, Chris Smith, and Jacob Weisberg; the Iowa guys, Mike Glover and David Yepsen; the Globies—Tom Oliphant, Marty Nolan, and the late David Nyhan; Tom Brokaw, James Carville and Paul Begala, Chris Matthews, Dan Rather, Tim Russert, Bob Schieffer, Leslie Stahl, George Stephanopoulos. I have learned so much from all of you.

Finally, thanks to my agent, booster, and social director Kathy Robbins—and to her husband, the writer, editor, and fencer Richard Cohen. Mark Glassman was a demon researcher and I'll bet he never forgets the weeks spent decoding the unruly brilliance of Pat Caddell. Peter Cove and Lee Bowes, Paul Gewirtz and Zoe Baird, Agnese and Gowher Rizvi, Fred Siegel, Ron Silver, Charlie and Sarah Stuart are close friends who listened to long rants about, and offered some terrific suggestions for, this book. I've been extremely lucky in parents and children—my parents, Miriam and Malcolm Klein, have been endlessly supportive. My children—Chris and Ann, Terry and Lindsay, Sophie and Teddy—are all brilliant politicians in their respective ways, and I suspect Zoe will be, too, with that lovely little smile.

As for Victoria, well, what can you say? Even though she **thinks** she doesn't know a whit about politics, she always seems to get the big things right, and the little things . . . and all those other things, too.

Index

★ ★ ★ ★

About the Author

Joe Klein is a political columnist for **Time** magazine. He is the author of five previous books, including **Primary Colors** and **The Natural.**

RH06